Creation and the Cross

The Mercy of God for a Planet in Peril

Elizabeth A. Johnson

ORBIS BOOKS
www.orbisbooks.com

ORBIS BOOKS
Maryknoll, New York 10545

Fathers and Brothers
MARYKNOLL™

Founded in 1970, Orbis Books endeavors to publish works that enlighten the mind, nourish the spirit, and challenge the conscience. The publishing arm of the Maryknoll Fathers and Brothers, Orbis seeks to explore the global dimensions of the Christian faith and mission, to invite dialogue with diverse cultures and religious traditions, and to serve the cause of reconciliation and peace. The books published reflect the views of their authors and do not represent the official position of the Maryknoll Society. To learn more about Maryknoll and Orbis Books, please visit our website at www.maryknollsociety.org.

Library of Congress Cataloging-in-Publication Data

Names: Johnson, Elizabeth A., 1941– author.
Title: Creation and the cross : the mercy of God for a planet in peril / Elizabeth A. Johnson.
Description: Maryknoll : Orbis Books, 2018. | Includes bibliographical references.
Identifiers: LCCN 2017039830 (print) | LCCN 2017048275 (ebook) | ISBN 9781608337323 | ISBN 9781626982666 (cloth)
Subjects: LCSH: Redemption—Christianity. | Ecotheology. | Restoration ecology. | Anselm, Saint, Archbishop of Canterbury, 1033-1109. | Atonement. | God (Christianity)—Love. | Creation.
Classification: LCC BT775 (ebook) | LCC BT775 .J64 2018 (print) | DDC 231.7—dc23
LC record available at https://lccn.loc.gov/2017039830

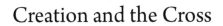

Creation and the Cross

Dedicated to

Robert J. Lombardo (1950–2017)

in memory of a life so beautifully lived

Contents

Introduction

How can we imagine the gracious, compassionate love of God for the created world? "The whole creation is groaning in labor pains until now," we read in the New Testament. Creation waits to be set free from its bondage to decay in order to share in the glorious freedom of the children of God, who are themselves groaning while waiting in hope for the redemption of their bodies (Rom 8:18–25).

Many theologians have written of human redemption. But how in our day can we understand cosmic redemption? At a time of advancing ecological devastation, what would it mean to rediscover this biblical sense of the natural world groaning, hoping, waiting for liberation? What would it mean for the churches' understanding, practice, and prayer to open the core Christian belief in salvation to include all created beings?

These are the questions that drive this book.

A formidable obstacle looms that would seem to end this exploration before it gets started: sin. In the course of giving public lectures on the subject, I have continually been asked in one form or another: "But what about sin?" Thoughtful listeners queried, "Didn't Jesus die to save us from our sins?" People pressed on, "Wasn't the cross an atonement for sin?" Following common teaching, people equated redemption with the pardon for sins said to be gained by Jesus' death. Since the natural world does not sin, theology would be foolish to include it in the blessing of redemption. Sin and the cross: the connection runs deep and powerful.

In truth, theologians would be foolish not to focus on sin. We human beings fail to love, both ourselves and others as ourselves. Relationships disastrously break down in individual lives and shared social life. Violence breaks out on international and domestic fronts. Voracious greed, racism, sexism, human trafficking, and other unspeakable injustices become solidified into social structures and create havoc. Suffering multiplies in a human world prone to selfish infidelity and hatred. Not content with harming our own species, human sin spills over into the natural world, ravaging habitats and destroying other species for personal and corporate gain. We profoundly need divine forgiveness. Out of the depths we cry for salvation.

Yet over the centuries Western theology's focus on sin became so intense that the wideness of God's saving mercy throughout the whole created world was by and large overlooked. Any connection between the cross of Christ and cosmic redemption came to seem esoteric. As a result, the natural world was ignored in doctrine, liturgical prayer, and ethical practice. It is hard to take cosmic redemption seriously if redemption is only about forgiveness of human sin. How did this come about?

Scripture offers multiple ways of speaking about salvation and diverse ways of interpreting the cross that do not lead into this *cul-de-sac*. Up to the Middle Ages no one way predominated. Neither did the church officially decide for one over the other. There never was an early council defining the terms in which Christ's redeeming work had to be understood, unlike specific decisions about his person. To this day the church in the East sees the incarnation as redemptive of all creation, and the resurrection of the Crucified as pledge of hope for all finite creatures who die.

Over time, however, a powerful current emerged in Western theology that favored a focus on sin and the cross. This was a juridical or legal way of thinking that interpreted sin as breaking a divine law. The work of redemption was a free and gracious act that nevertheless required something by way of penalty or recompense on the part of the law-breakers, similar to what happens in civil society. Such was offered by the death of Jesus, his body broken and his blood poured out for us. This current simply swept away concerns about creation's groaning.

In the eleventh century a theologian named Anselm framed up a cogent version of this juridical idea that locked it into place in the Western imagination. Finished in 1098, his treatise entitled *Cur Deus Homo* employed the formidable power of sweet reason to explain beyond a doubt why it was necessary for God to become a human being and die in order to save the human race. (The Latin title translates literally, *Why God Human*; or traditionally, *Why the God-Man*; or colloquially, *Why God Became Human*). His argument, called the satisfaction theory, made it clear that Jesus' death paid back what was due to God because of the sins of human beings, allowing divine mercy to flow. I sometimes think Anselm may well be the most successful theologian of all time, for what other theory has dominated theology, preaching, and liturgical practice for almost a thousand years? Joseph Ratzinger, a critic of this treatise, comments on its influence in words that are beyond dispute: it "put a decisive stamp on the second millennium of western Christendom, which takes it for granted that Christ had to die on the cross in order to make good the infinite offense that had been committed and in this way to restore the order that had been violated."

I invite you to explore an alternative to Anselm's influential theology. Drawn from a wide range of biblical sources, this alternative envisions the living God actively accompanying the world in its evolutionary and historical breakthroughs, its human sinfulness, and its universal suffering and death, with overflowing mercy that endures forever. Such a theology of accompaniment is but one way to understand redemption that will support planetary solidarity and work for ecojustice. A reader may walk along, knowing that there are also other trails.

Anselm's treatise is written in a winning style. I decided to adopt his style in order to present this "I am with you to deliver you" view of redemption with verve and ease for the reader. Since I will be working out a different way of thinking about the subject, I will not follow the steps of his argument in sequence. But the pattern Anselm established will show itself in at least four ways.

Structurally, *Cur Deus Homo* is divided into two books, each with about two dozen short chapters that add up to a total of forty-seven. For the sake of clarity in the reader's mind, I employ a greater number of books with titles that indicate their content. Each book will have fewer chapters, however, so that the overall number of chapters remains about the same. Footnotes had not yet been invented in Anselm's day so I will use them sparingly, but will give proper recognition to a wealth of sources at the end.

In addition to adapting his structure, I have employed Anselm's dialogic way of proceeding. At the Benedictine monastery of Bec in northern France where Anselm lived as a monk and served as abbot, a younger monk named Boso was wont to engage him in intense theological discussions, pressing his own questions for understanding. It seems Boso was also always carrying people's questions to his abbot and encouraging him to write pieces that would shore up people's faith. When Anselm moved to England as Archbishop of Canterbury, he summoned Boso "to help with the writing." When he traveled on church business, their exchanges continued via written correspondence.

In composing *Cur Deus Homo*, Anselm took as a partner this younger monk Boso and cast his argument in the form of their conversations. He explained his rationale this way:

Since investigations, which are carried on by question and answer, are thus made more plain to many, and especially to less quick minds, and on that account are more gratifying, I will take to argue with me one of those persons who agitate this subject; one who among the rest impels me more earnestly to it; so that in this way Boso may question and Anselm reply. (I.1)

At first Boso asks the kind of questions a carefully constructed "anyone" would ask. Since he is well-versed in religious matters through religious formation and life in a monastery, however, he soon does more than question. When he senses Anselm is backing away from the promise to explain things clearly, the student chides the teacher, pushing him back on track. As the two become more engrossed in the subject, he slips out of his role as simple inquirer and makes insightful contributions of his own. Anselm encourages him, "Speak on, according to your pleasure" (I.2). The treatise grows into a genuinely mutual investigation.

This method works very well. Readers can easily follow the argument in *Cur Deus Homo*. While not judging the quickness of mind of any readers of the present book (!), I have summoned up an imaginary interlocutor, Clara by name, who will interrogate, encourage, and challenge me while making her own contributions. With a name derived from the Latin word for clear and bright, Clara is a composite of the multitude of inquiring, insightful women and men students whom I have had the privilege of teaching for over half a century. Her persona is rounded out by a wide array of interested persons who have discussed these matters with me at public lectures and in different settings of academy and church whether face to face or by paper or electronic communications. I pledge that like Anselm "I will try to the best of my ability . . . not so much to make plain what you inquire about, as to inquire with you" (I.2). So in this way, to paraphrase Anselm, Clara may question and Elizabeth reply.

Beyond structure and dialogue, I also join Anselm in hesitating before the intellectual magnitude of the task. He professed to be overwhelmed by the number of related issues that needed to be mastered in order to do justice to his theory. There is so much to discuss, but time and space do not permit. He demurs, "I think this subject can hardly, or not at all, be discussed between us comprehensively, since for this purpose there is required a knowledge of Power and Necessity and Will and certain other subjects which are so related to one another that none of them can be fully examined without the rest" (I.2).

Given the ocean of writing about salvation in the past thousand years, including analysis of Anselm's treatise itself, I find my task even more daunting than his. In no way can I do justice to the mountain of scholarship on the subject. Many times I have felt like a water bug skating over the surface of a pond, seeing the enormous wealth of material below but not stopping or diving down to examine it, instead gliding above the depths to forge ahead and reach the goal: to interpret the cross and resurrection of Jesus Christ so as to include the full flourishing of all creation. Here I take comfort from Boso who cut off Anselm's excuses about all the required background with the reminder that the abbot could speak briefly about each idea in its proper place as needed to move the argument along, "and what remains to be said we can put off to another time" (I.2).

Finally, with Anselm I share an interest in reaching a wide audience of believers, seekers, doubters, and critics who are interested in this question, people whom today we would call educated lay persons and clergy with inquiring minds. Boso is the one who tips the reader off to this purpose. Anselm expostulates on why he is disinclined to undertake this project. Besides the needed background as indicated above, the subject lies beyond human comprehension, "for all that a person can say or know, still deeper grounds of so great a truth remain hidden" (I.2). In addition, he worried that like sorry artists who paint images of Christ in unseemly ways, his own verbal portrait should end up similarly rough and vulgar. Boso shuts down the delaying tactics with a clear statement of purpose. "But, to cut you off from all excuses, you are not to fulfill this request of mine for the learned but for me, and those asking the same thing with me" (I.2). Others may write more elegantly and insightfully if they do not like what you are saying, but "for me and those asking the same thing with me," be encouraged to get started.

Along with Anselm and many others I see it as one of theology's responsibilities to venture new understandings of faith that can take root in the Christian community's worship, preaching, teaching, spirituality, and practice for the good of the world. In our day this includes the very concrete good of the whole community of life on earth. This book is not a complete or definitive work on cosmic redemption, but a treatise that hopes to engage people in conversation about a central Christian belief in God who saves and how this belief affects life and practice at our crucial ecological juncture. In the process, we may discover that the beauty and power of our faith tradition is deepened by being rooted more firmly in the ecological reality of the earth.

So let us begin. Our planet stands at the door and knocks.

*

A word about format. At the back of this book the Notes section gives the references for direct quotations, according to the Book and chapter where the quotation appears in my text; this section also explains what lies behind an asterisk when it appears in the text. The Works Consulted section lists the major books and articles I used to think through and craft each Book; these works also provide guidance for further reading for anyone interested in digging deeper. I generally used the New Revised Standard Version of the Bible, except where other translations lend themselves more readily to the creation-centered meaning of the original language.

Book I

Wrestling with Anselm

1.1 *The question on which Anselm's whole work rests*

Clara. All my life I've been taught that Jesus died on the cross to atone for our sins; thanks to his death God forgives and saves us. I know many people who have turned away from this teaching, disliking the picture it gives of God acting like an angry father who needs to be placated. For myself, I don't see what this teaching has to do with the imperative to care for the earth and all its creatures, about which I am terribly concerned. So I would really like to explore the meaning of the cross for all creation, to connect the dots between them, if there are any. Such understanding would make my faith more vibrant, maybe even more believable, and definitely better for the earth.

Elizabeth. You are asking that we seek the meaning of a central matter of faith, which I am glad to do. One of the classical descriptions of theology is "faith seeking understanding." This is a never-ending task, for as cultures change new questions arise, making fresh understandings necessary lest faith be discarded like some outdated fashion. The phrase "faith seeking understanding" was crafted by an early medieval theologian named Anselm, who himself never stopped searching for the meaning of what faith believed. We will start with one of his major works that is particularly germane to your concern. Written in the eleventh century, it sets out a hugely influential argument about the cross that lasts to this day. No doubt it lies behind what you were taught about Jesus' dying for our sins.

Clara. Is it possible to get hold of this work?

Elizabeth. The treatise is easily available online in several translations. To read it with benefit you need to keep a sharp eye on the main question, because along the way Anselm does digress into other interesting issues.

Clara. In that case, it would be good to begin by laying out what his main question is.

Elizabeth. Identifying this question is tremendously important. Repeated twice in the opening pages of the treatise, it provides a key to the way Anselm will unfold his theory about the cross. Just as a blueprint determines how a house will be constructed, his opening question governs the steps of his treatise's argument. Does this make sense?

Clara. Yes, the way an architect designs a structure governs what gets built as a result. A blueprint for a small house with one bedroom will yield perhaps a lovely dwelling but one not ordinarily suitable for multiple families to inhabit in peacetime. I can see that the way a question is phrased opens up certain possibilities and shuts down others.

Elizabeth. This is why it is crucial to attend to the precise question that structures Anselm's treatise. He rightly states that the whole work rests upon it. The question asks why it was necessary for Jesus to die in order for God to forgive human beings their sins.

Clara. So he was concerned about the meaning of the cross for the human race, not for the whole of creation.

Elizabeth. Exactly. The natural world simply did not enter into Anselm's question. In person and by letter, many people had earnestly requested him to address what Christ's death on the cross meant for their soul's salvation. Knowing that many believers were pondering this in their hearts, he framed the treatise's initial question in very deliberate words. He set out to inquire "for what cause or necessity God became a human being, and by his own death, as we believe and affirm, restored life to the world, when he might have done this by means of some other being, angelic or human, or merely by his will" (I.1).

Notice how this way of asking the question already sets certain ideas in place. It assumes that Christ's death, standing alone as a specific event, is the means of restoring life. It takes for granted (and this is key) that this death is necessary, the only unknown being "why." It declares that despite stray thoughts about salvation being accomplished by some other agent or even the omnipotent will of God, this blessing had to be accomplished only by the death of God-become-human. Writing in Latin, Anselm explains that this question gives the title to his treatise *Cur Deus Homo*, or Why a God-Human.

To paraphrase the question: why and with what necessity did God become a human being, and *die*, to save human beings, when this might have been done some other way? The very structure of the question lines up a particular set of arguments, as we will see, about sin and human frailty, the need for restitution after offense, Christ's sinlessness that made him free of the punishment of death, and the greatness of divine mercy. In sequence they march to a conclusion with brilliant, rigorous logic. The cross of Jesus Christ, who is the *Deus Homo* of the title, is necessary for human salvation. If this person had not died, human beings would still be estranged from God. Anselm has built this answer into the way he set up the question. Note that within the framework of this question it is just about impossible to pay any attention to cosmic redemption.

1.2   *How feudalism shaped the satisfaction theory of atonement*

Clara. What strikes me in Anselm's question is the emphasis on the cross being necessary for human salvation. Today, myself and many others knowledgeable about the earth are asking a different question. We appreciate how the earth functions to sustain life; we are worried about clean water, the atmosphere heating up, and species going extinct. What does the cross mean in view of our ecological crisis? Can it make us realize that the whole created world is an intrinsically valuable part of God's redeeming work? Obviously, this way of thinking already starts us down a different, more creation-oriented road.

Elizabeth. We will consider your questions, but first we need to linger with Anselm and come to grips with how his view took such strong root and became the prevailing understanding of the cross. To appreciate his guiding question you have to place Anselm in his own cultural context. By the eleventh century European society had shifted from the law of the Roman empire, wherever it had extended, to a feudal system of justice. In the absence of the central authority of national states, the authority of a local ruler grounded and safeguarded the order of a whole region. His word was law. Violations of the law were more than simply disobedience to a rule; they were an offense against the dignity and honor of the feudal overlord. The crucial point is that these insults had an impact on society. Disobedience to the lord's word created disorder in the social fabric, or as we might say today, disruptions to the common good. To restore order, the law-breaker either had to be punished or had to pay compensation to rectify the situation. In Anglo-Saxon regions a graduated system of fines was actually devised whereby the offender paid due recompense for his or her criminal offense. This payback, called satisfaction, restored the honor of the lord, which in turn returned society to a peaceful, orderly operation.

The pattern ran through all levels of society. The amount of satisfaction required corresponded to the social status of the offended party, so that if one insulted a milkmaid less was due than if one somehow offended the lady of the manor. But in either case the requirement to restore the social order by means of some payment was non-negotiable. By Anselm's time the practice of satisfaction had become an integral part of the powerful feudal structure.

Clara. How did this cultural situation affect Anselm's understanding of the cross?

Elizabeth. What Anselm did, which is what we all do, is bring reality as he knew it into his theological reflection. Transferring the political arrangements of his society to the relation between God and the world, he imagined the cosmos as one great feudal society. Its good order depended on respect for the honor of the Lord of the manor, shown by obedience to his word.

Watch how this works in defining key terms. What is sin? "To sin is nothing else than not to render God his due" (I.11). Whatever the substance of the offense by which one violates the divine will, to sin is to refuse to give the honor that is due to God as Lord of the universe. As in feudal society, this act has consequences beyond the individual. A sinner "disturbs the order and beauty of the universe, as relates to himself, though he cannot injure nor tarnish the power and majesty of God" (I.15).

This sets up a situation that requires either punishment or some kind of satisfaction: "Satisfaction or punishment must needs follow every sin" (I.15). The reasoning runs like this: "For as one who imperils another's safety does not do enough by merely restoring his safety, without making some compensation for the anguish incurred; so he who violates another's honor does not do enough by merely rendering honor again, but must, according to the injury done, make restoration in some way satisfactory to the person whom he has dishonored" (I.11).

Transferred from the civic context, what is the religious meaning of satisfaction? "Everyone who sins ought to pay back the honor of which he has robbed God; and this is the satisfaction which every sinner owes to God" (I.11). One must pay back for offenses. The alternative would be sheer contempt toward the Creator, and an orderly cosmos tipping into chaos.

Clara. I don't see why God can't just cancel the debt and forgive sinners without requiring satisfaction.

Elizabeth. Boso also raised this excellent objection. One would surely think so, given the gospel narratives. Dwell on this pivotal point for a moment. All four gospels depict how in his teaching and practice Jesus revealed a different, non-feudal picture of the way God deals with sin. Think of the parables of the shepherd going after his lost sheep and the woman searching for her lost coin, both rejoicing with their neighbors when they find the one who has strayed, no satisfaction needed. Remember the parable of the forgiving father who runs out to embrace the returning prodigal son, throwing a party to welcome him back, no payback required. Recall the paralytic who, after Jesus assured him that his sins were forgiven, took up his pallet and walked away, no atonement given. Call up the story of the Pharisee and the publican in the temple; when the publican prays, "God, be merciful to me, a sinner," he goes home justified, nothing more required. Keep in mind Luke's depiction of Jesus himself, forgiving his executioners as his life ebbed away, no satisfaction needed.

In reasoning about the necessity of the cross, however, Anselm extracts the cross from the ministry of Jesus and interprets it against the background of his own feudal context. There is no escape from the iron-bound rules based on feudal society that control how he figures that God interacts with the world. Be very careful here: it is not that God is subject to some other law beyond the divine will. But not to punish sin or require satisfaction would go contrary to the dignity of divine being itself. In Anselm's argument, it would go against the way God exists in Godself, with dire results. For one thing, it would erase the difference between the guilty and the innocent. For another, it would free sin from being subject to the justice of the law. Both of these would result in cosmic disorder. But most egregious of all, with regard to God's own self, not requiring satisfaction would violate divine honor.

Clara. It's kind of strange that a loving God would put personal honor above all else.

Elizabeth. Once Anselm transferred the dynamics of feudalism to the theological relation between God and the world, the concept of honor took a leading role. It was, after all, the linchpin that functioned to make an orderly civic life possible. We are not talking about some kind of egotistic self-regard but about a beneficent authority over all else that preserves things in their rightful place, humming along. The feudal lord's honor functioned as the foundation of civic order; so too God's honor functions as the foundation of the order and beauty of the universe. If one thinks of God in the image of a feudal overlord ruling the cosmos, then it would be an improper exercise of mercy, amounting to acting unjustly, for God to let the sinner go unpunished or to ignore the necessity of satisfaction. Such an exercise would be tantamount to God's acting contrary to divine being itself. This would allow sin to be somehow exempt from control; lawlessness would break out; unrest and uprisings would pervade the world. But "God leaves nothing uncontrolled in his kingdom" (I.20). Satisfaction is required because the creature has taken away the honor due the Creator. It must be restored or else evil will undermine the whole created order. Indeed, although divine freedom and compassion are infinite, they operate in a way consistent with God's honor around which the orderly world revolves.

Given this worldview, Anselm hammers home his argument and Boso backs off his objections:

> **Anselm**: Therefore God maintains nothing with more justice than the honor of his own dignity.
> **Boso**: I must agree with you.
> **Anselm**: Does it seem to you that he wholly preserves

it, if he allows himself to be so defrauded of it as that he should neither receive satisfaction nor punish the one defrauding him?

Boso: I dare not say so.

Anselm: Therefore the honor taken away must be repaid, or punishment must follow; otherwise, either God will not be just to himself, or he will be weak in respect to both parties; and this it is impious even to think of.

Boso: I think that nothing more reasonable can be said. (I.13)

1.3   *Grim dilemma, gracious solution*

Clara. Even if we grant this view of things, can't sinners repent and receive mercy? They can make acts of contrition and perform religious acts of sacrifice that can atone for their sin. In this way can't they restore God's honor and get the world back on an even keel?

Elizabeth. Two factors prevent what you suggest from having the desired effect. The first is that as creatures human beings already owe the One who created them all their love and prayer and sacrifice in every moment. Anselm criticizes your view with this challenge: "But what do you give to God by your obedience which is not owed him already, since he demands from you all that you are and have and can become?" (I.20). Thus once you have sinned, even living a perfect life does not render to divine honor that "extra" bit required to make up for the offense.

The second factor is, if possible, even more intimidating. Recall that in feudal practice the satisfaction owed is proportionate to the dignity of the person offended. When humans commit sin, they offend the Creator and Ruler of the universe, God, whose dignity is infinite. Therefore, the satisfaction they owe is also infinite. And who can pay that?

Clara. At this point, it seems that the happiness for which people were created is beyond reach. We have sinned and stand condemned to eternal suffering, and nothing we can do will help. This is an awfully grim dilemma.

Elizabeth. Yes. Like yourself Boso made the anguished observation that human beings are snared in a predicament that they cannot escape. It is a brilliantly constructed dilemma. By sinning, they have offended the honor of God. Thus they owe the Creator, who is greater than anything they can conceive, infinite satisfaction for their sin. As the ones who have sinned they alone must pay this price, not the angels. Yet humans are finite, and only someone who is infinite, namely God, can actually make infinite satisfaction.

Clara. If "none but God can make this satisfaction," as Anselm writes, and "none but human beings ought to" (II.6), we are truly doomed.

Elizabeth. But there is one way out of the dilemma. If God became a human being and made satisfaction for sin, this would be an infinite act as well as coming from the side of sinners. The demands of the dilemma would be met.

Clara. Isn't Anselm clever! The solution is Christ, fully human and fully divine. I feel Boso's relief when he exclaims, "Now blessed be God!"

Elizabeth. Here is the gracious solution to the dilemma, a solution that Anselm had in mind all along. Basing his argument squarely upon the teaching of the Council of Chalcedon (451 CE) about the identity of Jesus Christ, his set-up has shown how only someone who in one person is truly God and truly human can jump into the breach. Being human, Christ makes amends as a member of the race that owes satisfaction. Being divine, his payment of satisfaction is of infinite magnitude. The stage is now set for human beings to be redeemed and cosmic order to be restored.

Clara. There still remains the question of why it was necessary that Jesus had to die. I would think that one act of love, one prayer, one tear would be enough to render the required satisfaction, because each of these, being done by his person, is of infinite worth. *Elizabeth.* Like every other human being, Jesus owed obedience to God. His every thought, word, and deed had to be in accord with divine will and pleasure. Therefore, if he had just lived a life of perfect goodness, this would not have made satisfaction for human sin. There would be nothing *extra* to pay back for offense against divine honor.

There is one thing, however, that Jesus did not owe. It was common understanding at this time that death came into the world as a result of the sin of Adam and Eve; all their descendants bore this punishment. Because Jesus was sinless, he did not deserve to die. Of his own free will he chose to do so, "delivering himself up to death for God's honor" (II.11)? God did not demand this of him. Since no sin was found in him, he ought not to die. But he voluntarily went the extra mile. The honor of God receives due recompense and the order of the cosmos is restored.

Clara. The trouble with this is that we know today death existed in the world of biological life millions of years before human beings emerged. Death is an intrinsic part of the evolutionary process of life. Sin or no sin, there is death on this planet.

Elizabeth. True, this is another place where Anselm's argument loses its hold on the contemporary mind. But for the moment let the eleventh century exist with its own lights. Here is what they thought: by dying on the cross in his human nature shared with all other people, Christ gave what he did not owe. The satisfaction that resulted was infinite, superabundant, due to his divine nature. Since Christ himself had no need of this abundance, he wished it to be bestowed on the whole human family, his brothers and sisters, those for whose salvation he became incarnate in the first place. "What more proper than that, when he beholds so many of them weighed down by so heavy a debt, and wasting through poverty, in the depth of their miseries, he should remit the debt incurred by their sins, and give them what their transgressions had forfeited?" (II.19). By making satisfaction for their sin, by paying back what they owed, Christ's death on the cross atoned for sin and saved the human race, opening up the possibility of their eternal happiness.

1.4 How great and how just is God's compassion!

Elizabeth. The treatise's original question is resolved. Why did God become a human being and die to save us, when this could have been accomplished in some other way? The answer: to make satisfaction for sin, which offended the honor of the infinite God. In truth, contrary to the question's wording, there was no other way. The cross was necessary as payment for sin.

Clara. I detect a sincere pastoral purpose in Anselm's satisfaction theory. He wanted to gladden the hearts of those who had questions, comforting their spirits once they saw how unimaginably great is the mercy of God, who personally took on the debt that humans owed.

Elizabeth. Your observation explains why the treatise draws to a joyous close. Although the dilemma made us think we were doomed, the cross of Christ reveals that God's compassion is "incomparably above anything that can be conceived" (II.20).

Clara. This is indeed beautiful. Within the constraints he has set up, Anselm shows that God's mercy is greater than we could ever have imagined!

Elizabeth. What compassion can exceed these words to the sinner doomed to eternal torments and having no way of escape: "Take my only-begotten Son and make him an offering for yourself" (II.20)? Christ's death can remit any debt, since his payment was greater than all debt. The generosity and magnitude of this scheme of human salvation brings Anselm to his knees in grateful tears. God's mercy is beyond what anyone could have expected, or deserves.

When I read this treatise with students in graduate courses, almost everyone is intellectually and even existentially moved by the power of the argument about divine mercy. We get swept away by the logic and end up almost speechless before the magnitude of divine goodness. The problem, of course, is the assumption, flawed at the outset, that God's offended honor needs to be recompensed with some kind of satisfaction, so that the cross becomes necessary. Even when problematic, however, the strength and intensity of Anselm's search for understanding of the faith remains.

1.5   *The flight of the satisfaction theory through history*

Clara. Anselm has surely made the case, in terms coherent with his culture, that the cross is our salvation. I can see why the logic of his argument has given it such a hold on the Western religious imagination. Still, feudalism did not last. How did his theory survive in a non-feudal society?

Elizabeth. Every author knows that one cannot control how others read what one has written. The text goes off on a trajectory of its own, sometimes appreciated, sometimes not; sometimes beautifully understood, sometimes interpreted differently or even distorted into something contrary to the author's intent; sometimes revealed to carry unexpected treasure when read in light of a new question.

This has surely happened with Anselm's *Cur Deus Homo*, a classic in its own right. As social patterns of governance changed away from feudalism, the innovative satisfaction theory became detached from its original context. Rather than disappear, however, the theory gained in importance and, not without some adjustment, found its way to the center of a full-blown theological system focused on fall and redemption. One life raft for its survival was the growth of penitential practices already gaining widespread acceptance in the medieval church. The theory became entwined with individual sacramental confession with penance set by the priest, for which the logic of the satisfaction theory gave intelligent justification. Promoting a heavily sinful view of the world, the theory also helped grow a public penitential system whereby indulgences could apply the satisfaction won by Christ to the debt one would have to pay off in purgatory. Not incidentally, this served to enhance the institutional church's juridical power, which controlled the dispersal of the satisfaction paid on the cross, giving the theory an even stronger grasp on ecclesial life.

The theory also lasted by generating new patterns of spirituality that focused on the cross, inspiring profound personal devotion to the crucified Jesus: he died for my sins, I owe him my love. Annexing the imagery of cultic sacrifice, the Council of Trent wove the theory into its teaching on the Mass as a sacrifice that made present once again Christ's atoning death on the cross for the sins of the world. Liturgical prayers were written that made this idea explicit during the Mass itself. Sacramental theology of the Eucharist developed extended explanations that generations of seminarians had to master; in this way the theory shaped the meaning of the ordained priesthood. Meanwhile, in the hands of the Protestant reformers Martin Luther and John Calvin and their interpreters, the theory morphed into a version that saw Christ's death not simply as payment of satisfaction but as a punishment undergone for human sin: he died in our stead. The so-called theory of penal substitution was worked out in numerous theologies of redemption right through the twentieth century.

Each of these developments deserves a closer look, but must remain among those things we leave for another time. The main point is that the satisfaction theory's view of the necessity of Jesus' death for salvation became entrenched in preaching, teaching, and piety, maintaining its dominant position for almost a millennium.

Truth be told, the shadow it cast almost eclipsed other elements of the gospel. Ironically, one of the casualties was the mercy of God as Anselm had understood it. Succeeding centuries had a much diminished sense of free grace liberally poured out in Christ.

1.6   *Critical assessments of the satisfaction theory in our own day*

Clara. As someone who lives in another century, even in another millennium, in a different culture, in a church decades out from the Second Vatican Council, in a world with pressing issues of justice, peace, equality, religious pluralism, and ecological well-being, I find that the satisfaction theory, while possibly compelling on its own terms and in its own time, just doesn't sit right with my mind or my heart. How can we think our way out of it?

Elizabeth. Your question brings us to the point where wrestling critically with the satisfaction theory both on its own merits and in its thousand year trajectory leads to new possibilities for a more holistic understanding of salvation.

Going forward let us not forget several positive elements in Anselm's treatise that have enduring value. For one thing, in terms of form, it stands as a model of doing theology in dialogue with one's own culture. It clearly responded to people's desire to understand what they were believing in terms familiar to their particular moment of history. For another thing, in terms of content, its whole goal was to demonstrate the mercy of God. Despite its now outdated assumptions and its transmutations in the hands of later thinkers, the satisfaction theory did not lose sight of the "for us," which in scripture is woven into the meaning of the cross. Thirdly, the treatise never lost sight of the heavy reality of sin. There is massive wrongness in the world, done by persons and pervasive in social systems, that wreaks havoc on the lives of human beings and other creatures. Anselm's cautionary words to Boso undercut any blithe theology of redemption: "You have not yet weighed the gravity of sin" (I.21). Christian hope finds its genuine meaning only in the midst of this appalling turmoil.

Clara. On balance, though, the scales today tip more heavily toward the problematic side of the theory, don't they?

Elizabeth. Yes they do. Consider the following criticisms arising from the standpoint of today's religious and moral sensibilities. They are the subject of vigorous contemporary discussion. A first criticism is that this theory presents a *disastrous image of God.* We have seen what Anselm meant to communicate about the mercy of God for a sin-laden world, but in the hands of less-gifted thinkers the nuances were lost. The satisfaction theory led to the awful idea of a sadistic God concerned with his own honor who becomes offended by sin and whose anger needs to be placated by the precious blood of his Son. Only a generation later Abelard objected, "how cruel and wicked it seems that anyone should demand the blood of an innocent person as the price for anything... still less that God should consider the death of his Son so agreeable that by it he should be reconciled to the whole world." In the thirteenth century Aquinas argued against Anselm that Jesus' death was *not* necessary but fitting, for we are saved not by some juridical exchange but by the greatness of Christ's love. In the same time period Duns Scotus objected, "What kind of God is this, in the image of a prince whose personal honor is the supreme law?"

Despite these and other theological criticisms, popular preaching nevertheless presented the necessity of the cross in such a way that it flat-out compromised the overflowing mercy of God. The development is epitomized in the famous sermon entitled "Sinners in the Hands of an Angry God," delivered by the colonial preacher Jonathan Edwards working in eighteenth-century New England. Christ appears as a victim of divine justice, crucified to satisfy the inscrutable demands of a vindictive God.

The hold that this interpretation of the cross, whether conscious or unconscious, continues to have on the Christian mind is pervasive. In the twentieth century Joseph Ratzinger took note of the vulgarized form of the satisfaction theory that shapes Western Christianity's view of redemption, finding it cruel, mechanical, and less and less feasible. The satisfaction theory, he wrote critically, has had this effect:

> [I]t looks as if the cross is to be understood as part of a mechanism of injured and restored right. It is the form, so it seems, in which the infinitely offended righteousness of God was propitiated by means of an infinite expiation. . . . Many devotional texts actually force one to think that Christian faith in the cross imagines a God whose unrelenting righteousness demanded a human sacrifice, the sacrifice of his own Son, and one turns away in horror from a righteousness whose sinister wrath makes the message of love incredible.

In sum, the satisfaction theory makes God morally repulsive.

Clara. My friend's grandmother in a nursing home heard the priest preach that God the Father so loved the world he sent his only Son to die for our sins. From her wheelchair she called out, "Strange family." Though I laughed when I heard the story, it made me think: even though we hear that it is love that sent the Son to the cross, it still ends up that God gets his pound of flesh, which does not sound like love at all.

Elizabeth. Anyone who understands love intuits the mistake preachers make when they say God, when offended, needs to be appeased by someone's death. This goes against the best instincts of the human experience of love, and sets an appalling example.

Clara. I have another reaction. I do not want to be saved at the price of someone else's suffering.

Elizabeth. In view of contemporary notions of virtue, a God who would require such a death seems morally primitive. Imagine planning such a thing as the agonizing death of an innocent person, or wanting or needing such a thing. How could anyone love and worship such a God? The satisfaction theory has eclipsed the God of unfathomable mercy in whom Jesus believed and about whom he fashioned parables and prayers.

Clara. But, in fairness, the theory did provide pastoral comfort for folk who were aware of human sinfulness, especially their own. The theory showed them that God had provided a way out of the grim dilemma.

Elizabeth. You are right about that pastoral issue. It is never far from my own mind. But what if the dilemma in Anselm's treatise were a false dilemma? Try to imagine this: what if God neither needed nor wanted the cross in order to save the world from sin? Imagine this another way: what if divine mercy pre-dated the cross? Or again: what if God did not want the crucifixion to happen but, when human sin had done its violent worst, met the disaster with the creative power of life in the resurrection? Unhitching divine mercy from the necessity of the cross does not necessarily leave people in their sin, but opens a different way to re-establish relationship with God.

Clara. Beyond the problem of depicting a sinister God, doesn't the satisfaction theory compromise divine freedom?

Elizabeth. It does seem to set a control on the way God must behave, compelling divine action in accord with the law that demands satisfaction for sin. But in truth the living God is under no such restraint, neither from the created order nor from the uncreated divine honor that supposedly grounds the order of the universe. Here is where the cultural working of feudalism becomes downright counterproductive to good theology today. Imagine this: under the satisfaction theory, the forgiving father in Jesus' parable would be obliged to tell the prodigal son that he had to work off his debt in the fields before rejoining the household. Instead we see an embrace, new clothes, a ring, a feast! The merciful love of God is not so constrained.

Clara. Against its own intentions, the satisfaction theory set off a trajectory of ideas and practices about an offended God whom sinners must appease, giving us a disastrous image of God. Detached from its later history, just as a theory on its own, what other criticisms does it draw today?

Elizabeth. To put it bluntly, the theory totally fails in view of the New Testament's teaching about salvation. Why? It completely omits the resurrection, and leaves out the entire gospel narrative of the ministry of Jesus. Thus, a second criticism—*resurrection is gone missing.* The renewal of biblical scholarship in our day has brought to light the stunning realization that the satisfaction theory focuses so strongly on the death of Jesus that it leaves out the resurrection. *Not once* does *Cur Deus Homo* even mention the creative action of God raising Jesus from the dead, which changes everything.

Clara. I am reminded of one of the apostle Paul's claims that "if Christ has not been raised, then our proclamation is in vain and your faith is in vain. . . . If Christ has not been raised, your faith is futile and you are still in your sins" (1 Cor 15:14, 17). But for Anselm, if Christ had not died then we are still in our sins. What a contrast.

Elizabeth. While the cross certainly occupied the minds and hearts of the early disciples, they could not think of it apart from the resurrection, which shed light retroactively on the meaning of this death. God raised Jesus from the dead: divine Love who created the universe now acted to create a new future for the one unjustly executed. This great paschal movement from death to life unleashed a new Spirit into history, which formed them into a new community to follow Jesus' way. In the presence of Jesus, the Crucified One who is now the Living One, his disciples proclaimed the good news that evil does not have the last word. Hope is born for a future for all others who have come to grief, for all the defeated and the dead, even as crosses keep on being set up in history. Talk about salvation!

The whole renewal of the Catholic liturgy since the mid-twentieth century, including the triduum of Holy Week with its extraordinary Easter vigil, focuses on the resurrection of the crucified as the heart of the good news. The satisfaction theory gives no support for this renewal. Basically, it truncates the good news of the gospel.

In addition to resurrection, *ministry is also gone missing*. The satisfaction theory overlooks the ministry of Jesus, which brought people joyful foretastes of salvation during his own lifetime. The gospels present these stories, but Anselm's argument completely omits them as if they had nothing to do with salvation coming from God in Jesus.

Clara. Jesus used the very word "salvation" when Zacchaeus came down from the sycamore tree and, moved by the grace of encounter, decided to become an honest tax collector. "Today salvation has come to this house," Jesus declared (Lk 19:9). I guess this means that besides forgiveness of sin, salvation also includes restoring people to right relations in their dealings with God and one another in the community.

Elizabeth. Jesus' preaching of the coming reign of God, by turns joyful and challenging, refreshed people's social situations as well as their relationship to God. His healings, exorcisms, inclusive table fellowship, and partisanship for marginalized people, interpreted by his preaching, already offered an anticipation of the world in which God will reign, a world without tears. Violent death was the price Jesus paid for this prophetic ministry, to which he was faithful with a tenacity that would not quit. Historically it was neither foreordained nor accidental but was carried out by the power of empire to which his movement posed a threat. He suffered for the way he loved God and neighbor, not because he needed to pay a debt to divine honor.

The very act of separating out the death of Jesus and giving it a significance independent from ministry and resurrection had the unfortunate effect of domesticating the cross. What got lost was the importance of the historical events that made Jesus' death a suffering through others and for others because of his critical preaching and radical behavior. What also got lost was how the resurrection put God's seal of approval on not just anyone but on precisely this crucified prophet and what he had done, whose way became a path of discipleship others could follow to find union with God. Detached from its context, the suffering and death of the cross became simply a necessary payment of satisfaction without which forgiveness is impossible. This is about as far from the biblical witness as you can get.

A significant fourth criticism is that Anselm's theory *sacralizes violence.* While the previous two criticisms uncover major weaknesses in the satisfaction theory in itself, the following three, like the first, address problems that have accrued as the theory marched its dominant way across the centuries.

Clara. If we are saved by this bloody death, then killing is somehow okay.

Elizabeth. By turning the historically unjust execution of Jesus into some kind of necessary good, the theory has offered a subtle but real religious justification for the evil of violence. Given the way divine honor is recompensed, it sets up violence as divinely sanctioned. Politically this translates into a blessing on the use of force, specifically the use of aggressive force by powerful people. The thinking runs this way: God used violence for a good purpose, so why shouldn't we? Such reasoning turns a manifest evil, the torture and execution of an innocent person, into a "good" that continues to harm other people. In a word, the atonement paradigm sanctifies violence.

Clara. This sticks in my throat. And it seems to make a mockery of Jesus Christ as a peacemaker who blessed the merciful and the peacemakers and taught a way of active non-violent love even of enemies.

Elizabeth. This criticism has become more acute in the aftermath of the murderous Nazi holocaust of the Jews, or Shoah. For centuries the libel that the Jews were responsible for Christ's death gave virulent strength to persecution of this people; the cross functioned as a cornerstone of anti-Semitism. By tying the necessity of this death into theology and church practice, the satisfaction theory did not lessen but added to the complicity of the cross in lethal anti-Judaism.

Clara. This is so tragically ironic. As a Jew himself Jesus would have been in the camps. It is hard to think beyond this horror.

Elizabeth. Can you think of a fifth negative consequence?

Clara. It seems to me that a *morbid spirituality* results. I think 5⟩
this theory promotes a spirituality that glorifies suffering as something of value, making us think that suffering, more than joy, is the best avenue to God. It makes enduring pain, even if inflicted unjustly, into an ascetic ideal that should be imitated. No one I know is attracted by this ideal.

Elizabeth. By leaving out the resurrection and ministry, the satisfaction theory's blinkered focus on the cross led to the idea that death was the very purpose of Jesus' life. He came to die. The script was already written before he stepped onto the world stage. Obviously, this idea robs Jesus of his human freedom, making his fidelity that led to the cross of little significance. But as you say, it also paints a positive glow around suffering.

Theology and spirituality in our day have by and large shifted to a more positive view of goodly human values and life on earth. But for centuries, and you can trace this in preaching and spiritual writing up through the twentieth century, suffering as such took on a haze of positive theological significance. The church became sin-obsessed; preaching emphasized guilt; life on earth was presented as a "valley of tears"; good people accepted suffering as divinely willed; a mystical, even masochistic dolorism colored the following of Christ.

Clara. I have heard homilies where the suffering of Jesus gets connected with obedience. For example, he had to go to Jerusalem to fulfill his Father's will that he should suffer and die. We are supposed to imitate him in his obedience. You already covered the problem of the disastrous image of a God who wills suffering to compensate for offended divine honor. But this makes it worse. I have to say that obedience to a male authority figure is not a big value in my life, let alone obedience to a male authority that wills my suffering. As a spiritual path, this is downright toxic.

Elizabeth. A sixth criticism is the introduction of an *ethic of submission in the face of injustice.* Take away the resurrection and the public ministry of Jesus, bring forth suffering, perversely, as a good in itself, and the cumulative effect is to allow actual injustice on the earth to continue without challenge. Edward Schillebeeckx offers a sharp insight about how this happened. When theology pondered the cross as a free-standing event, suffering became a way of avenging God's honor to our benefit, instead of the price Jesus paid for fidelity to his ministry. It appeared that God was pleased with the evil of killing an innocent person. God's act of overturning the judgment of the authorities by raising Jesus from the dead disappeared from view. In these ways the satisfaction theory "tamed" the critical force of the crucifixion, making it into a tool that integrates wrongful suffering into the way things necessarily are. While this may not be the exact significance that Anselm gave to his theory, it is the way it was preached and written about in many spiritual books. People were encouraged to suffer and endure injustice without resistance rather than challenge existing wrongful circumstances. Both Catholic and Reformation traditions have walked down this path.

Clara. Could you give some examples of this contemporary critique that would help us come to grips with its depth and reach?

Elizabeth. Theologies done in the light of the suffering of African American people, of the massive poverty of poor people in Latin America, and of women subordinated by gender, together make a convincing case.

The experience of slavery coupled with the legacy of racism in the United States opens a sharp angle of vision on the uses of the cross. Enslaved Africans were taught it was the will of God that they obey their "owners." If that entailed suffering, as it inevitably did, then the crucified Jesus should be their model. To the contrary, the music of the spirituals shows that enslaved people took comfort and strength from the cross because Jesus stood with them in their abject suffering, and through him the opaque power of God would win out. The cross as preached by white pastors, however, did not feed their resistance and survival strategies. Traditional atonement theory glorified suffering and was useless as leverage against oppression.

In the Jim Crow era, making the parallel with the cross all too real, mobs of God-fearing white Christians lynched over four thousand African Americans, hanging them from a tree. "Cursed is everyone who hangs on a tree," writes Paul of the crucifixion, citing the ancient law (Gal 3:13, citing Deut 21:23). Placing this curse in an American context, James Cone strips the cross of any ability to sanctify suffering; it was nothing less than a first-century lynching. In the United States Christ's suffering was re-enacted in the blood-soaked history of African Americans. None of that death is salvific. "What is redemptive is the faith that God snatches victory out of defeat, life out of death, and hope out of despair, as revealed in the biblical and black proclamation of Jesus' resurrection." Not silent suffering but political resistance to race murder is what the cross calls for. Only such active repentance can redeem the soul of America.

In view of African American women's historic experience of surrogacy, Delores William mounts a sharp criticism of the belief that Jesus took human sin upon himself and died in our place. Enslaved black women took the place of white women in doing domestic work, raising children, satisfying the sexual needs of their masters, and working in the fields. Such coerced surrogacy was oppression pure and simple, causing the death of personal identity. To take this despicable practice and make it a means of redemption distorts the very meaning of justice. Redemption "can have nothing to do with any kind of surrogate or substitute role Jesus was reputed to have played in a bloody act that supposedly gained victory over sin." Such an idea speaks no word of salvation to black women but encourages them to accept exploitation.

Clara. Connecting what I've learned in history classes with this subject, I'm realizing that the kind of Christianity that Portuguese and Spanish *conquistadores* brought to Latin America in the sixteenth century was steeped in the satisfaction theory, wasn't it?

Elizabeth. Indeed it was. They carried across the Atlantic a theology centered on the symbol of the suffering Christ crucified for our sins. As liberation theologians have shown, this image functioned to inculcate passivity in indigenous peoples. Enduring oppressive suffering, they could be pleasing to God if like Christ they accepted it obediently and did not open their mouths. Submission to authority became a religious ideal; obeying the colonial governor and the bishop was a means of obeying God. To protest or resist was to depart from the holy path walked by Christ. But if one accepted the sufferings of this life in the manner of the crucified Jesus who obediently submitted to a violent death, one would qualify for an eternal reward. Abetted by this theology, a small number of elites prospered while multitudes endured grinding poverty along with the violence necessary to maintain it through the generations. The crucified Christ functioned as a tool used to create a "crucified people," in Ignacio Ellacuría's powerful metaphor.

Preaching the gospel to millions of poor people suffering from systemic economic injustice, contemporary liberation theologians in base ecclesial communities have interpreted the following of the Jesus of the gospels to mean active engagement for justice. As happened to Jesus, such a following with all the love of one's heart might well lead to death; Archbishop Oscar Romero is a beloved example. But death is not the goal of discipleship. In company with Jesus, the community acts for justice with the hope that God will bring good out of evil; each small success gives a foothold to redeeming grace in the ongoing transformation of the world.

Clara. While women belong to all races, ethnic groups, and economic classes, their critique of the satisfaction theory also arises from their gendered experience, right?

Elizabeth. Yes. Feminist theologians have criticized the debilitating psychological effects fostered particularly on women by the satisfaction theory's interpretation of the cross. In a strange way the innocent Christ who suffered willingly on behalf of others has traditionally been held up as a model for women in a way different from men. It is women who are supposed to serve silently, obediently, without question, in imitation of the Crucified One. Such glorification of passivity undermines the agency that rightly belongs to women as adult human beings, all the while giving traditional expectations of women and their gendered roles in church and society a powerful divine gloss.

This kind of theology can prove intensely dangerous when domestic situations turn abusive, since holding up passive submission to victimization as a virtue undermines women's rightful ability to protect themselves from violent, battering partners. In this vein women have also critiqued the satisfaction theory for the kind of parent-child relationship it seems to portray. A psychological pattern of needing to placate an angry parent, of buying love and forgiveness through sacrifice, is debilitating to healthy child development. Furthermore, the notion of a father who needs the death of a son is abhorrent, no matter what benefit might accrue to others. Salvation is no excuse for child abuse on a cosmic scale. What is needed today, as Rita Nakashima Brock eloquently argues, is a "feminist redemption of Christ."

Clara. I think many people are still coming to grips with this critique. Turning Jesus into a passive victim of violence in some

kind of beneficial transaction with God has such hurtful consequences for our own ethical choices in the personal and political sphere. It really does cut the nerve of resistance. In imitation
of Christ, why would anyone try to eliminate unjust suffering? I
have to say, though, that I don't think Anselm had any intention of
depicting God as a child abuser.

Elizabeth. Of course not. But given its history of collusion
with oppressors by inculcating passivity, his theory has thwarted
self-determination, action on behalf of justice, liberation, and the
struggle for wholeness on many fronts.

Clara. Does every use of the cross apart from the ministry
and resurrection come in for contemporary criticism?

Elizabeth. Over time Latin American peoples created images
of the crucified Christ that were graphic in their portrayal of gro-
tesque suffering. In prayer and processions, they found and continue to find comfort in the solidarity the Lord of heaven and
earth had with their own egregious pain. The same intuition can
be found in the spirituals of enslaved African people in the Amer-
icas, which sing passionately of how Jesus is with them in their
struggles, knows what they are suffering, and gives them strength
and hope for freedom. Theology today finds deep wisdom in these
uses of the cross by the faith of the people, while deploring the
circumstances that make them necessary.

A seventh criticism highly relevant today is the *ecological
silence* maintained by Anselm. Given its focus on human sin and
the need to restore divine honor, the satisfaction theory obviously
neglects God's salvific presence in the rest of creation. It assumes a
view of the natural world as merely a stage on which the important
drama of human salvation is played out. Thus it fails to build up
faith convictions that lead to ecological commitments.

By contrast, as we will see, biblical themes of the community
of creation, God's covenant with all creatures of flesh on the earth,

incarnation, resurrection, and hope for a renewed heaven and earth where justice dwells open up a tremendous vision of salvation not only for humans but for all creatures who are other-than-human and the ecological niches in which they dwell and interact.

Clara. After this review of contemporary criticism it makes more sense to me why the satisfaction theory, for all its intent to argue for mercy, does not resonate with my religious experience. Each of these critiques on its own is compelling. Taken together, they are staggering. I can see why Mark Heim suggests that the cross should carry a label: "this religious image may be harmful to your health."

Where do we go from here?

Elizabeth. With respect for what Anselm accomplished according to his own lights—and doesn't every era, including our own, have its blind spots—we need to be clear that the satisfaction theory is not only inadequate but, frankly, erroneous. The mercy of God does not need the death of Jesus. Satisfaction is not due before sin can be forgiven. The death of Jesus is not necessary for salvation. Furthermore, the theory omits the bulk of gospel testimony about Jesus' ministry and resurrection. It has had deleterious effects on ecclesial practice and personal spirituality, undermined an ethic of social justice and peace, and ignored the broader community of creation.

How shall we begin to think of salvation in a different paradigm? How can we interpret the core connection between cross and salvation in a way that spells good news not only for sinful, struggling, dying human beings but for the whole community of life evolving on this planet? Humans are but one species, after all, although a key one, distinctive yet embedded historically and biologically in form and function within the broader community of life. What construal will do justice to God's redeeming care for the whole world?

1.7 *The question on which this whole work rests*

Elizabeth. For Anselm, if Jesus had not died, the world would still be estranged from God. There are, however, other ways of framing the question, which like a changed blueprint will lead to a different understanding and practice.

Today's growing ecological awareness of the world around us, both its wonder and fragility, presses us in a new direction, one that includes the human need for salvation within the wider groaning of all creation. The horizon of creation extends from the gorgeous galaxies expanding in time and deep space that we cannot even see, to planet Earth's ecosystems with millions of species of plants and animals evolving in interaction with land, water, and air. *Homo sapiens* is one of these species, capable of enormous cultural creativity and life-destroying violence. First we must ask: does all of this seething, beautiful life, among which are animals living satisfying lives, mean anything to the living God, Creator of heaven and earth?

John Muir, the nineteenth-century American naturalist, answered this question with a poignant story. Once when Muir was hiking in the Yosemite wilderness, he came upon a dead bear. He stopped to reflect on this creature's dignity: here was an animal with warm blood and a heart that pumped like ours, who rejoiced to feel the warm sun on his fur, for whom a good day was finding a bush filled with berries. Later he wrote a bitter entry in his journal, criticizing the religious folk he knew who made no room in their faith for such noble creatures. They think they are the only ones with souls, he complained, the only ones for whom heaven is reserved. To the contrary, he wrote, "God's charity is broad enough for bears."

If Muir is right, and I think he is, then all creatures are recipients of divine love. This love is not simply a generic benevolence but has the character of redeeming care for each individual creature and for species as a whole in their ecosystems. As with their origin that is from God, so too with their goal that is in God. The natural world in its evolutionary living and dying is destined for what scripture describes as a promised new heaven and new earth. Human beings are included as part of the whole community of creation. For Christian theology, the specific focus of seeking understanding about this matter gravitates toward Jesus Christ. We come then to the question on which this whole work rests, a question that is as rife with assumptions as is Anselm's and every other theology of salvation. The question is this: How can the life, death, and resurrection of Jesus Christ be understood as good news for the whole created world, including human beings, to the praise of God and to practical and critical effect?

Clara. For the curious mind, the gift of a new question is wonderful thing. The idea that the whole cosmos, the sun, the moon, and the stars, and the living world of animals and plants might be saved along with human beings is definitely different. Some might say that it isn't even all that important, although lovers of the earth, such as those who breathe a Celtic or Franciscan or Wesleyan spirituality, have always held it dear. How shall we proceed?

Elizabeth. I will not try to refute Anselm's argument point for point, nor to tweak it to make room for ecological interest. The hold that his theory in all its variations has on the deep-down Christian imagination is too powerful. Furthermore, the presence of the wide, evolving cosmos calls for a genuinely new paradigm, different from an anthropocentric concern with human sin in the context of feudal obligations. We need to turn the page on the satisfaction theory and allow it to take a well-deserved rest.

Given the rich pluralism present in scripture and the historical tradition as well as in contemporary methods of theology, there is no single way to arrive at an ecological understanding of salvation. In truth, the terrain has hardly been ploughed. One needs to figure out a line of reasoning that will be convincing to contemporary minds as well as faithful to what the church has believed and passed on.

Having tested a number of approaches, I propose to start with the biblical idea that the living God who creates the world is also the world's Redeemer and Savior, merciful toward all creatures. This belief, at once comforting and awe-inspiring, is found in the Jewish scriptures that Christians revere as part of their own Bible, which we might call the First Testament or the Christian Old Testament. It cannot be emphasized enough that the creating, redeeming Holy One of Israel is the God whom Jesus of Nazareth believed in, about whom he told stories, whose coming reign he preached, whom he called *abba*/father, and whose compassion his life story revealed in a compelling way. It is the same God. Without the Jewish scriptures and the people of Israel who produced them, the story of Jesus and the salvation which the community that believes in him announces, would make no religious sense.

We begin, then, with a prophet.

Book II

The Creating God Who Saves

*2.1   The historical context of Second Isaiah:
exile and release from captivity*

Elizabeth. "Comfort!" This astounding word, uttered through the oracle of a prophet, channels God's desire to save: "Give comfort to my people" (Isa 40:1).

From many rich biblical points of entry, I am making a wager that a close reading of the scroll of the anonymous prophet known as Second Isaiah will jumpstart our thinking about salvation in a very different direction from Anselm's satisfaction theory and its many variations. The scroll of this author comprises chapters 40–55 of the book of Isaiah as currently printed in the Bible. Proclaiming hope to a desperate people, the writing is magnificent, poetic, overflowing with beauty and assurance. Its basic message: have hope, because the infinitely good God who created heaven and earth is on the move to redeem you.

Clara. Why do you call this author Second Isaiah?

Elizabeth. Biblical scholars have figured out that the long book of Isaiah is most likely a compilation of the work of at least two and probably three different authors stitched together in sequence. Evidence comes not only internally, from analysis of their dissimilar literary styles, but also externally, from the different historical periods in which they wrote. Their chapters name different leaders and describe very different historical circumstances. Three sets of leaders, three time frames, three authors!

Clara. What situation prompted Second Isaiah to compose his work?

Elizabeth. In the sixth century BCE the Jewish people suffered a calamity of huge proportions. The Babylonian armies (from present-day Iraq), invaded the southern kingdom of Judah, the sole remaining functioning state of the people of ancient Israel. In a series of attacks they captured the capital city, Jerusalem, burned its walls and gates to the ground, ruined its buildings, and razed the great temple built by Solomon. The city was left uninhabitable. In successive waves they also rounded up large numbers of people, starting with the Jewish king and including his royal family and court, professional warriors, skilled workers, teachers, priests, and other leaders, and deported them to Babylon. Not everyone was taken away; estimates are that about 30 percent of the population, the poorest of the land, remained behind to till the devastated soil. But with the monarchy ended, the temple non-functioning, the cities wrecked, and the majority of people gone, for all intents and purposes the people of Israel ceased to exist as a nation.

Like captives and refugees of every age, the Jewish exiles found themselves trying to survive in a foreign land, yearning for home. This is the setting for Psalm 137, a lament that begins, "By the rivers of Babylon we sat and wept when we remembered Zion." Though goaded by their captors, the exiles hung up their harps on the willows and would not make music: "How could we sing a song of our God in a foreign land?" Memories of their homeland lying in ruins and their culture destroyed colored every day with sorrow. Unable to practice their own religion in the accustomed manner, living in and around the magnificence of a wealthy foreign city with its gardens, estates, canals, and stepped temples, the exiles' experience of loss and displacement also placed their faith in acute jeopardy. The Babylonian gods appeared stronger than Israel's own Holy One. The temptation to idolatry was strong.

Second Isaiah wrote near the end of this period of exile, which we know in retrospect lasted about half a century from 587 to 538 BCE. Now hope was in the air. The stronger Persian empire to the east was on the move; their armies would soon march against the Babylonians and no doubt defeat them. Given the Persian king Cyrus's track record of respect for conquered peoples, hope was rising among the exiles that his victory over their captors would allow them to return to their own homeland, there to rebuild Jerusalem and its temple under a central Persian administration. Second Isaiah's work is exuberant with expectation, barely able to contain its joy that exile might soon be over. He interpreted this as a new exodus. As in days of old when the Hebrews fled slavery in Egypt, liberation was in the air.

Clara. We read Second Isaiah's scroll very frequently during Advent, right? I always love the way it begins with the unexpected, almost unbearably tender word, "Comfort."

Elizabeth. The prophet utters that word as an oracle, channeling God's intent: "Comfort, O comfort my people, says your God" (40:1). Speak of comfort to the people, for this wretched situation is coming to an end. Abraham Heschel captured the significance of that opening line with his comment, "To comfort is to throw a glimmer of meaning into a cave of wretchedness." And surely Second Isaiah did so. To people weighed down by fear, weariness, grief, exhaustion, his scroll just shouts glad tidings. Look up! God is doing a new thing! The Holy One who powerfully created the world, marking off the heavens and weighing the mountains, and who at the same time acts like a tender shepherd feeding the flock, carrying frightened lambs in his bosom, and gently leading the mother sheep: this same holy God is coming to save you. Exile is ending. You are going home.

Clara. Prepare ye the way of the Lord!

Elizabeth. Exactly. Yet not everyone was comforted. Just as in an earlier moment of Israel's history some people freed from slavery yearned to go back to Egypt during their hungry trek through the wilderness, so too some exiles preferred their new surroundings. Empire has its seductive benefits. Not everyone wanted to return.

Clara. Human nature, I suppose. But can we pursue the message? In this fraught moment poised between captivity and freedom, the word of God bent on redeeming a defeated community bursts forth like a geyser from the hot depths of the earth. So that we may read with intelligence as well as heart, what are the precise meanings of the word "God" in this scroll, and what is the meaning of "redeem"?

2.2   YHWH the Redeemer of Israel

Elizabeth. Your query requires a bit of linguistic digging that will yield important insights. Basically, Second Isaiah uses two Hebrew words that refer to God, namely, El and YHWH. They bear distinctly different resonances.

First, El. This is the Hebrew form of the common word for deity in Semitic languages, which is *el* or *eloah*; one can see a cognate in the Islamic name for God, Allah. In the Bible El designates God in a general sense as the Almighty, the Most High, the Holy One, the Wholly Other. Standing alone the term appears some 238 times in biblical texts; in the compound form Elohim it appears some 2,600 times.

Clara. How do scholars translate El into the English language today?

Elizabeth. Simply as God. Starting in the third century BCE, Jewish scholars worked to translate the Hebrew text of their scriptures into the more broadly used Greek language to serve the needs of Jews living in the wider Mediterranean world. Known as the Septuagint, from the legendary seventy scholars who did the work, this version translates El with the Greek word *theos*, meaning God. Most English translations today take their clue from the Septuagint and render El with the word God.

Clara. What about YHWH?

Elizabeth. Far from a generic name for God, this is the cherished personal name of the God of Israel, a special name rooted in a history of liberation. It identifies God as the One who led enslaved Israelites out of Egypt to freedom.

Centuries before Second Isaiah wrote during the captivity in Babylon, oral and written traditions told of another captivity in Egypt where the numerous descendants of Abraham and Sarah were being worked to death as slaves. The exodus refers to their escape under the leadership of the siblings Moses, Aaron, and Miriam, followed by a covenant made with God in the Sinai wilderness and return to their ancestral land. To this day this move into freedom is at the center of Jewish imagination and piety, recounted in teaching and liturgy, remembered in daily prayers, taught to children, and celebrated annually around the family table at the spring feast of Passover.

The divine name YHWH came into being in connection with this event. To catch its significance, attend to how it first appears in the Bible. While shepherding a flock of sheep, Moses had an encounter with the Jewish ancestral God, the God of Abraham, Isaac, and Jacob, who was speaking to him from a burning bush. What he heard was a powerful description of God's self-involvement in trouble. The voice from the fire said: "I have seen the misery of my people who are in Egypt; I have heard their cry because of their taskmasters; indeed, I know well what they are suffering; therefore I have come down to deliver them" (Ex 3:7–8).

Biblical scholars point out that the word "know" in this text is the same Hebrew verb used for the start of the human family: "Now Adam knew his wife Eve, and she conceived and bore Cain" (Gen 4:1); some contemporary translations read "Adam made love to his wife Eve, and she became pregnant and gave birth." Obviously, "to know" in this sense is more than a cognitive exercise. It is an experiential, participating, even physical way of understanding.

Note the powerful sequence of verbs. This God of Sarah, Rebecca, Leah, and Rachel (we need to bring in the ancestral women) sees, hears, and grasps what people are suffering, and comes to liberate them. As is characteristic of God's action elsewhere, divine compassion works through human agency: "So come, I will send you to Pharaoh" (Ex 3:10).

The game of liberation is afoot. When Moses asks what name he should use for this God, the answer is mysterious: "Thus you shall say to the Israelites, I AM has sent me to you" (Ex 3:14). In Hebrew the term I AM, rendered YHWH or Yahweh in anglicized letters, comes from an archaic form of the verb "to be." It is a mysterious name. It can be translated "I am," or "I am who I am," or "I will be who I will be," or some variation of "I cause to be," or "I make exist," or "I make happen." For the Israelites, as for all peoples of that time, existence was an affair of community, of being with others, of being there concretely in action. Thus some scholars suggest the name actually means "I shall be there, as who I am, shall I be there with you." This four-lettered name, called the Tetragrammaton, is so sacred that out of reverence later Jewish tradition refuses even to pronounce it.

Clara. How does this name YHWH translate into the English language today?

Elizabeth. The Septuagint chose to translate it into Greek with the word *kyrios*, which in everyday language means sir, overseer, master, or lord; it can also mean a husband or a male idol. Drawing on that translation, English Bibles most often render YHWH as Lord. Estimates are that the holy name YHWH appears in the Bible over 6,700 times.

Clara. If this name, which is akin to a personal name and not a title, which is a verb and not a noun, is indeed mysterious in its original form, would it be fair to say that its meaning comes from what happens next in the narrative?

Elizabeth. Precisely. The content of the name YHWH is given by what this great God does next: end their oppression and liberate them into a new covenanted life. The freeing of slaves in events guided by YHWH reveals a radical divine identification with human suffering and the plight of the dispossessed found at the heart of Israel's birth story.

Clara. What an amazing reversal of the usual alliance between gods and kings. The great God of heaven and earth sides with a group of slaves against the royal power of the Egyptian throne.

Elizabeth. This choice is what fills the name YHWH with meaning. The God of Israel is not a generic God but one whose character bends toward those who suffer injustice, with intent to save. Israel knows its God by this name, a name attached to freedom: "I am YHWH your God who brought you up out of the land of Egypt" (Ps 81:10).

Clara. So centuries later, when Second Isaiah began to channel divine oracles to announce release to the captives in Babylon, he was not inventing a new God from scratch. His prophetic consciousness was drawing on this strong tradition of divine solidarity with the oppressed and giving it voice in a new moment of history.

Elizabeth. Well said. While biblical speech about God is found in multiple genres such as narratives, lists of commands, and songs of praise as well as in brief vignettes and fragmentary traces, the wide range of language never departs from this concrete reference point rooted in Israel's memory. An important programmatic text in the book of Exodus sets forth the understanding that grew from this seed, the freeing of slaves. On Mt. Sinai Moses encounters God through the medium of a cloud:

> YHWH passed before him and proclaimed: YHWH,
> YHWH, a God merciful and gracious, slow to anger, and
> abounding in steadfast love and faithfulness, keeping
> steadfast love for the thousandth generation, forgiving
> iniquity and transgression and sin. (Ex 34:6–7)

Time and again these descriptions of Israel's divine covenant partner are repeated throughout the biblical books. Merciful, gracious,
steadfastly loving, faithful, and forgiving: so profoundly consistent
is this understanding that Walter Brueggemann calls this text "a
credo of adjectives about the character of Yahweh."

Clara. It seems to me that such a notion of God underlies the biblical emphasis on justice. If the character of YHWH
is marked by compassion, then divine interaction with the world
bears a relentless ethical dimension shown in concern for the last,
lowest, and least.

Elizabeth. Divine identification with the plight of the dispossessed in the event of the exodus makes understandable the constant
return throughout the Bible to themes of God's special concern for
poor, powerless, oppressed, and marginalized persons. Gracious and
merciful, God acts to make a new future possible. Such compassionate concern also undergirds the great biblical ethic of hospitality:
"You shall not wrong or oppress a resident alien, for you were aliens
in the land of Egypt" (Ex 22:21); and more positively, "You shall
love the stranger, for you were strangers in the land of Egypt" (Deut
10:19). The people liberated from slavery must act in like manner
as the Holy One who delivered them.

Clara. I'm thinking of how this deep-rooted "credo" also
finds voice in Israel's prayer.

Elizabeth. It flowers in psalms of praise: "YHWH is gra-
cious and merciful, slow to anger and abounding in steadfast love.
YHWH is good to all, and compassionate toward all he has made"
(Ps 145:8). It appears also in psalms where a person in trouble cries

out to God for rescue: the insolent rise up against me and a band of ruffians seeks my life, "But you, O YHWH are a God merciful and gracious, slow to anger and abounding in steadfast love and faithfulness" (Ps 86:15). Based on the revelation flowing from the event of the exodus, these adjectives bear witness to YHWH's bedrock, reliable goodness and commitment that are everywhere assumed.

Clara. But this same programmatic text in Exodus goes on to speak of the wrath of God in terms that trouble many of us today. I will pick it up at the point of forgiving: "keeping steadfast love for the thousandth generation, forgiving iniquity and transgression and sin, yet by no means clearing the guilty, but visiting the iniquity of the parents upon the children and the children's children to the third and fourth generation" (Ex 34:7).

Elizabeth. Some commentators point out the limit to divine punishment here, which extends only to the fourth generation whereas divine steadfast love covers a thousand generations. Others reflect that the wrath of God maintains divine freedom, so that steadfast love and fidelity do not domesticate God. Still others see that the presence of this attribute prevents relationship with God from becoming permissive; people are held responsible for their actions.

The real issue, though, is how to understand divine anger in the context of overwhelming graciousness and mercy. The danger is that within a patriarchal, punitive setting, speaking of a wrathful God has been used to justify holy wars and torture, hostility to outsiders, and debilitating guilt in sensitive consciences. But righteous anger is a different breed of cat. It is profoundly ethical. It waxes hot in moral outrage because something good is being violated. Arising from love, it awakens energy to act to change the situation. Editing a powerful book of photographs of African American women, Barbara Summers was struck by the creative power of anger of even the most accomplished of these women: "A truly beautifying discovery for me was to find so much love in anger. It was a fist-up, death-defying love that challenged the unfair conditions of life and muscled in on injustice as it nursed both sides of a nation." This is not anger with the spirit of murder in it, but fury that is creative of life. Much feminist in-depth analysis, such as Beverly Harrison's influential essay "The Power of Anger in the Work of Love," makes clear that far from being the opposite of love, righteous anger is a vivid, moral form of caring that empowers transformation.

In the context of God's graciousness and mercy, divine anger functions for justice. It bespeaks a mode of caring response in the face of what harms beloved human beings or the created world itself. "The exploitation of the poor is to us a misdemeanor; to God it is a disaster," writes Abraham Heschel. Divine wrath is a worthy response. True, it lasts but a moment; true, it is instrumental, aimed at change and conversion. But it stands as an antidote to sentimentality.

Clara. I was thinking that visiting the parents' sins on the children down to the fourth generation takes on a disturbing resonance in our time of ecological distress. Extinct species will not come back again; a warmed up earth will not cool off any time soon; depleted water resources will leave millions of little ones subject to disease and early death. Future generations will pay the price of our indifference and greed.

Elizabeth. You make another telling point, as we understand today that much of the damage we are wreaking on the earth is irreversible. What is essential to grasp here is the insight into the living God brought to birth by the exodus. A God of astonishing creative power seen in the magnificence of the skies and the earth, YHWH is merciful and gracious, delivering people from the hand of their oppressors, forgiving sin, and interacting with the world with a relentless concern for justice. Such an understanding of God sounds a steady drumbeat throughout the Jewish scriptures, which, let us not forget, also functions as scripture for Christians.

Clara. This is a profound understanding of God. It makes sense that Second Isaiah would draw upon this tradition when announcing the hope of a new exodus to the distressed exiles in Babylon. YHWH's world is one of compassion, mercy, justice, and liberation; the prophet sings of this world against empire.

Before exploring how he does that, however, there are two matters I feel compelled to bring up about your explanation of God's name that vex myself and many other contemporary minds. The first arises from a post-colonial reading of the exodus narrative. The second concerns the gender of God.

Elizabeth. Let's discuss them one at a time.

Clara. While it is true that the exodus story has been a source of hope for communities struggling for freedom and justice, such as enslaved African Americans and base communities in Latin America, it has also served to oppress groups in other circumstances. Part of YHWH's promise of deliverance includes bringing the Israelites back to a land flowing with milk and honey. The problem is, this land was already occupied by other people. The exodus narrative comes to its end with the invasion of Canaan and the destruction of its inhabitants, although scholars doubt whether history actually happened that neatly. This has given imperial forces justification ever since. Puritan preachers, for example, were fond of referring to Native Americans as Canaanites, that is, people who, if they would not be converted, deserved to be conquered. Contemporary biblical interpreters from nations whose land, economies, or cultures have been colonized find the exodus narrative, if taken literally, to be a source of terror and violence. Its view of God favoring one people to the detriment of another can wreak havoc. How can we deal with this profound problem?

Elizabeth. First, know that there is no pure biblical text, untouched by its own context. There is ambiguity even in the most revered scriptures. Thus there is not just a casual but an absolute need for interpretation, for understanding why the text was written in the first place and posing questions to it from the religious and ethical struggles of today. Postcolonial interpretation, done by people who have suffered under Western imperialism in all its military, political, economic, and, yes, religious forms, views the biblical text from the margins rather than the centers of power. Done from diverse perspectives this rich work calls the conscience of victor nations to account.

Second, since the exodus narrative was written, our vision of the world has grown incredibly larger. The goodness of God glimpsed in that liberating story has also grown in scope to encompass the well-being of all peoples, and indeed of all creation. This has to be taken into account in all contemporary theology worth its salt. Second Isaiah already took giant steps in that direction with repeated emphasis on the community of Israel being given as a light to all nations and a conduit for God's blessing to the ends of the earth.

Aware of the ambiguity of the story and the need for interpretation, and consciously drawing on the weighty "credo of adjectives" described earlier, I intend to employ an understanding of the merciful and gracious God originally born out of the exodus story in order to provide a counterweight to Anselm's thesis that an offended God is in need of satisfaction. This can be done, I believe, without importing imperialistic interpretations. But at every step we must stay attuned to those who have been "burned" by the exodus story and support their interpretations that aim to release a blessing from difficult texts that have done much harm.*

Clara. This will take a lot of work, but it is a good road to set out upon. Now for my other concern. As someone committed to women's flourishing, I can't help but think how unfortunate the Septuagint translation has been when seen from the perspective of women's struggle for equal human dignity. By translating the mysterious name YHWH into *kyrios*, which comes into English as Lord, it took this relational, compassionate deity, whose name is a verb (!), who is utterly free and beyond any simple gendered categorization, and cast divine identity into the image of a ruling male person in a patriarchal society.

Elizabeth. Some scholars have suggested that the English translation "Lord" is unfortunate because it blurs the fact that YHWH is a personal name, not a title, and also because it renders the title in terms of masculine gender, which the original name does not in itself imply. Critical feminist analysis goes further, making clear that the problem is more severe than lack of intellectual precision. While it is commonly taught that God, who can be compared to nothing else, is neither male nor female but Creator of both in the divine image and likeness, most language about the divine summons up the image of a powerful male person. The biblical text does have female images of God, extensively so in the wisdom literature, but these are drowned out in the tsunami of Lords, repeated almost seven thousand times in English. The symbol of God functions. Language about the Lord has had the social and psychological effect of privileging men over women wherever these texts are used.

For that reason in what lies ahead I will take the liberty of using the unpronounceable proper name YHWH as closer to the biblical Hebrew text wherever the English title Lord appears in the Old Testament of the Christian Bible. The New Testament, originally written in Greek, follows the Septuagint in translating YHWH as *kyrios*, or Lord, a grammatically masculine noun that in practice refers to a male person. In the interest of gender inclusive language, I will take the liberty of using simply God for *kyrios*, except when the word becomes a title for Christ.

2.3   What it means to redeem

Clara. It remains but to explain the meaning of the term "redeem," one of the most important terms in Second Isaiah, and then we can turn to the text itself.

Elizabeth. Drawn from the world of commercial transactions in pre-exilic Israel, "redeem" was originally a practice in family law. It might happen that someone forfeits a piece of family property to settle a debt. Even worse, someone might place themselves into service as slave to a creditor in order to work off the debt. To keep the family and its possessions intact, the next of kin had a legal obligation to make good on the debt in order to win the release of the property or the freedom of the person. To redeem was to perform this transaction.

The one who did this was a redeemer, *goel* in Hebrew, a close relative who acted to set things right and restore the family's members or goods. As set out in the Torah, "If anyone of your kin falls into difficulty and sells a piece of property, then the next of kin shall come and redeem what the relative has sold" (Lev 25:25). To redeem, then, was an economic action of buying back done out of family solidarity. To be redeemed was to be delivered from the hands of outsiders. It was to be liberated and brought back into the family circle. This was a well-established custom in society and people were familiar with the practice.

Early in the story of Exodus, YHWH takes up this responsibility. Echoing the self-revelation at the burning bush, YHWH says again: "I have heard the groaning of the Israelites whom the Egyptians are holding as slaves, and I have remembered my covenant. Say therefore to the Israelites, 'I am YHWH and I will free you from the burdens of the Egyptians and deliver you from slavery to them. I will redeem you with an outstretched arm and with mighty acts of judgment'" (Ex 6:5–6). Hearing the groans, remembering the bonds, and then freeing, delivering, redeeming: YHWH is the subject of all these rich verbs, acting as next of kin who buys back Israel from slavery. A close covenant relationship hearkening back to Abraham and Sarah puts YHWH in this position of a relative with responsibility. Interestingly enough, no mention is made of what price is paid or to whom.

The idea of a God who redeems Israel and who therefore can be called the Redeemer became firmly fixed in Israel's religious imagination well before the disastrous exile in Babylon. In the dynamic way that language works, the technical meaning of redeem broadened out over time to include connotations of God's helping, rescuing, liberating, restoring, forgiving, showing steadfast love, comforting, taking away fear, and especially caring for the poor and defenseless. The language of redeeming also became associated with the act of saving. While in the same general family of meaning, the latter carries a distinct sense of healing from sickness and restoring to health, the opposite of which is perishing.

Clara. I heard in a lecture recently that the merciful love that leads God to redeem has a verbal resonance with women's experience of mothering.

Elizabeth. The act of redeeming is motivated by divine mercy or compassion (*rahamim*). If we knew Hebrew, we would realize that compassion is a cognate of the word for womb (*rehem*). When the people of Israel heard, "With everlasting love I will have compassion on you, says YHWH your Redeemer" (Isa 54:8), they understood that the redeeming God was pouring out on them the kind of love a mother has for the child of her womb. In Phyllis Trible's careful analysis, this journey of a metaphor from the wombs of women to the compassion of God is a powerful clue to divine being, unfolding as it does unsuspected female dimensions of the image of God whose mercy is greater than we can imagine.

Clara. Christians tend to use the word redeem mainly in connection with sin and the cross.

Elizabeth. The point here is to grasp its wider reference to God's merciful action toward a world in great need. As already mentioned, from its original financial meaning the verb "redeem" expanded and came to refer to rescue from physical, political, and spiritual bondage; from slavery, exile, and other kinds of oppression; from persecution, troubles, and enemies; from sin and from death. Individuals as well as the community as a whole were the beneficiaries of God's redeeming care.

This rich tradition flows into Second Isaiah who used it to awaken hope of redemption in people being held captive, based on the endearing *goel* relationship between YHWH and Israel: "But now thus says YHWH who created you, O Jacob, who formed you, O Israel: Do not fear, for I have redeemed you; I have called you by name, you are mine" (43:1).

2.4   *Healed, forgiven, redeemed, restored*

Clara. To think beyond the satisfaction theory, theology needs a rock-bottom, different view of the holy mystery of God, a God who is neither a feudal lord in need of satisfaction, nor an angry father, nor a punishing cosmic ruler. You are making a wager that Second Isaiah's poetic reiteration of the creating God who saves may begin to loosen the grip these theories have had on Western imagination.

Elizabeth. Well said. The scroll of this prophet is a magnificent mother lode of insight into the liberating, merciful God who saves, not because anyone deserves this or pays something to placate an offended deity, but because it is the very character of God to be extravagant with love. Written at a particular point in time, for a people humiliated, shamed, in forced exile, this scroll draws from deeply flowing themes in Israel's religious tradition and sends them forward with élan. The best thing anyone who is pursuing this issue could do would be to put down our dialogue and read the scroll of Second Isaiah itself (Isaiah 40–55).

Clara. Short of that, if you could present some key texts that we might ponder, it would help to make the point.

Elizabeth. In this scroll the announcement that God acts toward Israel with redeeming love flows like an unstoppable river. "Do not fear. . . . I will help you, says YHWH; your Redeemer is the Holy One of Israel" (41:14). The response called for is trust: "Do not fear, for I am with you; do not be afraid, for I am your God; I will strengthen you, I will help you, I will uphold you with my victorious right hand" (41:10). What lies in the future might seem terrifying: a long journey back to a ruined city and a land in tatters. But God, the Creator from the beginning, is pouring out divine energy to bring about a new creation. Crying out like a warrior in battle victorious against foes, and crying out like a woman in labor, gasping and panting to deliver a new life, YHWH shouts to help the people make a way out of no way. The rough path will be made straight, streams will flow in the dry land, and the wilderness will bloom. Whatever obstacle they face, be it raging rivers or burning flames, they will make it through, "for I am YHWH your God, the Holy One of Israel, your Savior" (43:3). This divine self-identification of God as Savior is followed by an extraordinary confession from YHWH's heart to a conquered, demoralized people: "you are precious in my sight, and honored, and I love you" (43:4).

The scroll gives God the title of Redeemer with a repetition that resounds like a mantra.

Thus says YHWH, your Redeemer, the Holy One of Israel: you think the Exodus was great? Open your eyes; I am about to do a new thing (43:14).

Thus says YHWH, the King of Israel and its Redeemer, besides whom there is no other god (44:6).

Thus says YHWH, your Redeemer, who formed you in the womb: I am YHWH who made all things, who alone stretched out the heavens, who by myself spread out the earth, the very same who declares that Jerusalem will be inhabited and the cities of Judah shall be rebuilt (44:24).

> Thus says YHWH, your Redeemer, the Holy One of
> Israel, who teaches and leads you in the way you should
> go (48:17).

> Thus says YHWH, the Redeemer of Israel, to one deeply
> despised, defeated and broken, but one who is neverthe-
> less chosen by God and cared for with a mother's intense
> love: "Can a woman forget her nursing child, or show no
> compassion for the child of her womb? Yet even if these
> should forget, I will not forget you" (49:7, 15).

> Indeed, "The Holy One of Israel is your Redeemer,"
> the very same one who is called "God of all the earth"
> (54:5).

> Who is this God, the Creator of heaven and earth? "I
> am YHWH, your Savior and your Redeemer, the Mighty
> One of Jacob" (49:26).

Notice that it is the Creator God who is called Redeemer
and Savior. These and other texts sing out an unequivocal assurance that the God who created the people is now acting as
Redeemer, claiming the people back from another's authority,
overcoming every obstacle to restore them to their own life in
God's covenanted family. This redeeming work clearly has a political dimension; people robbed, plundered, and taken into captivity
are being released to return to their native land.

At the same time, given that the exile was interpreted as
punishment for the nation's misdeeds, this moment of redemption also entails the forgiveness of sin, for the individual but also
for the whole community. More than a century earlier First Isaiah had tapped into the divine will to forgive with a vivid image:
"Though your sins be as scarlet, they shall be as white as snow"

(1:8). Now the Redeemer doubles down on forgiveness, not because the people deserve it but out of divine goodness: "I am the One who blots out your transgressions for my own sake, and I will not remember your sins" (43:25). Like the morning sun that burns off an early fog, the Redeemer says, "I have swept away your transgressions like a cloud, and your sins like mist; return to me, for I have redeemed you" (44:22). Though this historical disaster aroused feelings of being abandoned because of misdeeds, it is now time for glad tidings: "In overflowing wrath for a moment I hid my face from you, but with everlasting love I will have compassion on you, says YHWH, your Redeemer" (54:8). It remains but for the wicked to forsake their ways: "let them return to YHWH, that he may have mercy on them, and to our God, for he will abundantly pardon" (55:7).

A deep base note of appreciation for divine fidelity undergirds this prophet's work. The desire to redeem and forgive, to save and deliver, does not waffle but persists as an essential element of the very character of the God of Israel. It lasts in and beyond every catastrophe and every diminishment that finite creatures inevitably face. Here is the pledge:

> Lift up your eyes to the heavens,
>   and look at the earth beneath;
> for the heavens will vanish like smoke,
>   the earth will wear out like a garment,
>   and those who live on it will die like gnats;
> but my salvation will be forever,
>   and my deliverance will never be ended. (51:6)

This scroll closes with an invitation to come to a banquet where wine and milk, bread and satisfying foods will be served to everyone, and no payment is needed. A new future is arriving. Thanks to the steadfast love and faithfulness of God, Redeemer and Savior, the people will trek home in joy and peace. A new community will form in Jerusalem, healed, forgiven, redeemed, restored. As a final grace note, Second Isaiah declares that the rest of creation will take notice and rejoice: "the mountains and the hills before you shall burst into song; and all the trees of the field shall clap their hands" (55:12).

Clara. How wondrous the ways in which Second Isaiah has given expression to a most magnanimous view of God. It is in line with ancient tradition, but comes to new intensity in this historical moment of crisis.

Elizabeth. There is a crucial point to be gleaned for the theology of accompaniment we are working to establish as an alternative to the satisfaction theory. Let me state it as plainly as possible. More than five hundred years before Jesus' death on the cross, Second Isaiah proclaimed that the God who created heaven and earth was redeeming and saving Israel and forgiving their sin out of the infinite depths of divine compassion. This God is forever faithful and does not need anyone to die in order to be merciful. It is strange to contemplate how Christian preaching in the tradition of the satisfaction theory seems to assume that some seismic shift suddenly changed the divine character, so that Jesus' death was necessary to win favor for sinners. One hears that he came to die, and without the cross we would not be saved, as if at some point the flow of divine mercy were shut down, needing Jesus' death to start it up again. As we will discover, however, rather than making a necessary gift to placate divine honor, Jesus' brutal death enacts the solidarity of the gracious and merciful God with all who die and especially with victims of injustice, opening hope for resurrection amid the horror. If ever a healing balm could reach the depth of Christian soul wounded by the satisfaction theory, a close reading of Second Isaiah might begin the treatment.

Clara. Reading Second Isaiah I am tempted to respond with Anselm's own acclamation: "And so you see, God's mercy is greater than we could have imagined" (II.20).

2.5   *Even when you turn gray I will carry you*

Clara. Our exploration is guided by a question about the redemption of the whole cosmos. One of the delights of Second Isaiah is how closely the created natural world is involved with the salvific coming of God to the exiles.

Elizabeth. Among the prophets Second Isaiah makes the most extensive use of belief in God as Creator; citing one or another verse from this poetic scroll would hardly do justice to its interweaving of YHWH's creating and redeeming work. The key move is identifying Israel's Redeemer with "the Creator of the ends of the earth" (40:28) in the effort to encourage trust. The Holy One of Israel who is coming to free them is the very same God who created the heavens and the earth and all that dwells within them. No one else has stretched out the heavens, numbered and called the host of stars by name, laid the foundations of the earth, measured the seas, and set down the hills. Given that unfathomable accomplishment, a disheartened people sunk in hopelessness has every reason to trust God to fulfill the promise of release from captivity. "Who is like me?" (44:7). No one. Surely the Maker of the world is able to bring about a new saving future. YHWH creates and will set you free; you will fly away home like eagles. Creation texts are used to give grounds for hope.

Clara. The link forged between the creating and redeeming activities of God opens the door to bringing the natural world into the text in an organic way. It amazes me how many creatures are mentioned: the rising sun; all forms of water such as roaring waves, rivers, streams, and fresh springs; mountains and hills; deserts, rocks, and fertile earth; fish and all kinds of wild animals; jackals and ostriches; and a gorgeous array of trees: cedar, acacia, myrtle, and olive, cypress, plane, and pine together. All are party to the glad tidings of salvation.

Elizabeth. They not only witness what is happening to the exiles, but praise the Holy One of Israel who is doing such a new thing: "Sing, O heavens, for YHWH has done it; shout, O depths of the earth; break forth into singing, O mountains, O forest, and every tree in it! For YHWH has redeemed Jacob, and will be glorified in Israel" (44:23).

Clara. Besides giving the people reason to trust their redeeming God, Second Isaiah's gorgeous references to the work of the Creator seem to have an ulterior purpose, namely, to discredit the Babylonian gods who can neither create nor save.

Elizabeth. Remember that the exiles were surrounded by the worship of beautiful if strange gods, part of the religious system of the Babylonians who had conquered them militarily and ruined their country. These were great gods that legitimated the might of the victorious empire. Scholars speculate that over time some exiles felt the tug of temptation to honor these gods who seemed obviously stronger and more successful than their own YHWH. In multiple passages laced with understated irony, the prophet mocks these attractive images, contrasting them with the one and only God who has real power to save.

A carpenter selects a fine log. With part of it he kindles a fire to bake bread, roast meat, and warm himself; from the other part he carefully carves a god before whom he bows down and prays to be saved! How can he not comprehend that the thing he made from wood, half of which is now ashes, has no such power? (44:13–20). Wealthier folk hire a goldsmith to fashion a god which they then hoist onto their shoulders and carry forth to set in its place, and there it stands, totally immobile: "If one cries out to it, it does not answer, or save anyone from trouble" (46:7). A blacksmith fashions a god from metal, working it over the coals, using his own strength to forge its contours with hammers (44:12). But all of these artifacts made of wood, gold, or iron have to be carried around by their makers. Unfortunately these people are deluded; they "keep on praying to a god that cannot save" (45:20).

Clara. These descriptions of the Babylonian gods are ironic, even touched with humor. My one concern is that in our day of religious pluralism, this repudiation of idols might be taken as a warrant to mock adherents of other religions who fashion images strange to Christian eyes. True, it can be explained today that such images refer beyond themselves, so that people are not worshiping wooden or gold figures but the transcendent spirit they signify, similar to Catholic veneration for statues of Jesus, Mary, or Joseph. Still, history shows there has been little appreciation of such nuance. Many religious images were destroyed in the course of Christian mission, and their destruction aided and abetted the systemic oppression of the people who approached the divine through these ruined images.

Elizabeth. This is a crucial concern. It shows how vitally important it is to read biblical texts in their own historical context before attempting any further interpretation. Consider: here are the conquered people of Israel, forcibly deported, depleted of resources, living in a foreign land against their will. Is it not permitted for the oppressed to make fun of their oppressors, and thus diminish their power? The exiles are relatively small in number, without king, land, or temple, devastated in their identity, tempted to assimilate. Announcing a second exodus, Second Isaiah is fighting for the very soul of Israel, to be found in fidelity to the God of their religious tradition.

See how the scroll's contrast between deities works in such a situation. Using the name of the chief god of Babylon, Bel-Marduk, and his son Nebo, the prophet observes that idols of these gods have to be carried about. If they are too heavy for humans to lug about, they are loaded as burdens on weary animals, which sag under the weight. But the God of Israel is the one who does the carrying:

> Listen to me, O house of Jacob,
>> all the remnant of the house of Israel,
> who have been borne by me from your birth,
>> carried from the womb:

> even to your old age I am the One;
>   even when you turn gray I will carry you.
> I have made, and I will bear;
>   I will carry and will save.   (46:3–4)

The great Creator of heaven and earth, who holds sway over time saying, "I am the first and I am the last" (44:6), who holds sway over
space bringing salvation to "all the ends of the earth" (52:10), is
depicted as One who lifts up and cuddles a baby and carries an elderly
person who is no longer able to walk, faithfully loving them to the end.

Clara. What unexpectedly tender images. I quite like the
idea of being carried in the loving arms of God.

Elizabeth. Don't lose sight of the struggle between compet-
ing loyalties. In which God would you be smarter to place your
trust, Bel or YHWH? Truly, "There is no other god besides me, a
righteous God and a Savior. . . . Turn to me and be saved, all the
ends of the earth! For I am God, and there is no other" (45:21–22).

Clara. And here we have it again, the extraordinary idea that
the Creator of the whole world identifies with the fate of a little
unimportant group of people without rights.

Elizabeth. "For the mountains may depart and the hills be
removed, but my steadfast love shall not depart from you, and my
covenant of peace shall not be removed, says YHWH who has
compassion on you" (54:10).

2.6   *Partnering the redeeming work of God*

Clara. Do we need another element to round out the picture? I think of Moses and his siblings taking leadership roles during the original exodus. Who carries out the divine will to save in
the return from exile?

Elizabeth. Throughout the scriptures the divine work of
liberation and justice-making is ordinarily accomplished with the

help of people through whose agency YHWH's desire to save is carried out. With the Persian army on the move against their Babylonian captors, the people of Israel saw that the end of exile was in sight. Under the rubric of "the enemy of my enemy is my friend," they cast the Persian leader Cyrus in a very favorable light.

God roused this bird of prey from the east, writes the prophet, called him by name, and summoned him to service: "He is my shepherd, and he shall carry out all my purpose" (44:28). YHWH loves this pagan king and takes him by the right hand, ensuring victory so that he will set the exiles free and help rebuild the city and temple of Jerusalem. So strong is this king's role in the divine plan that the prophet calls him a messiah, one chosen for a special task: "Thus says YHWH to his anointed, to Cyrus" (45:1). The English term "anointed" is translated from the Hebrew word messiah; the Septuagint translated messiah with the word *christos*, Christ. Cyrus is God's messiah approaching to free the exiles.

Not that Cyrus is aware of any of this. It is the interpretation of the exiles who see their coming political deliverance through a religious lens. Even foreign leaders can do the work of God. In the words of the oracle spoken to Cyrus, "It is I, YHWH, the God of Israel, who call you by your name. For the sake of my servant Jacob, and Israel, my chosen, I call you by your name . . . though you do not know me" (45:3–4).

Clara. Second Isaiah also sees the people of Israel themselves acting like an agent of God's saving purpose. Because redemption is unequivocally meant for the whole world, they are to announce salvation to the ends of the earth.

Elizabeth. Their vocation comes to the fore in four passages usually called the Servant Songs, due to the repetition of the word "servant." In each poem, a certain figure is chosen and endowed with the spirit to bring God's teaching to the nations, or to restore justice on the earth, or to heal bruises and restore righteousness to many. The identity of this servant has been a source of intense discussion. A long tradition of Jewish interpretation sees it as the community of Israel itself, and a critical consensus of today's scholarship agrees. The second Servant Song makes this identification explicit, using the literary technique of personifying a whole group in a single representative person: "You are my servant, Israel, in whom I will be glorified" (49:3).

Choosing the servant from the womb, YHWH declares that it is not enough for the exiles to be restored. Rather, "I will give you as a light to the nations, so that my salvation may reach to the ends of the earth" (49:6). The light they are supposed to shine blesses others both concretely and symbolically, for the servant is sent to "to open the eyes that are blind, to free captives from prison, to release from the dungeon those who sit in darkness" (42:7). The nation itself has a mission, to witness before the entire world the marvelous deeds of the God who creates and saves. This call may entail great suffering, as the third and fourth Servant Songs describe. The servant will suffer terribly. But chosen as they are to bring blessings to the entire world, their suffering will redeem the nations and restore them to *shalom*. And "my servant Israel" will assuredly be vindicated.

Clara. Wasn't Jesus compared to the suffering servant?

Elizabeth. Yes, the fourth song in particular was later used by New Testament writers to make religious sense of the passion and death of Jesus, later called the suffering servant. It became one of many biblical sources pressed into service to shed light on the cross, as we will see; indeed, it was an enormously generative one. This shows how an evocative text can be open to interpretation in more than one direction. Let us be clear, however, that when Second Isaiah wrote his scroll, no one had an inkling that half a millennium later someone like Jesus of Nazareth would even exist, let alone that this member of their people would become central to a new approach to faith in the God of Israel. At the time the scroll was written, the song was describing the purpose of God's people, the covenant community. Their vocation has not been abrogated; as the Second Vatican Council declared, God "does not repent of the gifts He makes or of the calls He issues" (*Nostra Aetate* 4).

2.7 Sin forgiven

Clara. It is abundantly clear that Second Isaiah emphasizes the Creator God as God the Redeemer, freeing captives, forgiving sin, establishing justice, creating new possibilities of life, bringing salvation to the ends of the earth. This view blooms out from the root of the exodus experience and pervades the scroll of Second Isaiah. But one quick question. One swallow does not a summer make. Does this idea of God find support in biblical books besides Exodus and Isaiah?

Elizabeth. A simple answer would be that this is in essence the God of Israel. Every writer, even those most didactic or concerned with legal matters, takes this understanding for granted even if it is not explicitly stated. Prophet after prophet, even those most critical of the peoples' waywardness, sound the theme. Micah provides one good example: "Who is a God like you, who removes guilt, and pardons sin . . . who does not persist in anger forever, but instead delights in mercy . . . and will again have compassion on us, treading underfoot our iniquities. . . . You will cast all our sins into the depths of the sea . . ." (7:18–20).

The book of Psalms, the prayer and hymn book of Israel used in private meditation and public liturgy, stands as strong testimony to the enduring belief in God's redeeming mercy. There is an axiom in Christian theology, *lex orandi, lex credendi*, which translates from the Latin as "the law of praying is the law of believing." In other words, the way a community prays reveals what it believes. Applying this rule to the psalms holds up a mirror to Jewish faith.

Some of these hymns pour out praise for the magnificence of creation. Others, using a shared vocabulary with Second Isaiah, remember with gratitude the saving work that freed the people from slavery and continues to nurture the community throughout history. As passionate devotional works, a number give voice to a felt personal relationship with the Holy One who saves: "May the words of my mouth and the thoughts of my heart find favor in your sight, O YHWH, my rock and my redeemer" (Ps 19:14); or again, "Into your hands I commit my spirit; you have redeemed me, O YHWH, faithful God" (Ps 31:5).

Most assuredly the idea of God as Redeemer is a bedrock of Israel's faith.

Clara. In contrast to the satisfaction theory, can we say that forgiving sin was an important part of this bedrock understanding?

Elizabeth. The people of Israel were keenly aware of their behavior that broke the covenant, both as individuals and as a community. Not ducking responsibility, their prayers acknowledged guilt and prayed for forgiveness. Consider Psalm 25, steeped in assurance of mercy:

> Be mindful of your mercy, YHWH, and of your
>   steadfast love,
>   for they have been from of old.
> Do not remember the sins of my youth or my
>   transgressions;
>   according to your steadfast love remember me,
>   for your goodness' sake, YHWH! . . .
> For your name's sake, YHWH pardon my guilt, for it is
>   great. . . .
> Turn to me and be gracious to me,
>   for I am lonely and afflicted.
> Relieve the troubles of my heart
>   and bring me out of my distress;
> Consider my affliction and my trouble,
>   and forgive all my sins. (Ps 25:6–7, 11, 16–18)

Psalm after psalm testifies to how the cry for forgiveness is met: "Then I acknowledged my sin to you, and I did not hide my iniquity; I said, 'I will confess my transgressions to YHWH and you forgave the guilt of my sin'" (Ps 32: 5).

Perhaps the most well-known prayer with this theme is the so-called great penitential psalm, used annually in the Christian liturgy of Ash Wednesday which opens the season of Lent:

> Have mercy on me, O God,
>   according to your steadfast love;
> according to your abundant mercy,
>   blot out my transgressions.
> Wash me thoroughly from my iniquity,
>   and cleanse me from my sin. (Ps 51:1–2)

As the prayer goes on, the act of washing gives graphic expression to the felt need for pardon: sprinkle me with hyssop, wash me whiter than snow, create a clean heart in me. It is possible that the linguistic resonance of mercy with the womb noted earlier summons up the image of a mother pouring out merciful womb love for her dirty child by scrubbing away at grease, grime, blood, paint until the little one's body is restored to huggable good order. In any event, the one who prays this psalm hopes for the joy of salvation, so that praise and right living can get back on track.

Clara. The connection between redeeming and forgiving sin is an important aspect of the paradigm we are trying to build, and it is already in full flower in the faith of the Jewish scriptures.

Elizabeth. Exactly. It becomes explicit when the psalmist cries "out of the depths" to YHWH, for if God remembered iniquities and did not forgive, who could stand? "But with you is forgiveness" and fullness of redemption. Therefore, even more than sentinels on night watch wait for the dawn, I wait and hope. "For with YHWH there is steadfast love and great power to redeem, and he will redeem Israel from all its iniquities" (Ps 130).

At the cost of repeating myself, I want to note that in all these psalms there is no need for anyone to die. When a person turns to God from a wrongful path, divine forgiveness of sin is a gift generously given, pressed down and overflowing, because of the goodness of the God who loves them: "as far as the east is from the west, so far God removes our transgressions from us" (Ps 103:12). No satisfaction is needed.

2.8   The God of the Christian Old and New Testaments is the same God

Clara. To take stock of how our thinking about salvation is developing, can we sum up where zeroing in on Second Isaiah has taken us thus far?

Elizabeth. Certainly, but I want to emphasize what everyone who ponders and teaches the Jewish scriptures will readily admit. The God of these sacred writings cannot be neatly categorized. Not only are the books diverse in literary genre, historical context, and theological insight, but the subject referred to as G-o-d is incomparable, untamed, beyond imagination. This God cannot be captured in the net of our concepts; no single portrait will suffice. Consider how the Bible presents God as transcendent yet immanent; self-revealing yet unknowable; all powerful yet grasping with feeling what slaves are suffering; merciful yet demanding repentance. In a word, God is incomprehensible, free, as the name YHWH, I AM, I will be what I will be, declares.

At the same time, this is not a generic deity. The divine character becomes especially clear in situations where people are treated unjustly. In solidarity with those who are suffering, the Creator and Redeemer of the world is a relentless opponent of oppression, even by legitimate powers. Restoring wholeness to damaged people has social and political dimensions. It also entails spiritual dimensions, comforting wounded spirits, sowing hope, and forgiving sin. Related to the world in overflowing love, delight, and compassion, the Holy One of Israel generously does all this and more in surprising, joyful ways, opening up an unexpected future. A steady drumbeat throughout the biblical books keeps the exodus credo of adjectives front and center: "a God merciful and gracious, slow to anger, and abounding in steadfast love and faithfulness, keeping steadfast love for the thousandth generation, forgiving iniquity and transgression and sin" (Ex 34:6–7a). Walter Brueggemann's summary can hardly be bested when he observes that this grammar "saturates" the imagination of Israel.

Clara. Obviously, every theologian has to make choices out of this wealth of material, has to choose which books, texts, angles of vision to emphasize. The choice is made with intent, to develop an argument.

Elizabeth. I chose Second Isaiah's way of propounding the heritage and hope of Jewish faith because it offers such a beautiful and compelling contrast to the medieval feudal lord whose offended honor needs to be recompensed according to the satisfaction theory. Such a profoundly different view of God the Redeemer is a first step toward a different interpretation of the cross, one that opens redeeming care to the whole created world. Living in the sphere of God's gracious love, our response should be to love back, with mutual regard and care for one's neighbor.

Clara. I have to say this here because some readers are probably thinking it. An older way of approaching the Bible sees the Old Testament featuring a God of wrath, versus the New Testament's God of love.

Elizabeth. This is so sad, an ignorance born of faulty preaching and teaching. As early as the second century Marcion tried to discredit the Old Testament on the basis that the New had superceded it, but this move was rejected by church authorities. Still, many Christian scholars in the past have pictured Judaism, especially the Judaism that Jesus inhabited, as decadent, degenerate, and legalistic, which gave them the opportunity to extol how Jesus revealed a merciful God. Such a description is a caricature, and not an innocent one. Its presentation of noxious stereotypes goes hand in hand with prejudice against the Jewish community.

Clara. It also indulges a lazy but all too common way of thinking that boosts one's own status by putting down others. Of course one can pick out a text of divine wrath in the Jewish scriptures and play it off a text of love in the New Testament. But one can also do this in reverse, choosing words about God's anger in the book of Revelation and contrasting it with Second Isaiah's theology of God who comes to redeem.

Elizabeth. Done in either direction it is an illegitimate move that misreads both Testaments, both of which bear witness to the same God. Judaism, like Christianity, is a religion of grace.

Clara. This is especially important to emphasize lest what I think of as this first stepping stone you have laid down gets forgotten when we move to the next, the story of Jesus. Because the New Testament takes no other god to be God except the creating, saving God of Israel, right?

Elizabeth. The integrity of this connection cannot be emphasized enough. The God of Exodus, Second Isaiah, and the Psalms is the God to whom Jesus prayed, whose festivals he celebrated, whom he taught his followers to address as "our Father." In Knight and Levine's succinct sentence regarding God, "There is no personality shift between the Testaments."

As evidence, ponder the song Mary of Nazareth, the mother of Jesus, sang, telling of her joy in "God my Savior." Where did she get such an idea that God was her Savior? From the Jewish scriptures, of course. The God in whom she rejoices brings the powerful down from their thrones and lifts up the lowly, helping his "servant Israel" and remembering mercy through the generations according to the promise first made to Abraham (Lk 1:46–55). Read again the canticle of Zechariah, father of John the Baptist. Replete with references to divine mercy, it begins with the praise, "Blessed be the Lord the God of Israel, for he has looked favorably on his people and redeemed them" (Lk 1:68–79). The source for thinking that God redeems? Jewish religious tradition, oral and written.

"Jesus brought no new concept of God," Brevard Childs argues, but demonstrated in action and in a new setting God's redemptive will for the world. Far from being provisional, Jewish religious insight is part of the very warp and woof of New Testament understanding.

The topic of creation provides a prime example. There are very few explicit texts about God as Creator in the New Testament. Internal textual evidence indicates that the authors writing about Jesus simply took Jewish creation faith for granted. Drawing on this established belief, they occasionally refer to God's creative work that made the world in the beginning, that feeds the birds and clothes the flowers in beauty today, and that will bring about a transformed heaven and earth in the future. To put it plainly, Christian faith in God the Creator rests squarely on the faith of Israel, which is everywhere presupposed.

This is not to say there is simple continuity without development. The early church's expanding christological interpretations of Jesus led the community to view the God of Israel in light of its own relationship to Christ, which in turn led to new insights and formulations about God in trinitarian terms. Nevertheless, the First Testament's view of the God who creates and saves shaped the early church's interpretation of Jesus in an intrinsic and irreplaceable way. The God whom Jesus revealed and even embodied as self-expressing Word is none other than the God of Israel. "In times past God spoke to our ancestors in many and various ways by the prophets, but in these last days he has spoken to us by a Son. . . " (Heb 1:1). It is the same God who speaks, abounding in steadfast love and faithfulness.

Book III

Jesus of Nazareth King of the Jews

3.1   The importance of knowing the gospels are narratives of faith

Clara. From the religious depth and richness of the Jewish scriptures, the Old Testament of the Christian Bible, we have lifted up a central belief about the merciful God who liberates, comforts, saves, redeems. What comes next?

Elizabeth. Within that same Jewish tradition we focus on Jesus of Nazareth, a mystic and prophet who made the presence of this God vividly concrete amid the joys and hopes, griefs and anxieties of early first-century Israel, and paid a terrible price. After his death his disciples came to believe that he was the Christ, the Messiah, God's own Son, God's own Word made flesh; but there was a time during his actual life before any of this was thought about or articulated. The next step in working out a theology of redemption that encompasses all creation is to access that period. This means tapping into the story of Jesus from an historical angle. By showing that Jesus was put to death for reasons that had nothing to do with making satisfaction for sin, the heat of this history will melt Anselm's theory like an ice cube on a hot day, and make room for the natural world to enter the picture.

Clara. Obviously the major source for the life, ministry, death, and resurrection of Jesus is the Christian New Testament, specifically the four gospels. How did the faith of Matthew, Mark, Luke, and John shape these narratives? And how does knowing the faith character of these gospels provide a tool to access the historical angle?

Elizabeth. It is crucial to grasp what the last two centuries of biblical research have made clear, namely, that the gospels are faith documents, not simply eyewitness reports of what actually happened. They were written by members of the early church to inspire the faith of others. John's gospel states this purpose with utter clarity. Stories about what Jesus said and did were written down "so that you may come to believe that Jesus is the Messiah, the Son of God, and that through believing you may have life in his name" (Jn 20:31). The gospels are written from faith for faith, as scholars are wont to say.

Clara. This characteristic is clear when it actually works, when for example you are moved by a good sermon preached on a gospel text. The story can lift your mind and heart to God and inspire your life in a certain direction. The religious purpose is also evident if you take up a gospel story and meditate on it yourself, seeking a deeper relationship with God or incentive to live more fully. When encountered in faith, these gospels radiate spiritual encouragement and challenge.

Elizabeth. That is their true nature. They are spiritual texts, shot through with belief in Jesus Christ. This does not mean, however, that they are divorced from history. The gospels' inspiration flows from a figure who lived as an actual person on this earth, not a character in a novel. In fact, there is historical evidence in Jewish and Roman writings outside the New Testament that Jesus of Nazareth did indeed exist and was put to death under Pontius Pilate. He is not a figment of someone's imagination. But the gospels were written by people whose interest was not simple reporting. They remembered him with love and wrote out of deep faith commitment to spread good news.

Clara. It would help to review how these faith-filled gospels came into being. Knowing that story will help to explain why you will use here an historical method of interpretation.

Elizabeth. The gospels came into existence through a dynamic process of composition. Try to imagine the years of the first century divided into thirds. Jesus' actual life spanned approximately the first third of the century. During his brief public ministry what he did and said was witnessed by disciples, Jewish men and women who traveled with him during his ministry in Galilee and went up to Jerusalem with him at the end.

After his death these disciples remembered his words and deeds and, as happens with almost every beloved or noteworthy person, interpreted them in view of the final impact of his life. In particular, their Easter encounters with him after his death cast a powerful light on his significance. In retrospect they saw more meaning than when the events first occurred. During the middle third of the first century, treasured memories about Jesus circulated orally in various communities of disciples. Like filaments of wool they were spun forward through the decades, interwoven with insights generated by resurrection faith, by new experiences of the Spirit poured out in the community, and by the needs of the fledgling Christian mission.

The final third of the century saw these memories, now shaped by the developing faith of the early church, collected into coherent narratives called gospels or "good news" scrolls. Writing in different places, each author composed a portrait of Jesus Christ from a different theological perspective and with the challenging needs of a particular local community in mind. The scholarly view today is that Mark wrote first, and then Matthew and Luke relied on his outline and added their own sources, including a scroll of Jesus' sayings they had in common. Toward the end of the first century John drew from a different set of traditions altogether.

Written in the light of the resurrection decades after the events they narrate, the gospels are documents rooted in historical memory filtered through layers of faith interpretation in rapidly changing circumstances.

Clara. What an interesting story of composition. I must say these stages do open the gospels to a richer, less prosaic kind of interpretation. But this can be a little unsettling to someone used to reading them as regular history.

Elizabeth. It may help to know that the Second Vatican Council (1962–65) affirmed such an approach to the gospels. Summing up the enormously complex back-story of the gospels' composition, it taught that when the evangelists wrote about what Jesus said and did, they did so with a "clearer understanding" that resulted from the events at the end of his life, his crucifixion and resurrection. Enlightened by the Spirit, the council teaches, the four authors wrote faithfully, "selecting some things from the many which had been handed on by word of mouth or in writing, reducing some of them to a synthesis, explaining some things in view of the situation of their churches, and preserving the form of proclamation, but always in such fashion that they told us the honest truth about Jesus" (*Dei Verbum* 19).

The honest truth they are telling is a truth of faith, on which they have staked their lives. This makes them valuable texts for the church to this day. Selecting, reducing, explaining, proclaiming, the one act they are not engaged in is disinterested reporting.

Clara. This explains why it will not do to simply take a passage and read it in a literal fashion without interpretation, as if it were an exact transcription of an event. In our culture with live filming of important events available as they happen, I find this the hardest thing to remember and practice when dealing with the gospels. If I read that Jesus said or did this or that, my mind plays a video of it happening in exactly that way. But the text is depicting what Jesus said and did colored by insights from developing oral tradition over time in the early church and shaped by the different theologies of the evangelists.

Elizabeth. To help sort this out, biblical scholarship uses criteria that have proved workable on other ancient documents to distinguish how different layers of original event, interpretive memory, and theological composition, or Jesus, early church community, and evangelist, intersect in gospel texts. Though the results are never without controversy, it becomes possible to work back from the text to get a glimpse of the actual figure of Jesus in his own time and place, before Christian belief existed.

Clara. This helps to explain something I've wondered about. In Mark chapters 8, 9, and 10 Jesus tells his disciples of his coming death, each time in greater detail. The first text declares that he will suffer, be killed, and after three days rise again; the next adds the point that he will be betrayed; the final time we hear that he will be mocked, and spit upon, and flogged. I've never understood why the disciples did not "get it" when these events happened. But Mark composed his narrative long after Jesus was crucified. Would it be fair to say he drew on the community's memory bank and inserted these particulars "after the fact"? This would help explain why the disciples did not understand what was going on.

Elizabeth. Exactly. Scholars call these texts "predictions after the event." While it is quite possible that Jesus shared a sense that his life was under threat as the end drew near, the disciples retold that moment with the added particulars they knew about once the actual event took place.

Clara. Do the long accounts of the end of Jesus' life, called the passion narratives, have the same character?

Elizabeth. They do. They are dramatic narratives structured to bring out theological interpretations of the historical fact of Jesus' suffering and death. One example: given the political situation of the early Christian communities, which were trying to make their way in the Roman empire although their founder was executed by Roman authorities, the passion narratives bend over backwards to exonerate the Roman governor Pontius Pilate. But he held the power of life and death. Jesus' crucifixion was his decision.

We will be using historical critical methods in this Book III to paint a picture of Jesus the Jew under Roman rule. This historical angle will go a long way toward reconnecting the meaning of his death to the ministry that preceded it and the resurrection that followed. Telling the story this way sets up strong resources to loosen the satisfaction theory's grip on our imagination. With the historical situation in view, theologizing about the meaning of the cross can blaze a different trail.

3.2   Jesus the Jew under Roman rule

Clara. A small historical detail can open the door to the larger picture we seek. While each gospel recounts different last words of Jesus, all four tell that as he hung dying by order of the Roman governor, the indictment affixed to the cross accused him of a crime that many today find puzzling. Consider:

> Over his head they put the charge against him, which read, "This is Jesus, the King of the Jews." (Matt 27:37)

> The inscription of the charge inscribed against him read: "The King of the Jews." (Mk 15:26)

> There was also an inscription over him, "This is the King of the Jews." (Lk 23:38)

> Pilate also had an inscription written and put on the cross. It read, "Jesus of Nazareth, the King of the Jews." (Jn 19:19)

So all four are in agreement about the offense for which he was executed.

Elizabeth. John's gospel adds the detail that the charge was written in Hebrew, Latin, and Greek so that multi-cultural passers-by outside the walls of Jerusalem could read it, no doubt to be warned off from committing the same crime. Christian crucifixes today often add the Latin in abbreviated form: the letters INRI stand for *Iesus Nazarenus Rex Iudaeorum.*

Clara. What does this brief script reveal about the historical context of Jesus' death?

Elizabeth. First, it brings to light the presence of Roman authority in Israel. After living for a time under enlightened Persian rule following their return from exile, the Jewish people had endured a succession of conquering empires. Most recently in 63 BCE the general Pompey had invaded Israel, taking over the small nation and making it a province of the powerful Roman empire. Unlike the Babylonian invasion that forcibly deported Jewish populations into exile, Roman law allowed people to remain in place. Its domination took the form of installing Jewish client kings to govern in its name, maintaining a military presence, and demanding stiff taxes.

While people were allowed to worship their own gods, the empire had zero tolerance for opposition to its rule, meeting any semblance of resistance with stiff counter-force. One instrument of intimidation was the cross, a form of punishment used specifically to execute those who were guilty of threatening the state either by direct rebellion or by inciting others. In addition to ensuring a torturous and ignominious death for the rebel, crucifixion was a spectacle of warning to others. Its cruelty was meant to serve as a deterrent to those who might consider acts of treason against the empire.

Jesus was not the only one ever crucified, including on the day of his own death. The first century Jewish historian Josephus, one of those who wrote that Pilate condemned Jesus to the cross, gives plentiful other examples. Varus, the Roman legate of Syria, crucified two thousand rebels in 6 CE as part of his effort to pacify the Jewish countryside. During the final Jewish revolt in 70 CE when the Roman army besieged Jerusalem, the general Titus captured any residents trying to escape and crucified them in view of the city walls. As Josephus wrote, he hoped "that the sight of it would perhaps induce the Jews to surrender in order to avoid the same fate. The soldiers themselves through rage and bitterness nailed up their victims in various attitudes as a grim joke until, owing to the vast numbers, there was no room for crosses, and no crosses for the bodies." The crucifixions in Israel were paralleled in other conquered lands and in Rome itself, wherever sedition reared its head.

Nevertheless, popular resistance ran through some groups of Jews and occasionally broke out in open revolt. Keep in mind the disastrous date of 70 CE, a few decades after Jesus' death. Then a Jewish uprising was crushed by Roman troops who burned the city of Jerusalem and destroyed the temple once again, leaving only its outer western wall that stands to this day. The nation was wrecked.

Jesus of Nazareth was born into these tumultuous political conditions. The cross and its script reveal that he was a Jewish person living under the rule of the mighty Roman empire.

Clara. I understand your point that as a Jew he was governed and executed by the Romans who had conquered his own nation. But could we think more concretely about Jesus as a Jew? The Jewishness of Jesus tends to fade in Christian preaching that emphasizes the risen Christ's presence in today's community as a focus of faith and moral inspiration. But as a human being on this earth, Jesus of Nazareth was Jewish in biological, ethnic, cultural, and religious senses. What details might help our imaginations grasp this identity?

Elizabeth. Born of a Jewish mother, Jesus was counted among the people descended from Abraham, the people freed from slavery in the exodus. All the gospels assume this; two even take the trouble of listing in detail the line of ancestors from which he descended. The gospels depict his parents as observant Jews;

they gave him a popular Jewish name and followed Torah instruction about the birth of a male child, including the ritual of circumcision. The gospels also depict the family celebrating the annual festival of Passover, at times making pilgrimage to Jerusalem for the feast, which their first-born son continued to do in his adult life. Jesus taught in synagogues, or Jewish halls for meetings and prayer, throughout the northern province of Galilee. He also taught in the temple in Jerusalem, the one rebuilt after the Babylonian exile and more recently renovated into magnificence by King Herod. He honored the Sabbath and kept it holy, at times arguing about its proper observance, arguments common at this time among people who wanted to understand how best to follow God's holy law. In obedience to Torah he even dressed Jewish. A woman who had been suffering from hemorrhages for twelve years came up behind him and, seeking healing, "touched the fringe of his cloak" (Matt 9:20). These are twisted cords tied on the four corners of the outer garment, as called for in the Torah: "You shall make tassels on the four corners of the cloak with which you cover yourself" (Deut 22:12). The purpose was to remind the wearer of the teachings of YHWH, "who brought you out of the land of Egypt, to be your God" (Num 15:38–41).

As part of the community of Israel Jesus of Nazareth prayed like the Jew that he was, communing with the mystery of God through the Jewish prayer tradition, including the psalms of thanksgiving, lament, longing, and praise that formed the religious matrix in which he lived. Two gospels show him praying one of these psalms in his death agony, indicating he knew the words by heart: "My God, my God, why have you forsaken me?" (Ps 22:1).

When challenged to choose the greatest commandment, this prophet from Nazareth quoted the Torah's book of Deuteronomy: "The first is, 'Hear O Israel, the Lord our God, the Lord is one, and you shall love the Lord your God with all your heart and with all your soul and with all your mind and with all your strength'" (Mk 12:29–30, citing Deut 6:4–5). To this he added another Torah commandment that flows powerfully from belief in this God: "The second is this, 'You shall love your neighbor as yourself.' No other commandment is greater than these" (Mk 12:31, citing Lev 19:18). To even make such a choice Jesus had to be familiar with Torah, and to have spent time mulling its meaning in his own life.

The close band of male and female disciples who traveled with him around Galilee and up to Jerusalem, the crowds who came to hear and be healed, the religious leaders with whom he tussled over teachings of the law: all were fellow Jews. If you read the gospels with this point in mind, it becomes clear that Jesus was embedded securely and coherently in the world of late Second Temple Judaism.

Clara. So it is important to understand that this actual Roman subject was truly a Jew. This historical fact fits in with the church's teaching that Jesus was truly human, doesn't it? Historically there is no such thing as a universal human being, only concrete persons born of particular gene pools with discrete characteristics and living in specific times and places. As a genuine human being Jesus had to be particular. He is not a generic person but Jewish.

Elizabeth. This is a point with irreplaceable significance. Historically, it situates his life and that of his original followers in the turbulent first-century conditions prevailing in Israel that brought him to the cross. Theologically, Jesus' rootedness in the people of Israel explains the later New Testament use of the Jewish scriptures to interpret him in a religious sense. Apart from his Jewish identity Jesus' story does not make sense either historically or theologically.

Clara. Many people are surprised to learn this. I will never forget one student who challenged the idea in class, saying that Jesus might have been Jewish during his lifetime, but just before he died on the cross he became a Catholic.

Elizabeth. Such an anachronistic misunderstanding! There was as yet no Catholic church. Whether the result of poor preaching and teaching, a tribal identification with the church, negative stereotypes about Judaism, or some combination, who can say. But historically Jesus was not a Persian, a Roman, a Greek, or an Egyptian. He was a Jew.

The script on the cross shows that the power of the Roman empire intersected with the life of this deeply religious Jew in a disastrous way.

3.3   *Three powerful ideas in circulation: kingdom of God, messiah, resurrection of the dead*

Clara. It seems to me that the gospels, written in the first century, ask a great deal of twenty-first-century readers. They employ intensely Jewish ideas that would be quite familiar to people of the time, though remote from our own culture. Before we plunge into the Jesus story, could we hear about three ideas that together are going to play a major role: the kingdom of God, messiah, and resurrection of the dead? They are deeply interconnected, and knowing how they were "in the air" could give us a tool to follow the story with a more enlightened understanding.

Elizabeth. The kingdom of God lies at the heart of Jesus' preaching. His opening words in Mark's gospel place this idea front and center: "The time is fulfilled, and the kingdom of God has come near; repent, and believe in the good news" (1:15). Throughout his ministry Jesus created parables about the kingdom; taught his disciples to pray "thy kingdom come"; and went throughout cities and villages "proclaiming and bringing the good news of the kingdom of God" (Lk 8:1). This is a symbol that just reverberates with joyful anticipation.

Clara. I have to say that the phrase "the kingdom of God" does not stir my heart with excitement today. Besides having patriarchal, hierarchical overtones, it simply does not connect with us who live in democratic societies as something greatly to be desired. *Elizabeth.* Understandable. But think of it in this first-century way. In a world made up of many kingdoms where power and wealth reigned to the harsh disadvantage of those without either, the kingdom of *God* meant wondrous changes. For this was the kingdom of the redeeming, saving God of Israel. Slaves would be freed, exiles returned home; springs would flow in the desert, abundance mark the fields; justice would be established and mercy reign. In a word, the symbol refers to the state of the world when the will of God is finally and fully honored: compassion and kindness will abound, joy and peace will break out, and all creation will flourish. Jesus' use of this particular symbol was inherently subversive. His announcement turned the usual operations of the kingdoms of this world on their heads. God's way of ruling was the opposite of the empire's Caesar.

Recognizing the cultural disconnect, however, some scholars today suggest that synonyms for kingdom such as reign, rule, or realm of God might serve better. Others opt for Ada María Isasi Díaz's suggestion of the kin-dom of God, which points to the warm, encompassing Latina experience of family and community to which all will belong. To my mind, Edward Schillebeeckx makes a compelling suggestion by way of a paraphrase: Jesus' announcement that "The kingdom of God is at hand" is actually a shout that announces "Salvation is on its way from God!" This captures something of the heads-up, joyful dynamic of the proclamation.

Clara. How did this symbol function in its first-century context?

Elizabeth. This was a period of intense political turmoil, including popular unrest and occasional armed confrontation. In the teeth of the suffering caused by foreign oppression, hope in God assumed a particular orientation. It became an intense expectation that the God who liberated the Israelites from slavery and who restored the exiles to their homeland would soon

transform the whole world with a final act of salvation. This hope
was carried in kingdom language: the rule of God is near, which
means the creating, redeeming God is coming to set the world
to rights.

As should not be surprising in a complex Jewish society,
there were different versions of what the coming reign of God
would entail. Various groups envisioned some or all of the following elements in different combinations: the city of Jerusalem
and the temple restored in a final renewal; the nation ruled by a
new monarch descended from David who would ensure peace
and prosperity; oppressors overcome and their idolatry crushed;
justice established for the poor; the wicked punished; the righteous who suffered vindicated; the dead resurrected to new life;
suffering and travail replaced by everlasting joy; the Spirit of God
poured out on all flesh; the blessing of redemptive peace poured
out not only on Israel but on the whole world. Any or all of these
was something greatly to be desired.

Clara. I am tempted to say, in a word, "Comfort!" This fleshes
out one powerful religious idea circulating at the time that lies at
the center of Jesus' preaching. What about the idea of the messiah?

Elizabeth. Messiah, or the anointed one, would be the person who inaugurated God's reign. Not everyone expected a messiah, but messianic hope was well-established and often discussed.

Past texts had identified the anointed one with the current
king, or a prophet, priest, or warrior, or even the entire people of
Israel; we have seen how the pagan king Cyrus could be gifted with
the title. Running through all uses, however, is a primary reference
to David, king of Israel. As head of a future idealized kingdom, the
Davidic messiah would defeat enemies and reign over a restored
Israel at peace among the nations. The figure appears in correlation with the hopes of the poor, for the messiah will be a righteous
judge who will impart justice to widows and orphans, defend the
weak, and bring about reconciliation. By the early first century,

the messiah was hoped for as a herald of the arrival of God's kingdom. The very mention of messiah summoned up hope for a radical change in the present political order, an eschatological or final hope for the redemption of the world.

Clara. During Jesus' ministry didn't some people think he might be this expected figure?

Elizabeth. Indeed they did, or at least they suspected or hoped so. Recall the question John the Baptist in prison sent his disciples to ask: "Are you the one who is to come, or are we to wait for another?" (Matt 11:3). What complicated the situation is that, as Josephus writes, in those unsettled times there were a number of other candidates for the role, popular leaders thought to be the divinely appointed messiah who would deliver Israel from the Roman yoke. Some of these possible messiahs promoted violence; some attracted large numbers of followers.

Clara. So even if they did call Jesus the Messiah, there would be others with a similar claim.

Elizabeth. Right. After his death and resurrection, however, the disciples thought of him in this role without ambiguity. Translated into Greek as *christos,* Christ, it became a preferred way of alluding to him. These days we often miss the original meaning since it seems to function like a last name, as if Jesus were the child of parents with the family name Christ. But it is a title that signifies a vital role in the coming of God's reign.

Clara. You said that people also hoped for resurrection of the dead as part of the coming kingdom of God. I have always thought of this belief as a Christian innovation.

Elizabeth. Scholars today are discovering the deep roots of hope for resurrection in Jewish scripture and prayer. It grew out of a convergence of a number of biblical themes, chief among them trust that the liberating God of merciful love would prove faithful even beyond death. This hope began to wax strong in the prophets. During a political crisis in the eighth century BCE, Isaiah uttered an oracle from YHWH promising, "Your dead shall live, their corpses shall rise. O dwellers in the dust, awake and sing for joy!" (Isa 26:19). The flavor of hope is even more palpable in his poetic vision of a mountain on which God will spread a feast for all peoples of rich food and well-aged wine, and then "will destroy on this mountain the shroud that is cast over all peoples . . . will swallow up death forever . . . will wipe away the tears from all faces. . . . This is YHWH for whom we have waited; let us be glad and rejoice in his salvation" (Isa 25:6–9).

The hope that God *will swallow up death forever* found dramatic narration in Ezekiel's vision of the dry bones coming back to life and being clothed with flesh, written during the exile in Babylon. While the primary image refers to the people being restored from exile, the great rattling reassembly of the bones culminates in the promise, "I will bring you up from your graves, O my people. . . . I will put my spirit within you and you shall live" (37:12, 14). Some psalms began to incorporate this vision so that it entered into Israel's prayer: "Our God is a God of salvation, and to God, YHWH, belongs escape from death" (Ps 68:20).

Israel's continued oppression by foreign forces was the catalyst that racheted this hope into vivid expectation of what would happen on the last day when God's kingdom would finally come. The thinking went that if God is just and merciful, then those who have been ground down under the heel of power would be especially cherished. During the persecution under Antiochus Epiphanes in the second century BCE, the scroll of Daniel spelled out what scholars consider the first clear reference to resurrection as such in the Bible. In a time of great anguish, there will be deliverance: "Many of those who sleep in the dust of the earth shall awake, some to everlasting life, and some to shame and everlasting contempt. Those who are wise shall shine like the brightness of the sky, and those who lead many to righteousness, will shine like the stars forever and ever" (12:2–3).

Death is inevitable; it cannot be avoided or minimized. But the God of life can graciously rescue even the dead. Resurrection of the dead takes its place in this kind of summoning up of a large, audacious vision of the world's redemption.

Clara. By Jesus' time, the resurrection was still not universally accepted but was hotly disputed among various Jewish groups, right?

Elizabeth. Recall how the gospels famously depict the Sadducees, who opposed the idea, arguing with Jesus using the story of a woman who had to marry seven brothers in sequence after each one died. They asked, "In the resurrection, whose wife will she be?" Applying the burning bush story, where the voice from the fire self-identifies as the God of Abraham, Isaac, and Jacob, Jesus argues that God therefore "is not God of the dead, but of the living; you are quite wrong" (Mk 12:18–27). He thus places himself in agreement with the Pharisees on this question.

Clara. I've always thought that when the seventh brother died, this poor woman must have said, "What a relief."

Elizabeth. Touché. But to the point: for those who held to it, the resurrection of the dead was a rightful, even necessary, element anticipated in connection with the coming reign of God. John's gospel story of the raising of Lazarus shows how the idea was definitely in the air with this exchange: "Jesus said to her, 'Your brother will rise again.' Martha said to him, 'I know that he will rise again in the resurrection on the last day'" (11:23–24). Hope was abroad that the God who delivered out of slavery and exile would definitively redeem Israel, working, in some versions, through the agency of a messiah. To right the wrongs of history, the righteous who suffered unjustly would be vindicated and the dead would be raised. This was a profoundly hopeful vision, with power to lift sagging spirits in disastrous times.

3.4   A ministry that blazed like a meteor

Clara. Having set the scene with the political and religious background, especially noting Roman oppression and Jewish hope for God's reign, can we now draw on the gospels for a picture of Jesus' ministry? In the churning of expectations that marked early first-century Israel, the carpenter of Nazareth's decision to leave his home and embark on a public ministry set many wheels in motion. It's amazing how much happened in so short a time!

Elizabeth. The length of Jesus' ministry was actually quite brief. Launched after he was baptized at the hands of John in the Jordan River, it lasted about one year according to the synoptic gospels or three years in the gospel of John. Like a meteor he blazed across the Jewish sky and was gone. But length was not of the essence. Here was a mystic on fire with the love of God, a prophet who preached the coming of God's reign as a blessing for suffering people. He made an impression.

Jesus began his public ministry with the message that the reign of God was near. Far from being a distant, some-fine-day event, it was already dawning. In fact it was taking root concretely in and through his words and deeds. Jesus was serving as advance agent of God's redemptive power; his mission established a foothold for this blessed reign, even as evil continued to hurt and destroy. This shines through in an early scene. Standing to read in his hometown synagogue of Nazareth, Jesus was handed the scroll of Isaiah. His choice of text reverberated with the sense of God who redeemed the exiles: "The Spirit of the Lord is upon me, because he has anointed me to bring good news to the poor. He has sent me to proclaim release to the captives and recovery of sight to the blind, to let the oppressed go free, to proclaim a year of favor from the Lord" (Lk 4:18–19, citing Isa 61:1–2).

Clara. Jesus' ministry went forward under this banner. What do we see him doing?

Elizabeth. Scholarly consensus holds that certain activities were typical. With headquarters in the fishing town of Capernaum on the lake, he traveled around Galilee with a band of men and women disciples and drew interested crowds, some enthusiastic, some hostile. He taught in homes, in synagogues, on hillsides, from a boat on the shore of the Sea of Galilee. Many sick people knew his healing touch; many possessed by destructive spirits were restored to peace. He comforted the sorrowful and gave assurance of forgiveness. With the learned Pharisees he debated the meaning of Torah. A special grace note were the meals he hosted with a mixture of companions, honorable and not so honorable. The joyous fellowship of the shared table offered a foretaste of belonging characteristic of the coming reign of God. Probably a bit uproarious, these meals brought on the criticism that Jesus was "a glutton and a drunkard, a friend of tax collectors and sinners" (Matt 11:19).

Clara. What a time they must have had!

Elizabeth. As for teaching, using his gifts of creative imagination Jesus spun colorful epigrams and parables that illuminated the coming reign, giving a glimpse of how the compassion of God's boundless goodness would turn the world upside down. A farmer sowing seed, the seed itself growing, weeds mixing in, a woman kneading flour, a treasure hidden in a field, a merchant finding a fine pearl, a shepherd finding his lost sheep, a woman finding her lost coin, a father forgiving a prodigal son, a net in the sea catching fish, lamps filled with oil or wretchedly empty, a king giving a wedding banquet, a Samaritan helping a wounded traveler, an employer crazily generous with salaries: all awaken a sense of the presence of God coming to redeem. All bring to life the insight into God of the prophet Hosea that Jesus quotes in defense of his hungry disciples, "I desire mercy and not sacrifice" (Matt 12:7, citing Hos 6:6). In response, the human heart was called to love as God did—yourself, your neighbor, even your enemy.

Clara. Do you think Jesus was attuned to the wonders of the natural world?

Elizabeth. It would be anachronistic to attribute to this first-century prophet the environmental concerns of twenty-first-century people. But he did grow up in Galilee, a fertile region where farming, fishing, and animal husbandry were main occupations. Clearly he was attuned to the natural world in this rural context. His preaching is filled with references to the processes of seeds growing, vineyards bearing fruit, and fig trees leafing out, and to the ways of wandering sheep, foxes, and nesting birds. Jesus knew how to read the clouds to predict the next day's weather. Speaking movingly of the beauty of wildflowers and the vitality of birds of the air, he encouraged listeners to learn from them lessons of trust. He went so far as to declare divine concern for one dead little bird: "Are not two sparrows sold for a penny? Yet not one of them will fall to the ground without your heavenly Father knowing it" (Matt 10:29). Jesus' whole ministry was centered on the coming of the reign of God. Given that this God is the Creator who loves the whole world, this means nothing less than the flourishing of all creation.

Since the reign of God is especially attentive to the needy and outcast, Jesus showed a partisanship for suffering people that we can today interpret as extending to encompass the earth and its myriads of distressed species and ecosystems. His ministry reveals a wideness in God's mercy that includes all creation.

Clara. Can we link Jesus' ministry back to the scroll of Second Isaiah? Maybe one way to interpret the impact of Jesus' activity would be to say that in the name of the gracious God of Israel he was announcing comfort, and giving people practical tastes of release from captivity in their own situation?

Elizabeth. That is one beautiful summation. In his own prayer and study of the Jewish scriptures Jesus encountered the ineffable loving God who is gracious and merciful, full of steadfast love and faithfulness, "YHWH, your Redeemer, the Holy One of Israel" (Isa 43:14). The joyful good news that the reign of this God was near propelled his words and shaped his deeds.

3.5   Naming God

Clara. One thing puzzles me. You have been insisting that the merciful God of the Jewish and Christian scriptures is the same God. But most Christians think of Jesus teaching about God as our Father, not the God of Israel. For the sake of understanding salvation differently from the satisfaction theory, this seems to me a vital point to clarify.

Elizabeth. Biblical scholars generally agree that drawing on a minor tradition in the Jewish scriptures, Jesus at times called God *abba*, father. I say minor in the sense that it is not a frequent usage. However, when it is used, the identification between the Holy One of Israel, the liberating, merciful YHWH, whose name by now was reverently not pronounced, and a good father, whose name can be said, is unmistakable.

Consider how Isaiah sees God's creative work shaping us into being: "Yet, O YHWH, you are our father; we are the clay, and you are our potter; we are the work of your hand" (Isa 64:8). The same literary phrase connecting YHWH and father in the act of creating is used with reference to the divine work of saving and liberating: "O YHWH you are our father; from of old your name is our Redeemer" (Isa 63:16). Singing of YHWH's steadfast love, a psalm celebrates the covenant with David who in turn cries out, "You are my father, my God, the Rock of my salvation" (89:26). In beautiful cadences Psalm 103 praises YHWH who works vindication and justice for all who are oppressed, and who like a loving father forgives the peoples' sins:

> YHWH is merciful and gracious,
>> slow to anger and abounding in steadfast love. . . .
> He does not deal with us according to our sins,
>> nor repay us according to our iniquities.
> For high as the heavens are above the earth,
>> so great is his steadfast love. . . ;
> as far as the east is from the west,
>> so far he removes our transgression from us.
> As a father has compassion for his children,
>> so YHWH has compassion for those
>> who fear him. (Ps 103:8–13)

When the disciples asked Jesus to teach them to pray, he expanded this tradition from the Jewish scriptures with a prayer to "Our Father who art in heaven," the father in this context being YHWH whose name is to be hallowed, whose kingdom is coming, whose nearness bestows the blessing of bread, forgiveness, and deliverance from evil. The originality of this prayer lies not in its petitions, all of which reflect Jewish themes, but in their combination and trusting address to "our" father who, being the God of Israel, can be relied upon to hear and respond from the unfathomable depths of divine graciousness.

Clara. When I read the gospels, it seems that Jesus uses the name "father" almost all the time. Yet upon reflection, his language about God is not monolithic but diverse and colorful.

Elizabeth. The parables are a rich source for Jesus' speech about God. Stories about the reign of God or the kingdom of heaven spun from Jesus' imagination range over human experiences to illuminate divine ways. The kingdom of heaven is like a mustard seed, a king who gives a marriage feast, a bakerwoman kneading dough: all point to God in the indirect ways characteristic of Jewish speech. The kingdom of God itself is a circumlocution for YHWH, unpronounced, whose reign approaches.

With regard to the term father itself, careful word count shows that God is referred to as father in the gospels with increasing frequency: some 4 times in the first gospel Mark; 15 times in Luke and 49 in Matthew who wrote next; and 109 in John. The count may vary slightly, but that is the pattern. As James Dunn concludes, it is scarcely possible to dispute that "here we see straightforward evidence of a burgeoning tradition, of a manner of speaking about Jesus and his relation with God, which became very popular in the last decades of the first century." Calling God "father," in other words, is a matter of theological development in the early church rather than abundant use by the actual Jesus who lived.

Clara. When Christians pray the "Our Father," we think of the Father who is being addressed in the framework of the holy Trinity. For some it seems a stretch to think Jesus was referring to the God of the Christian Old Testament.

Elizabeth. Remember that it is the same God. The powerful Jewish understanding of God whose name is a verb, the great I AM who is Creator of the world and Redeemer who delivers the poor from oppression, shaped Jesus' life and flowed into his teaching and ministry. At times he called this God *abba*, father, in his native Aramaic tongue. In light of their own experience of grace, subsequent generations gave voice to new insights about Jesus and his relationship to God, which today's Christians inherit. But this is a later development. In the early first century this prophet from Nazareth did not wake up in the morning and say the Nicene Creed, going forth to the day with the clear knowledge and assurance that he is "one in being with the Father." That very language reflects a Hellenistic, not a Jewish, mindset, to say nothing of having been written three centuries later.

Clara. You like to quote Vatican II's teaching that Jesus "worked with human hands, thought with a human mind, acted by human choice, and loved with a human heart" (*Gaudium et Spes* 22).

Elizabeth. Indeed, and the human mind he thought with was an early first-century Jewish mind. There is great value in allowing him the integrity of his own historical life.

3.6   Facing death

Clara. Toward what turned out to be the end of his ministry, Jesus set his face toward Jerusalem, as Luke's gospel puts it, and decided to take his message to the nation's capital. Can we say his death was a consequence of his mission? As I see it, if he had decided to go back to the carpenter shop, he probably would have lived a lot longer.

Elizabeth. From an historical point of view it is true to say that Jesus died as a result of his mission to which he stayed faithful with a courage that would not quit. His words and deeds sharpened hope in the reign of God that spelled salvation for all, especially for suffering and marginalized people. Going up to Jerusalem for the festival of Passover signaled that Jesus was bringing passionate hope for God's saving reign into the very center of the nation. In first-century Israel dominated by Rome, this was a dangerous thing to do. Jesus died as a consequence of fidelity to his ministry.

Clara. This does not mean that Jesus intended or wanted to die, does it?

Elizabeth. Quite the opposite. He was announcing the coming of the kingdom with great joy, in hope that people would repent and believe in the good news. Indications were that this was happening among some people, including his band of followers. Life abundant was the goal.

Clara. When opposition and even danger arose, why did he not stop?

Elizabeth. Jesus' ministry arose from a deep-rooted sense of vocation: of who he was, of what he was called to do, of his purpose in life in relationship to God. It would have been a denial of his own deepest self, his own basic commitment, to quit. Fortunately and unfortunately, present times give us far too many examples of good women and men who have stayed the course in similar manner, doing the work of love despite danger. I think of Doctors without Borders in Syria; Dorothy Stang in the Amazon rainforest; Stephen Biko in South Africa; Dietrich Bonhoeffer in Nazi Germany; Oscar Romero and companions in El Salvador; Yolanda Ceròn Delgado in Colombia.

In a letter written weeks before her death in El Salvador in 1980, Jean Donovan, the lay missioner from Cleveland, expressed the way such commitment works with simple eloquence:

> The Peace Corps left today and my heart sank low. The danger is extreme and they were right to leave. . . . Now I must assess my own position, because I am not up for suicide. Several times I have decided to leave El Salvador. I almost could, except for the children, the poor, bruised victims of this insanity. Who would care for them? Whose heart could be so staunch as to favor the reasonable thing in a sea of their tears and loneliness? Not mine, dear friend, not mine.

When a mission gets its grip on your heart, you faithfully stay the course, regardless. Your own integrity, felt in a passionate sense of right and wrong and love for others, prevents you from doing otherwise.

Clara. Do you think he knew he might meet a violent death?

Elizabeth. Jesus was not stupid. The times were dangerous. The fate of the prophets was a recurring motif in Jewish rhetoric. He had before him the example of John the Baptist, whose powerful preaching had influenced his own entry into public ministry and who now lay buried without a head. Going up to Jerusalem would draw Jesus' ministry into a spotlight. It is not possible using critical historical methods to know what was in his mind. But simply musing, it is reasonable to surmise he was aware of the danger. It is also possible that he discussed with his disciples the likelihood of a harsh outcome to his life and, in the manner of the psalms, expressed hope in God for rescue. Such a conversation could even be thought probable, given their relationship and shared life. Whatever he thought privately and discussed with his followers, the bottom line was that he decided to go.

An uncanny parallel lies in the final speech Martin Luther King, Jr. delivered in a crowded church on April 3, 1968. Warned not to go to Memphis to support striking sanitation workers but going anyway because "the issue is injustice," King ended by eloquently expressing a sense of danger to himself combined with trust in God and hope for the people:

> We've got some difficult days ahead. But it really doesn't matter with me now, because I've been to the mountaintop. And I don't mind. Like anybody, I would like to live—a long life; longevity has its place. But I'm not concerned about that now. I just want to do God's will. And He's allowed me to go up to the mountain. And I've looked over. And I've seen the Promised Land. I may not get there with you. But I want you to know tonight, that we, as a people, will get to the Promised Land. So I'm happy, tonight. I'm not worried about anything. I'm not fearing any man. Mine eyes have seen the glory of the coming of the Lord.

The next day he was shot to death.

Given this calculus, theologians today tend to underscore the radical freedom and passionate love with which Jesus stayed the course regardless of its consequences. A certain integrity, being true to himself, and a keen sense of responsibility, being passionately true to his calling before God on behalf of others, all motivated by love, led him on. He walked his mission, come what may. Allow his heart to abandon the people? "Not mine, dear friend, not mine."

Clara. Even if Jesus had a sense he might run afoul of the authorities and be put to death, it doesn't mean he interpreted his death with Christian insight, does it?

Elizabeth. It is highly unlikely that the actual Jesus who lived interpreted his death in terms of the models later developed by the New Testament, such as reconciliation, sacrifice, or redemption. In radical fidelity to God and in service to people whom he loved, he stayed the course and was crucified to death. Doctrinal interpretation came later, and was then retrojected into the way the story of Jesus was told. It is vitally important not to rob his life of its real historical character, the worries and creative decisions, the joy and final terror.

3.7 *Suffered under Pontius Pilate, was crucified, died, and was buried*

Clara. By every measure of historical investigation, it is commonly agreed that Jesus of Nazareth was executed by crucifixion on the orders of the Roman prefect Pontius Pilate. What historical details set the stage for his condemnation of Jesus?

Elizabeth. Early in the first century Rome had deposed the Jewish client king in Judea for incompetence, and replaced him with an appointed Roman governor, called a prefect or procurator. The southern province of Judea thus came under direct Roman rule, with the prefect answering directly to the emperor. Pontius Pilate held this colonial post from the years 26–36 CE. For most of the year he lived in the harbor town of Caesarea Maritima on the Mediterranean coast, commanding three thousand troops garrisoned with him. On the three major pilgrimage festivals (Booths in autumn, Passover in spring, Pentecost in early summer), he would march with his troops from the coast up to Jerusalem to reinforce the smaller contingent of Roman troops stationed permanently near the temple. This public show of force was intended to restrain the multitudes who were gathering from every direction for the feasts. "For it is on these festive occasions that sedition is most apt to break out," as Josephus remarked.

By all accounts Pilate was a mean character, deliberately and unnecessarily provocative of Jewish religious sensibilities. The Jewish philosopher Philo of Alexandria described him as "a spiteful and angry person," a man of "inflexible, stubborn, and cruel disposition," whose administration was marked by "venality, violence, thefts, assaults, abusive behavior, and frequent executions of untried prisoners, and endless savage ferocity." Rome ultimately removed him from office due to troubles stirred up by his belligerence.

One of privileges of the Roman prefect was to appoint the Jewish high priest. This was a political plum of a post with both religious and civic duties. In addition to presiding at services at the temple in Jerusalem, the high priest was responsible for keeping peace in the temple precincts. For this purpose he commanded several thousand temple guards, who also acted as a police force for the city of Jerusalem. Together with his council of chief priests, the high priest was in charge of overseeing the collection and delivery of the all-important taxes to Roman authorities. Positioned in the middle between the Jewish populace and the Roman governor, if the high priest did his job well a tenuous peace would hold, with rebellion held down on the one side and bloody military reprisals restrained on the other. Inevitably, the dynamics of such a position allied the high priest's judgment and primary loyalty with the empire, rather than with fellow Jews seeking freedom or redress of grievances.

At the time of Jesus' execution, Caiaphas was the current high priest. He and the former high priest Annas together held office for seventeen years; their longevity in office gives some indication of how well they walked their tightrope of a job.

Clara. What brought Jesus to their attention?

Elizabeth. Two things. A general though not unanimous agreement among biblical scholars points to Jesus' entry into Jerusalem when crowds hailed him as the messiah, coupled with his subsequent action overturning the tables of moneychangers in the temple.

The festival of Passover drew huge numbers of people to the city to celebrate God's deliverance of Israel from slavery. They sang as they approached, in hopes of new liberation still to come. As a prophetic preacher of the coming kingdom of God and healer of the sick in God's name, Jesus had drawn crowds throughout Galilee. Now as he came toward the city, festive crowds of pilgrims hailed this charismatic figure as a messianic king, one whose work heralded the coming kingdom of God. The golden age when David reigned would be restored and even surpassed when the people lived as God's independent covenanted nation. Soon! The crowds acclaimed Jesus: "Hosanna! Blessed is the one who comes in the name of the Lord! Blessed is the coming kingdom of our ancestor David!" (Mk 11:9–10); "Blessed is the king who comes in the name of the Lord!" (Lk 19:38).

Clara. Listening to these cheers against such a highly charged background gives me the chills. The crowds heralded Jesus as the hoped-for messiah. What a challenge to imperial domination! Led by Jesus, the arrival of God's kingdom would overturn Roman rule.

Elizabeth. Any Roman colonial governor worth his salt would want to discourage the possibility.

Clara. How did Jesus' action in the temple add to the danger?

Elizabeth. Sometime after entering the city, according to the synoptic gospels, Jesus entered the temple precincts and performed a symbolic act. He overturned the tables where pilgrims exchanged the coins of their own lands for the type of shekels accepted for temple use; with the shekels they could buy animals for sacrifice. Christians have interpreted this scene as a "cleansing," as if there were something wrong with this trade. In actual fact, however, these exchanges of buying and selling were essential for temple worship to continue. Its central act of sacrifice had always required a daily supply of suitable animals.

In the tradition of prophets before him, Jesus was enacting a prophecy of destruction and renewal. He was acting out symbolically the eschatological hope that this temple and its religious services would be destroyed by God and cede its place to a new temple coming from heaven at the end of days. The glorious time of restoration was fast approaching. The kingdom of God is at hand.

Clara. Any Jewish high priest worth his salt would be hostile to such an action. I see that the pieces are now in place for the crime tacked onto Jesus' cross.

Elizabeth. Exactly. You were right earlier to urge us to understand the linked themes of the kingdom of God, the messiah, and the resurrection of the dead, as well as the situation of Roman occupation. All these lay the groundwork.

Observed by Roman soldiers patrolling on high alert, crowds acclaiming Jesus as harbinger of the messianic kingdom would provoke Pilate's concern: this could mean rebellion. Passover crowds swirling around this charismatic figure in the temple, taking in his teaching and symbolic action, would elicit the chief priests' sharp attention: this could lead to a riotous demonstration with bloody Roman reprisal sure to follow.

At some point the chief priests met in council saying, "If we let him go on like this, everyone will believe in him, and the Romans will come and destroy both our holy place and our nation." The high priest Caiaphas's decision was utterly pragmatic: "It is better for you to have one man die for the people than to have the whole nation destroyed" (Jn 11:48–50). Events moved swiftly and the end came in a matter of hours. Most Christians know the main points.

Clara. These would include a final meal with his disciples; betrayal of Jesus' location by a disaffected member of his inner circle; stealth arrest at night by the temple guard; the high priest handing him over to the prefect; Pilate's decision to crucify; the decision carried out by Roman soldiers.

Elizabeth. "Jesus of Nazareth King of the Jews." The trial scenes in the gospels are shaped by later Christian determination to show that Jesus was innocent of the charge of sedition. But there it stands in three languages. It identifies him as a messiah, poised to incite rebellion against Roman rule. Jesus met the fate of an enemy of the empire. The message to the holiday crowds was not subtle: back off, settle down, give up your hopes for the coming kingdom, or this will also be your fate.

Clara. But Jesus did not advocate a violent overthrow of the Roman emperor.

Elizabeth. He need not have called for violent insurrection in order to have been perceived as politically disruptive. Preaching the hope of God's coming kingdom with its new order of peace and justice put the current order under threat. The fact that large numbers of enthusiastic people responded to his prophetic message would mark him as dangerous. As Paula Fredriksen points out, "In the tinderbox of early first-century Palestine, crucifixion of such a prophet would be a prudent Roman response."

Clara. And so he was crucified, his life wrenched away by barbaric violence to maintain the rule of arrogant power, as has happened to so many other human beings before and since.

Elizabeth. His physical suffering can only be imagined. A group of women disciples stood keeping vigil, but there was no hope. The gospels depict Jesus bearing the condemnation and violence inflicted on him with a spirit of surrender to God. Mark and Matthew depict the utter dereliction of Jesus as the righteous sufferer who has been abandoned, praying a psalm: "My God, my God, why have you forsaken me?" Luke presents Jesus like a trusting martyr commending his spirit to God: "Father, into your hands I commend my spirit;" John's Jesus controls the situation in a unity of will with the Father: "It is finished." What is historically most likely is that the last sound he made on earth was an agonizing scream: "Then Jesus gave a loud cry and breathed his last" (Mk 15:37). A desolate cry without words.

Clara. To me, this historical approach is so helpful to faith.

Elizabeth. We need to dwell near the cross and feel the weight of its historical negativity in all honesty. This was a real death. One morning Jesus was a living, breathing, warm human being and by nightfall his body was lying cold and still in a grave. Hewing closely to history, the Apostles' Creed gives a succinct summary: he "suffered under Pontius Pilate, was crucified, died, and was buried."

The manner of his death, furthermore, was scandalous. One of thousands crucified over the years by the unjust exercise of political power, Jesus was not just dead but publically disgraced. His movement shattered. His company of disciples scattered. The dreams of those who loved him and believed his message that God's reign was near went down to dust. "We had hoped," said the disciples on the road to Emmaus several days later, but that hope was gone along with him, smeared with shame.

Clara. There is a depth of evil here, found also in the violent deaths of multitudes of people throughout history, that no theory or theology or theodicy can justify.

Elizabeth. Hold onto this moment. It is not erased by what came next.

3.8 "But God raised him up, having freed him from death" (Acts 2:24)

Clara. After the devastating fiasco of the crucifixion, if nothing else happened we would be left with the memory of one more good person crushed by the unjust powers of this world. The question pressing itself on a religious heart would be why evil is so powerful. But something more did happen according to the disciples. What can be said with relative assurance?

Elizabeth. Two aspects of what ensued bear up under the scrutiny of historical methods. The first has to do with Jesus' burial place. That the tomb was found empty seems likely, though not absolutely so, because it would have been difficult to preach that he was risen from the dead if people could go and observe his corpse. In addition, the gospels report that the discovery was made and announced by women, not the likeliest of witnesses in a patriarchal culture; this indicates a memory of women's involvement that could not be erased. The empty tomb, however, does not prove anything; it could have been empty for many reasons. One gospel narrates that the chief priests paid the guards generously to say that "his disciples came by night and stole him away while we were asleep," an explanation that had staying power (Matt 28:13).

Besides the empty tomb, a second historically observable development is an obvious change in the behavior of the disciples. Turning from grief to joy, from fear to bravery, they coalesced into a community with a mission. In their own telling, they attributed this change to the encounters they had with the crucified Jesus now alive in God. The evil provoked by the message of God's own coming rule became the condition of a yet more radical deed: God raised the Crucified One. Whether or not Jesus actually was raised cannot be established with the tools of historical research. At this point we move into the language of faith. But what is historically certifiable is the disciples' faith; they embarked on a course of mission on the strength of powerful experiences that they interpreted as encounters with the crucified Jesus risen from the dead.

Clara. It is curious how at this point the gospel stories go in all different directions, unlike the story of the passion, which follows a generally agreed upon sequence.

Elizabeth. The unexpected nature of the Easter appearances coupled with their staggering revelation created a colorful prism of different testimonies. Individually and in groups, indoors and outdoors, at the tomb, in the Jerusalem upper room, on the shore of the lake in Galilee, along a road, at an inn, on a mountain, first Mary Magdalen and the women who had kept vigil at the cross and then Peter and various men of Jesus' company encountered and interacted with the one who had been crucified.

Some recognized him immediately, some did not. The way they described these encounters was also varied. He called them by name, passed through walls, conversed at table, walked with them along a road, cooked breakfast for them on the shore. They recounted his message that breathed peace and encouragement: "Do not be afraid" (Matt 28:10). And across the board they took note of the charge to carry on the mission—to Mary Magdalen: "Go and tell" (Jn 20:17); to Peter, "Feed my sheep" (Jn 21:17); to the disciples, "Go into all the world and proclaim the good news to the whole creation" (Mk 16:15).

The point of these stories, for all their bewildering diversity, is the same. The disciples are testifying that Jesus became present to them in a new way beyond the distance of time and space forged by death. He was not annihilated by death but transformed to new life by the Spirit, and able to inspire them with peace and boldness. Peter articulated what they believed had happened: "But God raised him up, having freed him from death" (Acts 2:24).

Clara. Why did they articulate these post-crucifixion experiences in the language of resurrection?

Elizabeth. As daughters and sons of Israel they had this interpretation ready to hand. Recall that the resurrection of the dead was expected, at least in some quarters, as an aspect of the coming kingdom of God at the end of time. With power to set hearts on fire, the near approach of God's reign was part of Jesus' teaching. As thinking, believing people hoping in a Jewish manner with a thirst for salvation, the disciples used the kingdom language of life for the dead to express their own surprising religious experiences of Jesus after his death. He is risen! And if so, the kingdom is arriving. The redemption of the world is dawning.

Clara. Could one raise the objections that not everyone has been raised, only this one person? And that the last day did not come, but day kept following day?

Elizabeth. Absolutely. The early church grappled mightily with this issue. At first they expected the final day at any moment. After a while they began to figure out that what happened to Jesus was just the beginning of the end, like a flare sent up from the future, full of promise for everyone else. About twenty-five years later the apostle Paul presented this solution using an agricultural metaphor: "Christ has been raised from the dead, the first-fruits of those who have fallen asleep" (1 Cor 15:20). The end of the world hasn't happened yet, but the risen Jesus is a pledge of what is in store for all the dead.

Clara. First-fruits! This reminds me of what it is like to plant a summer garden and watch it grow and pick the first tomato when it ripens.

Elizabeth. Any gardener knows it is a wonderful moment when that first tomato is plucked. Part of the joy of the first-fruit lies in the fact that it is not the only one, but signals that the harvest is beginning; there are plenty more to follow. In a similar manner, the disciples came to see that resurrection signals the opening act of the final age of redemption. It discloses the ultimate direction of human history, and indeed of all creation, when the dead will be raised.

Clara. The risen Christ, the first tomato!

Elizabeth. Just so! The disciples proclaimed the good news of salvation with vigor and joy on the strength of their belief that God raised Jesus from the dead, and the gift to this one historical person gives assurance of what lies ahead for all. This first-fruits theme finds careful if unusual expression in Karl Rahner's words: "We are saved because this human being who is one of us has been saved by God, and God has thereby made his salvific will present in the world historically, really, and irrevocably."

Clara. I have to say that resurrection seems very hard to imagine.

Elizabeth. You are absolutely right. There really are no words or images that can do justice to what resurrection entails. What happens after death is no longer accessible to inquiry by us whose lives are bounded by the constraints of time and space. Artistic and literary attempts to describe resurrection fail utterly, stained glass windows and Easter cards to the contrary notwithstanding. Notice that the gospels do not give any actual descriptions of Jesus being raised from the dead. There were no witnesses. The texts are modest and do not luxuriate in speculation.

What the disciples affirm without any imaginative embroidery is that they have had a religious experience of encounter with Jesus alive in a new way thanks to the creating God who saves. No other conceivable power is stronger than death. From the historical point of view, the disciples' Easter experiences are a new Jewish faith experience of the liberating, compassionate God, the Redeemer of the burning bush, who sees, hears, and knows what people are suffering and comes to deliver, this time from the last enemy—death.

3.9   *Resurrection: theological reflections*

Clara. Apart from what can be said using historical methods, can we take a deeper look into what resurrection means theologically? Perhaps start with what it does *not* mean.

Elizabeth. On the one hand, this event does not refer to the simple physical resuscitation of a corpse, although imagination often follows that route. To be resuscitated would entail being restored to earthly life as we know it, as happened with Lazarus. This would mean Jesus would have to die again, like poor old Lazarus did. However, the risen Jesus is alive in God in a new way: "Christ, being raised from the dead, will never die again; death no longer has dominion over him" (Rom 6:9). Resuscitation does not get at what happened here.

On the other hand, neither does resurrection mean simply that Jesus' cause lives on, or that he lives on the memory of those who loved him. This view is memorably carried in the phrase, "Jesus rose into the kerygma," meaning that he rose into the disciples' faith and came alive in their preaching. Their word, passed down through generations in the church, keeps the memory of Jesus alive as example, inspiration, and a way to God. But valuable and even dangerous as such remembering might be, such a position does not come close to taking away the dominion of death.

A third contrast should be made with Greek anthropology that held the idea that humans have an invisible, incorporeal soul that will survive death while the body decays. In biblical anthropology, though, human beings are a psycho-physical unity, not a dualistic composite of body and soul. Death takes the whole person, through and through, no part escaping. If the crucified Jesus is raised from the dead, the possibility does not reside in an eternal element that is part of his make-up.

Consequently, the biblical notion of the resurrection of the dead is profoundly *theocentric*. It is a God-crazed idea. It believes in God's loving, creative power that will restore the whole person as a psycho-physical-social reality, body and soul, to a new transformed way of being. To believe that Jesus is raised from the dead rather than being objectively resuscitated, or subjectively remembered, or passing through death unscathed with an immortal soul, is in essence a radical act of faith in God.

Clara. So many people find this hard to get hold of. They think it is weird or spooky.

Elizabeth. It is enormously helpful to see the way early Christians connected resurrection with creation. The logic of the connection allows this impossible hope to make more sense. Paul forges this link in a quick line: God "gives life to the dead and brings into existence the things that do not exist" (Rom 4:17). There it is. Just like that, you can see that if the living God can create the world to begin with, then God can create anew in death. Why ever not? No future existed before the world began; no future exists for a dead person. But divine creative action that occurs "in the beginning" continues to act through time and up to the end, which becomes a new beginning. It is the same loving, creative, divine action.

Clara. So belief in resurrection is a form of creation faith.

Elizabeth. There is a profound correlation between the two. Even earlier than Paul an unforgettable Jewish mother found courage in the same connection. Losing her seven sons one by one to torturous deaths during the persecution under Antiochus, she encouraged them to stand firm. Remembering how each one felt in her womb during pregnancy, she expressed a daunting belief: "It was not I who gave you life and breath, nor I who set in order the elements within each of you. Therefore the Creator of the world, who shaped the beginning of humankind and devised the origin of all things, will in his mercy give life and breath back to you again, since you now forget yourselves for the sake of his laws" (2 Macc 7:22–23).

Miserable death does not have the last word. Abounding in loving-kindness and fidelity, the Creator who calls into being the things that do not exist can also give life to the dead.

Clara. I begin to see the substance of the claim made by Walter Kasper, which at first hearing sounds preposterous: "Easter faith is not a supplement to belief in God . . . it is the entirety and essence of that belief."

Elizabeth. In truth, belief in the resurrection is actually belief in God. Logically speaking, it is faith in God all the way through to the end. "In the beginning" the Spirit of God moves over dark chaos and God speaks the word of creation: "Let there be." In the resurrection, the Spirit of God moves again over the body of death and God speaks the same word anew: "Let there be." Just as God freely created all that exists out of nothing, God can freely bring new life out of the apparent nothingness of death. Easter is nothing less than a new creative activity of God that pledges a blessed future of the whole cosmos.

Clara. In this framework, shifting the focus from God to the crucified Jesus, what other understanding does theology venture to offer?

Elizabeth. At the outset we must caution ourselves that ordinary language is inadequate to the event being described, which goes beyond history and human experience. None of us yet knows what it is like to live beyond death in the glory of God. No one actually saw Jesus rise from the dead. While the gospels describe the empty tomb, none attempts to explain exactly how it got that way. "Christ rose in the silence of God," wrote Ignatius of Antioch. Less explanation rather than more is the rule, since we are dealing here with a mystery that we cannot completely fathom.

That being said, theology does dare to seek some understanding. One of the preferred categories often pressed into service is that of transformation. For Jesus himself, the resurrection does not undo his death, as if he hadn't suffered and been cut off from life, but it creates a new future. As Karl Rahner argues, it is not as if in death he just changed horses and rode on. Rather his unique life receives permanent, redeemed, final, and definitive validity in new life with God. Since then the past salvation event in Jesus Christ becomes, through the power of God's Spirit, a constantly new presence for all times. We must relinquish any imaginary model of how this happens; it is incomprehensible and known only in hope. But this hope holds that the crucified Jesus is alive in God.

Given the dualism that remains in Christian thinking, it is important to emphasize that this is not simply a case of the immortality of the soul. Jesus does not shuck off his bodiliness like a suit of clothes and rise heavenward, so to speak, as a purely spiritual being. Resurrection affirms new life of the whole enfleshed person Jesus, transfigured beyond death. In a deeply material way, the Easter appearances disclose the divine depth-dimension undergirding all flesh, which opens novel possibilities for the body itself.

But again, imagination fails us. When pressed about the kind of body the dead are raised with, the apostle Paul pointed in exasperation to the difference between a seed and the full-grown plant that emerges after the seed is planted, splits its outer covering, and is transformed into something unimaginably different (1 Cor 15:35–38). In essence, Jesus' whole historical person in all dimensions is pervaded by the vivifying Spirit and made whole in a completely new way.

In this view, both the Easter proclamations that "he is risen" and Easter narratives of the empty tomb and appearances to the disciples point to God's living Spirit acting on behalf of the crucified Jesus, transforming him to new life in glory. Sharing in divine life, he now is present in the way God is present and known in the way God is known, through minds and hearts imbued with faith to "see" a hidden presence.

This is why the resurrection appearances were not objectively tangible events that could be captured in a photo shoot. God made the risen Christ manifest in religious theophanies, or manifestations of his person from the hidden depths of divine mystery. The disciples became aware of his risen presence not with objective sight, the way they used to see him on the hillside before his death, but with insight that drew on their memory of him in light of new revelatory religious experiences. These moments of disclosure may indeed have had a physical component, the disciples' sight being itself clarified, intensified, given visions by the Spirit to perceive the risen Christ. But Jesus really died. The risen Christ encounters them from the other side of the awful event that definitively ended his historical life. The disciples recognize him with the eyes of faith.

The resurrection starts on earth with Jesus dead and buried, and ends up in God with Jesus the Living One transformed by the power of the Spirit. Alive in God, his presence is no longer bound by earth's limits but partakes of the omnipresence of God's own love. Christ is now present in word and sacrament and wherever two or three gather in his name. True to the pattern of his ministry, he also approaches, mysteriously revealed and concealed, in the hungry, the thirsty, the sick, the homeless, those in prison, the very least of those in need. Ultimately, through the power of the Spirit, Jesus is with the whole community of disciples, indeed with the whole community of creation, though every hour, until the end of time. Is this true? All explanations aside, it has to be a lived truth, seen in the lives of those who are participants in Christ's ongoing work in the world.

Clara. I think the insight of Book II about the God of Israel, Creator and Redeemer, who stretches out the heavens and the earth and approaches to lead the exiles home, comes roaring back in this paschal event. The rough path will be made straight, streams will flow in the dry land, and the wilderness will bloom; whatever obstacles you face, like raging rivers or burning flames, even excruciating death, you will make it through, "for I am YHWH your God, the Holy One of Israel, your Savior . . . and I love you" (Isa 43:3–4).

3.10 *The cross revisited*

Clara. I am thinking back to how the disciples were devastated after the crucifixion, their beloved Jesus ruinously killed, their hopes dashed. How did they view the cross now, in the light of their Easter experience?

Elizabeth. They made three fundamental moves. First, they fused the cross and resurrection into one hopeful symbol. This does not mean they thought the resurrection gave Jesus' life a happy ending. As an historical event his life ended violently by political execution. But going forward, the followers of Jesus, first Jews and then Gentiles, did not ponder the cross in isolation, let alone judge Jesus' crucifixion in itself to be a saving event. An unjust death at the hand of empire is not salvific! The resurrection, however, revealed God's power even over the most horrible form of death. Jesus' loving fidelity unto death met God's creative power of life. This is what is essentially salvific. The two moments condensed into a fundamental sign of salvation.

The cross is such a dramatic event that at times it is referred to by itself in a kind of shorthand. Even then, reference to the cross in a faith context is always made with belief that God had raised Jesus from the dead. While Paul waxed eloquent about the cross as the wisdom of God, for example, he stated unequivocally, "If Christ has not been not raised, your faith is futile and you are still in your sins" (1 Cor 15:17). As David Tracy puts it, "Cross and resurrection live together or not at all." It is the resurrection of the crucified that reveals God at work to save.

Clara. I am dumbfounded by what a searing light this sheds on Anselm's satisfaction theory, making it clear that the problem lies not only in the way his theory was used in subsequent centuries. The very structure of the argument itself, focused on the cross alone as saving because it gave God payment for a debt, is fundamentally in error, to say nothing of how it omits the essential salvific import of the resurrection.

Elizabeth. Let us look at the second move the disciples made after they fused the cross with the resurrection. They allowed it to cast a strong light back on Jesus' whole life, giving it saving significance. It is crucial to note that God did not raise just anyone from the dead. It was this particular person, who had engaged in a passionate ministry proclaiming the good news of divine compassion and showing what this meant especially for poor and suffering people. It was this particular person who had been put to death as a consequence of his ministry. The resurrection showed that the God of Israel endorsed this prophet and what he said and did. This act of divine graciousness affiliated God with Jesus. It showed him to be God's beloved, the one who revealed God's own heart.

Clara. The resurrection put God's seal of approval on the crucified Jesus and his life. What a striking point!

Elizabeth. Such loving divine confirmation overturned the judgment of the judges who found him guilty and deserving of death. It revealed that Jesus is the one whom the God of Israel favors, whose ministry, teaching, and way of acting coheres with the heart of YHWH, gracious and merciful. As he healed the sick and brought good news to the poor, the longed-for salvation of the messianic age was already beginning in his lifetime, through his person and activity. It continued to arrive now in the community of disciples who carried on his mission.

The third move that the disciples made in light of the first two was to identify Jesus as the expected messiah. Recall that the resurrection of the dead was expected to be part of the arrival of the reign of God, and that the messiah would herald its arrival. In short order the disciples connected the dots. Already during his ministry the possibility had circulated that Jesus might be the one who would restore the nation. His crucifixion obviously put a stop to any such thoughts. But the resurrection lifted the Crucified One into the role of the Christ, the person chosen by God to usher in a new age of redemption. In figuring this out, the disciples rethought the messianic role of political leadership of the nation. They broadened the reach of that role to include others in addition to the people of Israel. In short order the role of Christ expanded in service to the salvation of the world.

Clara. What an irony. Since the resurrection confirms the truth of his whole life as God's beloved, and reveals him to be the messiah, then the charge on the cross is true. Jesus of Nazareth King of the Jews!

Elizabeth. The point for our purpose is this: the disciples came to grasp that the gracious God of Israel who frees slaves, leads exiles home, and hears the cry of the poor had gone the unimaginable distance of offering salvation to the world through the life, death, and resurrection of Jesus the Christ. This was the good news they started to announce.

3.11 *Salvation: a double solidarity*

Clara. Telling the story of Jesus' life, death, and resurrection (fused!) using historical methods opens up a different angle of vision. It makes astoundingly clear that the satisfaction theory was not present in the unrolling of events. It beggars belief to think that this Jewish prophet who announced and enacted the joyful reign of the gracious and merciful God of Israel decided to go to Jerusalem to die in order to pay back the debt sinners owed to the offended honor of God, who could not forgive sin without the death of an innocent man. Not in your wildest dreams.

Elizabeth. What our trek through the scriptures gives us instead, to use alternative language, is a theology of accompaniment. It fosters the idea of salvation as the divine gift of "I am with you," even in the throes of suffering and death. Redemption comes to mean the presence of God walking with the world through its traumas and travail, even unto death. This theology entails a double solidarity, of the actual Jesus who lived with all who live, suffer and die, and of the resurrecting God of life with the ministering and crucified Jesus. The two solidarities are actually one as the story takes place, but we will consider them separately for the sake of clarity.

Clara. Regarding the first aspect of solidarity, it seems relatively simple to connect Jesus' own arc through time with all other human beings insofar as he is one of our race. I have always loved the way the letter to the Hebrews says that he was made like his brothers and sisters in every respect. "Because he himself was tested by what he suffered, he is able to help those who are being tested" (2:18). In other words, Christ knows from the inside what it is like to be human, and so he is able to sympathize with our weakness.

Elizabeth. Sharing our flesh and blood, he tasted death. By the grace of God he tasted it for everyone, so that the power of death itself and fear of death might be overcome. Those whom Jesus is not ashamed to call brothers and sisters can in turn call him "the pioneer of their salvation" (Heb 2:10). This is not just an objective solidarity, but a loving connection of the most intimate kind.

Liberation theologies today give a certain specificity to this solidarity, highlighting a powerful connection between the cross and the suffering of countless victims of injustice throughout history. "To die crucified does not mean simply to die, but to be put to death," presses Jon Sobrino; it is to suffer a death actively inflicted by unjust structures. In the United States what some call the nation's "original sin" of racism, expressed in structures and deeply rooted attitudes, plagues the lives of the black community. In Latin America millions of people live severely impoverished lives in economic and political circumstances maintained by military violence. Across the globe there are people pressed into slavery for the profit of others, refugees from conflict, victims of war, of economic aggrandizement, of ecological disaster, and of institutionalized violence of all kinds; some suffer domestic violence, rape, bullying, or persecution because of race, gender, sexual orientation, religion, or migrant status. So many are afflicted. To this litany of grief add those who suffer myriad existential setbacks, mental or physical illness, and the searing grief of bereavement.

Jesus' crucified death places him in solidarity with this desolation. Through that placement the cross of the risen Christ stands in history as an anguished if contradictory sign that, rather than abandoning them, the living God is present in the bleakest moment, accompanying them, intending to save.

Clara. Why do you call it contradictory?

Elizabeth. Because instead of associating divinity with power and glory, the cross also locates the living God with Jesus in the blood and guts of suffering. Even when experienced as absence, God is with him and with them, accompanying them through the anguish.

This is the second aspect of solidarity, and is an insight with teeth. To those who believe, the call from the depths of their relationship with God is to bend every effort to stand with God in solidarity with those who suffer; to right the wrongs, counter injustice, relieve the pain, and create situations where life can flourish. Then a resurrecting word can gain a foothold in this fractured world.

Clara. What you just said about God accompanying Jesus through the anguish—this goes directly counter to the satisfaction theory's view that divine honor required this death to pay the debt due because of sin. But did sin have anything to do with the cross?

Elizabeth. In one sense the tradition is right to say that Jesus died because of sin. But this refers to very specific sinful human actions of unjust judgment, torture, and execution, of death meted out by violence at the service of the power of empire. The story of Jesus told as accompaniment makes clear that there is no master plan in the divine mind to engineer his death in order to garner satisfaction for everyone else's sins. The cross was in no way necessary. Think about it. Wouldn't such an idea be blasphemy? It would ascribe to God, gracious and merciful, an evil that was done in the course of human injustice. How contradictory can you get?

Not even remotely did Jesus' death satisfy divine honor; it dragged that honor into the dust. Nor did Jesus' crucifixion change

God's attitude from anger to being appeased, as more popular atonement theologies would have it. I dare say that if the will of the living God had been carried out that "good" Friday, Jesus would not have been crucified.

The double solidarity of Jesus with those who suffer and of God with Jesus structures a theology of accompaniment so that it brings the presence of God who saves to the fore. Keep in mind that we are talking here about the same God who creates and delights in the world; the same God who sides with slaves against the might of Pharaoh, with exiles against their imperial captors, and now with a crucified prophet against the Roman empire; "a God merciful and gracious, slow to anger, and abounding in steadfast love and faithfulness, keeping steadfast love for the thousandth generation, forgiving iniquity and transgression and sin" (Ex 34:6–7). We are talking about the same gracious God, "your Savior and your Redeemer" (Isa 49:26), whom Jesus called father, whose compassion flashed out from the picturesque parables Jesus made up, and was tasted in the challenge and joy of his multiple interactions. Toward the end of the New Testament we read the bold statement that "God is love" (1 Jn 4:8). This is a pithy summary of all that has gone down in the history of revelation up to that point. God loves the world and, like any good lover, wants the beloved to flourish.

Given the negativity of the cross, the creative power of the loving God showed itself once again in an unexpected new way by (unimaginably) raising Jesus from the dead. But God neither needed nor wanted the cross. True, this evil was encompassed by providential action, by God writing straight with crooked lines. True, in an antagonistic world suffering borne in the loving struggle for the good of others can bear fruit. But in itself, violent death is not what God desires.

Schillebeeckx puts it bluntly in a statement that has caused some controversy but that I think gets it right: "we are not redeemed *thanks* to the death of Jesus but *despite* it." Rightly do we praise the fidelity of Jesus to his mission, and the love with which he went forward. But keeping a laser focus on the essence of the satisfaction theory in contrast with biblical testimony, we have to say that God did not need or want Jesus to suffer.

Clara. Let me raise an objection. Jesus died in desolation on the cross. The human power to destroy did its worst. Why did YHWH, his loving *abba*, not intervene?

Elizabeth. You raise here the thorny issue of theodicy, why evil exists in a world created by a good and great-hearted and all-powerful God. In my judgment the issue can never be resolved. None of the reasons adduced ever go the distance toward explaining the mystery of iniquity, why so many creatures are harmed. The question itself gets on the right track, however, when you realize that the relation of God to the world does not work like magic. To put this in medieval terms, God is not a being among other beings but Source of all beings. And God does not act like a bigger and better secondary cause, weighing in like any other created factor, but is the ultimate Creator of all causes. As such, God works in and through created causes, that is, in and through the free agency of secondary causes that operate according to their own norms and processes. Ordinarily, for all practical purposes, God does not intervene.

Clara. What this means is that when human creatures make bad decisions or act unjustly, when we sin, God does not prevent the effects. History proceeds with its own chaotic dynamic. This gives accompaniment an even sharper meaning.

Elizabeth. God is there, accompanying those who are suffering. The Creator is the Savior; in Jesus this becomes dramatically personal. Whether or not one feels divine presence, and in the depths of agony or despair one usually does not, God does not abandon.

Clara. God does not intervene, but neither does God abandon. The awful event of the crucifixion is the crux of this idea, isn't it?

Elizabeth. If any words dare be spoken, they would be words of hope that God was there, keeping vigil with the dying Jesus, accompanying him through his death. This was not apparent. The crucifixion, like too many other horrific scenes throughout history, showcases the anti-divine, an apparent silence instead of the loving presence of God. But in crying out the great "why" in protest against God's forsaking him, Jesus showed he had not abandoned God. That prayer carries the fragile, burning hope that God had not abandoned him either. Their mutual fidelity, symbolized in the women who stayed, is the one positive element on which the whole story turns.

Clara. So we can understand salvation as the presence of the living God companioning us in travail. This changes everything, doesn't it?

Elizabeth. Seeing the cross fused with the resurrection, faith can affirm that the creating God was with Jesus in this disaster. When human evil had done its worst, something more was in store for the person who had lived in history. Jesus died not into nothingness but into the arms of his loving God, the Redeemer of Israel, his *abba.* Death did not have the last word. Through the double solidarity of Jesus with those who suffer and of God with the crucified Jesus, a blessed future opens in hope for the rest of the world. In the tangle of our lives, graced fragments of personal, social, and ecological flourishing give foretastes of this blessed life, the fullness of which is still to come.

The liturgy of the Easter Vigil employs a wealth of symbols to point to this joyful truth: new fire struck from darkness, the paschal candle lit, the flame spreading throughout the community, an exulting song, ringing bells, green branches and flowers, water of baptism, oil of confirming, bread and wine of Eucharist. God raised Jesus from the dead, and the gift to this one historical person gives assurance of what lies ahead for all creation.

Never the cross in isolation: it has no causality with regard to the gracious will of God to save. But take the cross in relation to the ministry of the one who was crucified and raised from the dead: the whole event inscribes into history the powerful love of God who is with creatures in their agony, bent on redeeming the world. This is what the story of Jesus reveals.

Clara. "For I am with you to deliver you, says YHWH" (Jer 1:8). Maybe amid the power of injustice, destruction, suffering, and death at loose in our tumultuous world, a quiet "alleluia" can be heard.

Book IV

Interpretations Blossom

4.1 "Those who loved him did not cease"

Elizabeth. In the decades following the life, death, and resurrection of Jesus, the original band of disciples and then those who joined them bent every effort to understand what had happened and what they were called to do as a result. This was a period of intense creative interpretation. Inspired by the Holy Spirit they shared memories of Jesus, they prayed, they searched the scriptures, they conversed, they argued, they broke bread, they traveled on mission, they made decisions, they wrote letters and gospels, and they lived according to the "way" of Jesus, all while trying to discern the religious meaning of what had taken place and was still taking place. The writings of the New Testament let us listen in.

Clara. Speaking of this period, a passage in Josephus's *Jewish History* written in the late first century has always caught my interest. Shorn of later Christian interpolations it reads like this:

> At this time there lived Jesus, a wise man. For he was a doer of startling deeds, a teacher of people who receive the truth with pleasure. And he gained a following both among many Jews and among many of Greek origin. And when Pilate, because of an accusation made by leading men among us, condemned him to the cross, those

who had loved him previously did not cease to do so. And up until this very day the tribe of Christians, named after him, has not died out.

This view of how the community of disciples kept on loving Jesus touches my heart. More than half a century later, an outside observer presents loving Jesus as a main characteristic of the "tribe." It seems so simple, yet drives everything else.

Elizabeth. Jesus of Nazareth whom they had loved and followed had been cruelly put to death and no longer walked with them as in the days of his historical life. This was a shock. Yet in their community they experienced his continuing, encouraging presence as the risen Christ through the power of the Spirit. This was also a shock. Something extraordinarily significant had happened. The God who freed enslaved people from Egypt, who led exiles home from Babylon, who was gracious and merciful, abounding in loving-kindness and faithfulness, this God was doing a new thing. It shifted their overall view of the world. It upset their habitual ways of acting and thinking. It raised new questions. Who was Jesus really? How should they respond? The need to understand was a pressing, immediate challenge.

As might be expected, the early disciples turned to their Jewish scriptures with prayerful urgency. These sacred texts provided them with teachings, prophetic oracles, images, narratives, and religious wisdom that helped shape their interpretation of Jesus' life and destiny. One early insight held that the cross placed him in the long tradition of prophets who were persecuted for proclaiming the word of God. Another insight placed Jesus among the company of righteous people who suffered unjustly but received vindication from God. Soon, other important interpretations began to accrue.

As their mission expanded, believers who were no longer Jewish but Gentiles drew on their own Hellenistic religious traditions prevalent around the Mediterranean world. Everyday experiences of political, social, and family life also provided good metaphors to illuminate the religious significance of what was taking place through Jesus. By the end of the first century the Christian movement had burst forth with an extraordinary array of images, motifs, models, ideas, and themes to express the saving meaning of the "good news." And yes, love was at the heart of it.

Clara. This is so interesting. I wonder what we would have done in a similar situation. But this was the first century, and from Jewish to Gentile communities the scene kept changing. If you could quickly sketch how the situation evolved it would be helpful, because the Jesus movement ended up in a different place from where it started.

Elizabeth. Soon after Easter the disciples gathered in Jerusalem. As good Jews they continued to worship in the temple while "breaking bread" at home with gladness of heart. They lived with intense expectation that the last day of the old world order would soon draw to a close and the reign of God would dawn. However, the world kept on turning and that final day did not arrive. The delay of its arrival pushed them to a new conclusion, namely, that it would come soon, and in the brief time remaining they had to announce the good news to all of Israel. A period of energetic, committed mission resulted in the gospel being proclaimed in synagogue communities along the coast and beyond that into Jewish communities of the diaspora (the Jews who had emigrated, mostly to the trade centers of the Roman empire). Not too many Jews responded positively to their preaching.

Traveling missionaries began to encounter a number of interested Gentiles who wanted to join the Way. This raised the absolutely crucial question of whether these people had to convert to Judaism before joining the Christian community through baptism. The path through Judaism would include the requirement of circumcision for men. During a ground-breaking meeting of early church leaders in Jerusalem, it was decided that there was no need for anyone to convert to Judaism to join the community of Jesus' disciples. They had only to avoid idolatry and the sins associated with it: "It seemed good to the Holy Spirit and to us to impose on you no further burden than these essentials" (Acts 15:28). Subsequently, Gentile women and men joined the movement in large numbers. They brought with them different religious backgrounds which created new possibilities of interpretation beyond the patterns the early disciples saw in the Jewish scriptures.

A significant shift in thinking occurred in tandem with these changing circumstances. The early disciples were all Jews who shared a hope for the coming reign of God, which would bring about the restoration of Israel under a messiah from the line of David. In light of their personal experiences of the risen Christ and what they were learning from the success of their mission among the Gentiles, leaders in the budding communities reinterpreted the biblical promises of salvation to Israel. Instead of focusing on political aspects of the nation's restoration under a messianic king, they expanded hope of redemption to the whole world. In Christ the blessing given to Abraham and his descendants would overflow to the Gentiles. God's loving-kindness and faithfulness manifested in covenant mercy toward Israel, and while still including the covenant people, would offer salvation to the entire world.

The first generation of disciples began to die out, and then the second. In the unthinkably tragic catastrophe of 70 CE, the Roman army destroyed the city of Jerusalem and wrecked the temple. To this day Titus's arch still stands in the Roman Forum in Italy, showing the menorah and other sacred vessels of Jewish temple worship being marched in triumph down the processional route of the empire's capital. With Jerusalem a smoking ruin and its inhabitants scattered, the nation of Israel once again ceased to exist. With no more temple, priesthood, or animal sacrifices on the altar, the Jewish religion itself could have disappeared. A brilliant shift to a rabbinic form of Judaism centered on home and synagogue saved the tradition. As far as the community of believers in Jesus Christ was concerned, a remnant might have remained in the locale, but Jerusalem was no longer the center of the movement. All the gospels were written elsewhere, after that cataclysm, with full awareness of the disaster.

By the end of the first century all twenty-seven writings that now comprise the New Testament were in circulation, though their compilation into an approved list or canon was a process that took several centuries more. All transcribe the creative meditations of the first apostolic generations about the "gospel," by which they meant the dynamic power of good news centered through the Spirit in Jesus that opened up new experiences of God's mercy, shaped their community life, and inspired a practical way of love following the Way of Jesus.

During this time the cross continued to be a scandalous embarrassment. Somehow the disciples had to figure out how God had chosen to work through this folly. The fundamental arc of belief from the Exodus through the Jewish prophets to post-resurrection writings affirms the same conviction, that God is good and will prevail over evil, redeeming all creation. For Christians, Jesus Christ is at the center of this hope. But how to interpret the cross?

4.2   *The power of metaphor: salvation*

Clara. There is so much scholarship about this formative first century, isn't there? But to stay on track, we need to concentrate on ideas about salvation. As you have shown, Jesus loved faithfully to the point of death. In turn, through the power of the Spirit, God sustained him in and beyond the impenetrable situation of death. Enlivened by this same Spirit, first-century Christians gave creative voice to their understanding. What kind of language did they use? Did they focus on the satisfaction theory? Or talk of it at all? If not, how did they speak about redemption?

Elizabeth. Virtually every commentator points out that the New Testament has no logically articulated theory of salvation. No one composed a systematic explanation of how the life, death, and resurrection of Jesus, let alone the cross taken by itself, redeemed the world. There is no single doctrine. There is no Anselm in the first century. There are no theories, syllogisms, or tightly reasoned arguments. New Testament texts were not written in objectively academic language.

While the disciples did not theorize, what they did do was find metaphors in holy scripture as well as everyday life that illuminated their religious experience of the good news and helped them communicate it to others. Their writing is like poetry, a brief phrase here, a more extended reflection there, a flash of discovery here, a whisper of insight there. All the vivid metaphors hold that the saving God had acted through what happened to Jesus, but none try to rationalize precisely how this works. When pushed to their logical limits, the illuminating metaphors inevitably break down.

Clara. Didn't Aristotle, that great abstract philosophical thinker, praise this form of image-rich speech? He wrote, "The greatest thing by far is to be a master of metaphor. It is the one thing that cannot be learned from others. It is the mark of genius" (*Poetics*, 1459).

Elizabeth. It certainly marked first-century preaching and writing about the cross and resurrection. And with good reason. Metaphor can be used to illumine something that cannot be adequately described in everyday empirical terms. It is a figure of speech that takes the literal meaning of one known thing and extends it to shed light on something less accessible, like love or mental illness: "Shall I compare thee to a summer's day?"; "You are my sunshine"; "He fell into the trapdoor of depression."

We cannot confidently deduce further claims from metaphors. Consider Romeo's seeing Juliet on the balcony: "But soft, what light through yonder window breaks? It is the east and Juliet is the sun." Clearly, the metaphor shows her as the light and center of his life. But it does not mean that she is literally over ninety million miles away or has a core temperature of twenty-seven million degrees Fahrenheit. She is not the sun in that sense. Attempts to draw inferences from metaphors are always tricky and prone to crash into irrationality.

In this vein, recent developments in literary studies emphasize the power of metaphor to express central religious truths that are not completely open to rational analysis, because they are dealing with the holy mystery of God. "A mighty fortress is our God": how better to express divine strength and safeguarding? Unlike theories that may be mutually exclusive, a rainbow of metaphors can refract the same religious reality. Unlike defined concepts, metaphors also have an immediate emotional resonance, deepening their hold on human minds and hearts.

Clara. And you are saying that this was the situation for first-century believers in Jesus Christ, yes? They were dealing with new experiences of the mystery of the living God. So they used metaphoric images and comparisons to put the good news into evocative language ordinary people could understand in their own culture.

Elizabeth. Exactly. They pressed many different metaphors into service to express God's saving presence in Jesus' cross and resurrection. These motifs also became building blocks of their new community. With a strong focus on God's saving love in Jesus Christ and a hope that opens up the future, the language gave assurance that the community was on the right track.

Not all metaphors used in the New Testament appeal to twenty-first-century people, nor do they have to. Appreciating what they were doing, we can creatively add to the repertoire of salvific references with comparisons from our own culture; good preachers do this all the time. The point here is to understand the nature and power of the figurative language used in the New Testament, to respect it, and to avoid reducing the power of metaphor to flat literal language. Anselm's satisfaction theory turned a social practice into an ontological treatise, with terribly unfortunate effects. Surrounding his theory with a host of other metaphors can loosen the grip of his view so that more vibrant language about salvation can take center stage, some that may benefit the good of the earth. There are inspired alternatives.

Clara. In this discussion of salvific language, aren't we already using a metaphor? Isn't "salvation" itself already a metaphor?

Elizabeth. Indeed it is, so let us start here. The religious meaning of salvation has roots in the medical art of healing or curing. A medical practitioner brings people safely through an illness and restores them to health: he or she saves them. Over time in everyday usage the content of "to save" expanded beyond physical healing, with meanings that included to deliver, to rescue from danger, to help in distress, to protect or keep safe and sound, to preserve, and to make well and make whole. It meant restoration of physical and mental health and social well-being along with spiritual health. It meant healing in a comprehensive sense.

We have already seen how the prophets and psalms speak of the God of Israel as the Savior who acted again and again to save the people of Israel. A classic text in Isaiah portrays the dimensions of this salvation in gorgeous metaphors:

> Say to those who are fearful of heart, "Be strong, fear not. Here is your God . . . who comes to save you." Then the blind will see, the deaf will hear, the lame will leap like a deer, those who cannot speak will burst into song; the waters will flow in the desert, the dry haunt of jackals will become a swamp, the grasses will turn green;

a straight road will lie ahead, no lions will attack; the
redeemed shall walk home singing; "everlasting joy shall
be upon their heads, and sorrow and sighing shall flee
away." (Isa 35:4–10)

This is what it means to be saved.

The whole New Testament bears witness to the experience
of salvation coming from God in Jesus through the power of the
Spirit. The God of Israel, gracious and abounding in kindness, has
once again freely reached to people in distress through this carpenter from Nazareth, Jesus the Christ. In tune with his life, death, and
resurrection and the ongoing experience of the Spirit poured out
in their community, the disciples knew themselves to be healed
and at peace with God; this flowed into a profound mission to love
their neighbor in solidarity with Jesus' care for all.

Some New Testament authors connect salvation very
strongly with being restored from the ravages of sin; some do not.
The apostle Paul is clearly one who does. His letters tell us precious
little about the ministry of Jesus, but he was exuberant about how
through Jesus' death and resurrection God saves human beings
who are in a situation of mortal danger because of sin. Jesus "was
delivered over to death for our sins," he writes, "but raised to life
for our justification" (Rom 4:24). The cross may be foolishness
and a stumbling block, "but to us who are being saved it is the
power of God" (1 Cor 1:18).

Unlike Paul, the synoptic gospel writers do not restrict salvation to the paschal event but see it flowing through the ministry
of Jesus and the church's later preaching of the good news. Jesus'
healing work, his message, and way of life were already experienced as salvific, for this gift of graced wholeness has as much to
do with life on earth fully flourishing as with forgiveness of sin
and other spiritual blessings. In recent decades scholarly attention
has focused especially on Luke, author of a gospel and the Acts of

the Apostles, with strong debate over the thesis that his theology, unlike Paul's, does not connect the cross with the forgiveness of sin.* While seeing that the cross took place in accord with a divine plan for Christ's glory, Luke does not give it any kind of atoning significance.

Clara. This is kind of stunning, to discover that not all New Testament authors connected the cross with the forgiveness of sin.

Elizabeth. The point is that New Testament interpretations are diverse. If you read Luke through the prism of Paul, you will conflate them and miss the difference.

Clara. So salvation became a metaphor through which the disciples viewed these events: the gospel "is the power of God for salvation" (Rom 1:16), that is, for healing the world and making it whole. What other metaphors did they press into service? Scrolling through our biblical heritage might help to expand our imaginations beyond the satisfaction theory.

Elizabeth. Rather than proceeding author by author, a broad overview will highlight the seriously creative interpretations at play. In addition to the medical metaphor of salvation, we will consider military, diplomatic, financial, legal, cultic, and familial metaphors used by the disciples, as well as motifs drawn from biblical creation and servant texts. In the end we will see that this wealth of material simply does not admit of being sutured together into a coherent theory, at least not without disfiguring surgery.

4.3   *Military and diplomatic metaphors*

Elizabeth. The dramatic experience of victory on a field of combat serves as one metaphor for salvation in the New Testament. In the cross and resurrection of Jesus Christ, God triumphs over evil. The most obvious enemy to be defeated is death itself, a universal fact of human and all biological life over which no one has ultimate power. Isaiah had already proclaimed that God "will swallow up death forever" (25:8). Paul paraphrases that text at the end of a great riff on the resurrection of the dead:

> When this perishable body puts on imperishability, and this mortal body puts on immortality, then the saying that is written will be fulfilled: "Death has been swallowed up in victory." Where, O death, is your victory? Where, O death, is your sting? The sting of death is sin, and the power of sin is the law. But thanks be to God who gives us the victory through our Lord Jesus Christ. (1 Cor 15:53–57)

There were other enemies besides death to contend with. First-century cultures believed in the existence of supernatural spirits of various ranks that could wreak havoc with peoples' lives. These were called fallen angels, devils, rulers of this age, authorities, principalities and powers; Satan was their leader. The letter to the Ephesians describes it this way: "For our struggle is not against enemies of blood and flesh, but against the rulers, against the authorities, against the cosmic powers of this present darkness, against the spiritual forces of evil in the heavenly places" (6:12).

Clara. A more contemporary idea is that these principalities and powers can refer to structured forces of political, economic, social, and ecological injustice, not visible as single objects to the naked eye, but powerfully destructive of people's lives and the natural environment. Such forces may well be the demons of the present.

Elizabeth. The New Testament holds that the death and resurrection of Christ has broken the power of these evil forces. Talking about hardship and distress, persecution and the sword, Paul uses the language of victory when he writes: "In all these things we are more than conquerors through him who loved us." More than conquerors! And then the victory theme rings out: "For I am convinced that neither death, nor life, nor angels, nor rulers, nor things present, nor things to come, nor powers, nor height, nor depth, nor anything else in all creation, will be able to separate us from the love of God in Christ Jesus our Lord" (Rom 8:37–39).

One famous study by Gustaf Aulén declared that this dramatic motif of conflict-victory, expressed in a variety of forms, is not only the predominant idea in the New Testament but held pride of place for the first thousand years of Christian history. Aulén called it the "classic" view of salvation, a vigorously positive sense of God's victory in Christ that brings divine blessing, grace, forgiveness, and new life continuously poured out through the Holy Spirit. Its importance led Aulén to craft a new title to underscore the redeeming significance of Jesus crucified and risen: *Christus Victor.*

Clara. In contrast with the metaphor of being victorious in battle, is there another image of winning out over conflict that is a bit more peaceful?

Elizabeth. The metaphor of reconciliation serves this purpose. To reconcile means to restore relationships that have frayed. Differences may have divided people, or even nations, but being reconciled makes peace, restores harmony, buries the hatchet, so to speak. The disciples pressed this idea into service to express what God has effected through the cross and resurrection of Jesus: "In Christ God was reconciling the world to himself, not counting their trespasses against them, and entrusting the message of reconciliation to us," writes Paul (2 Cor 5:19).

Note that the working of this metaphor carries an important nuance. Disputes in personal and social relationships usually involve antagonism between two or more parties. Sometimes, however, estrangement is only on one side. One party becomes disaffected to the point of hostility while the other party continues to love and hope for a vibrant, peaceable relationship. Such could be the case with parents who love a rebellious child, or one partner who continues to love the other who strays. Such is the case envisioned here, with human beings alienated by their own uneasiness and rebellion from God who, rather than being alienated, never stops loving them. Through the life, death, and resurrection of Jesus, God reaches out to estranged folk and restores them to peaceful union with Godself.

In the relation between nations, reconciliation often means making peace after war. This usually requires the effort of diplomatic mediators. Scholars see this kind of diplomatic effort at play behind New Testament usage, with Jesus acting as the mediator. In face of all the uproar of a fractured world, while we were still alienated, redeeming grace created a situation where we can become friends of God again. "For if while we were enemies we were reconciled to God through the death of his son, much more surely, having been reconciled, will we be saved by his life. And so we boast in God through our Lord Jesus Christ through whom we have now received reconciliation" (Rom 5:10–11).

Clara. I can feel language straining here. Paul seems to be trying to articulate something good being experienced by the community. He does not explain how this is done, but affirms that through the cross and resurrection God put to death our own fighting hostility that made us aliens, strangers, afar off, having no hope.

Elizabeth. This breaking down of one-sided enmity and making peace extends far beyond the human race to include all hostile powers in the universe. The early Christian hymn in Colossians sang of it in these words: "through him God was pleased to reconcile to himself all things, whether on earth or in heaven, making peace through the blood of his cross" (1:20). Far from being simply an anthropocentric blessing, God's peace embraces whatever is hostile or fussing in the whole fractious universe.

Clara. I was once able to visit one of the best museums in the world, found in Oslo, Norway. It features people who have won the Nobel Peace Prize and shows photos, videos, and texts of their acceptance speeches. It left me dumbstruck and grateful to see how these women and men contended with the hostile forces not only of military violence but also of social injustice, political repression, and ecological devastation in order to bring about *shalom*. In the light of the New Testament view of reconciliation, giving this award to Jesus the Peacemaker might be appropriate.

Elizabeth. What an idea! Like the *caveat* that attends all recipients of the prize, giving Christ such a medal would come with the recognition that history continues in a violent world, so that the fullness of reconciliation has yet to take place. Still, the work of peacemaking offers a rich metaphor for salvation. With a foretaste of the fullness to come, believers can say of Jesus Christ, "he is our peace" (Eph 2:14).

4.4   Financial and legal metaphors

Clara. In addition to healing, victory, and peacemaking, the disciples also employed the financial transaction of redeeming someone, well-known to them from everyday practice. I recall that in civic society the act of redeeming was a business deal in which a family member paid a price to buy back the freedom of a relative who was in servitude to pay off a debt; sometimes they bought back family property. The freed person or land was restored to the payer's family, which became whole again. In scripture the practice of buying peoples' freedom already functioned powerfully to characterize God's work of liberation in the Exodus out of Egypt and the return of exiles from Babylon. Now the disciples used it of what transpired in Jesus.

Elizabeth. By the first century the practice was also commonly used for the emancipation of slaves. Either the slave would save up money, or someone acting on his or her behalf would come up with the right amount. The same kind of exchange could take place to ransom a prisoner of war or someone captured in battle. Money was handed over in exchange for freedom. This practice became a strong metaphor ready to hand to help interpret the cross and resurrection. Here God the Redeemer was at work once again to deliver people from bondage and bring them into a new relationship. The disciples named various oppressors that held them in bondage including sin, death, the law, the devil, the powers and principalities of this world, estrangements of all kinds. In Christ, God was redeeming or buying back the freedom of those heavily burdened, in order to acquire them as a newly dedicated people.

Clara. The question of price arises here, especially in view of Anselm's theory that the cross paid a debt. The metaphor does not suggest that divine honor is owed satisfaction because of sin, does it?

Elizabeth. Quite the contrary. Instead of receiving payment, God is the agent doing the paying. Early uses of the metaphor of redeeming did not speculate about what it cost to buy back our freedom or to whom God paid the fee. There was no point-for-point correspondence between the everyday practice and what went on with Jesus' death and resurrection. "You were bought with a price," writes Paul; "therefore glorify God in your body" (1 Cor 6:20). The metaphor worked by alerting readers to their change of status without going into details: "You were bought with a price; do not become slaves of human masters," but remain in the household of God (1 Cor 7:23).

In Mark's gospel, after the mother of James and John seeks a place of prominence for her sons among the disciples, Jesus' teaches about service using himself as a stunning example. Rulers among the Gentiles lord it over others and tyrannize their subjects, but it is not to be so among his followers. The great must be servants and the first must wait on others, just like Jesus who "came not to be served but to serve, and to give his life as a ransom for many" (Mk 10:45). Here the gospel depicts Jesus as a family member who offers his own self as the payment needed to redeem others. Clearly a piece of Markan theology, this saying sweeps the whole course of Jesus' life into the purse that wins freedom. Later authors worked the metaphor more specifically, seeing the cross as the high price that was paid. Toward the end of the first century one elder made the connection explicit, writing to a community under pressure that they were redeemed "not with perishable things like silver or gold, but with the precious blood of Christ, like that of a lamb without defect or blemish" (1 Pet 1:19). Still, as in the working of metaphor, the recipient of the payment is not specified. The image is not one that displays *how* God redeems us from bondage by the cross, any more than "Juliet is the sun" portrays who Juliet is. The metaphor focuses on the community's grateful relationship to God as those who are freed, ransomed, redeemed. To think otherwise is to literalize the metaphor, a theoretical blunder.

Clara. I've always thought the famous hymn written after his conversion by the slave trader John Newton is the best expression of what it means to be redeemed:

> Amazing grace! how sweet the sound,
> that saved a wretch like me.
> I once was lost, but now am found,
> was blind, but now I see.

He might just as well have sung something like:

> I once was enslaved, my spirit bound,
> redeemed, I now am free.

Elizabeth. Redemption uses an ancient financial custom to signify that divine mercy springs people free from sin of all kinds, personal, interpersonal, social, and institutional; delivers them from death and fear of death; and liberates them from bondage to be in turn persons of redeeming grace toward others whose lives can be a living hell. Rather than detailing a mechanism by which this happens, the metaphor gratefully celebrates the result.

Clara. It is interesting that despite its later influence, redemption is not the most prevalent metaphor in the New Testament, which does not even call Christ a Redeemer.

Elizabeth. It is simply one among many metaphors that point to the cross and resurrection as good news. "Since all have sinned and fall short of the glory of God, they are now justified by his grace as a gift, through the redemption that is in Christ Jesus" (Rom 3:23–24).

Clara. You have moved us to the next motif. In addition to redemption, this text also employs the motif of being justified. What does this mean? I know from friends that it is a legal metaphor, and that it is of major importance in the Protestant tradition, though it does not get much play in Catholic piety or theology.

Elizabeth. To be justified is to be acquitted. Used especially by Paul, this is a metaphor derived from a judicial procedure. Picture it: a law court is in session. Sinners are in the dock. Sitting enrobed as judge is the divine Maker of heaven and earth. To the astonishment of all, the accused are declared not guilty. The verdict is one of acquittal! In technical terms they are justified. In truth, they do not deserve this verdict. But the mercy of God declares and even makes them not guilty, motivated not by the merits of the defendants but by the depths of divine love. Later theology was to call this the sheer gratuity of grace, a gift given because God is good.

This metaphor has roots in the Christian Old Testament where the prophets at times depicted YHWH involved in a lawsuit with a rebellious people: "YHWH rises to argue his case; he stands to judge the peoples" (Isa 3:13). With a profound quality called righteousness, not odious self-righteousness but the uprightness of being true to oneself, YHWH manifests covenant mercy in these trial scenes by acquitting and vindicating the people: "I am the One who blots out your transgressions for my own sake, and I will not remember your sins" (Isa 43:25). This is not cheap grace, for the people need to change their ways. But such an acquittal sets up a new situation, a new salvific beginning in relationship to God, not just for the individual but for the whole community.

Knowledgeable about the scriptures, the apostle Paul was also acquainted with jurisprudence as practiced in the Roman empire. In a creative leap he linked the two and applied the juridical metaphor to the paschal mystery. The love of God that renders this verdict of "not guilty" is proved through "Christ Jesus who died, yes, and who was raised, who is at the right hand of God, who indeed intercedes for us," as if Christ were acting as a defense attorney (Rom 8:34). Sprung from jail, we are released into new, hopeful relationship with God. "Therefore, since we are justified by faith, we have peace with God through our Lord Jesus Christ" (Rom 5:1).

Clara. The inconsistency in Paul's use of this metaphor is interesting, isn't it?

Elizabeth. Yes. At one point our justification is due to Christ's death: "we have been justified by his blood" (Rom 5:9). At another point it is due to the resurrection: Jesus "was put to death for our trespasses and raised for our justification" (Rom 4:25). It is always God who justifies, but how this exactly works is unclear—more evidence, if such were needed, that no rational, systematic theory is being proposed but simply a motif that shines a spotlight on something wonderful.

Clara. It seems that consistency is a good quality for theories. But to seek consistency from a set of varying metaphors that yield a spread of insights really does miss the point.

Elizabeth. A further angle of great interest emerges in an essay on Paul's use of forensic metaphors in his letter to the

Romans. The author, Andrie du Toit, draws attention to the social situation of some of that letter's recipients. A substantial number of them would have been slaves or ex-slaves; their encounter with the Roman justice system would not have been happy, to say the least. "Since they belonged to the lower echelons of Roman society, many of them would have suffered from the sharp edges of the Roman judicial system [which did not offer equal treatment before the law]. They certainly would not have dreamed of any special favors." Instances of pardon did occur, but these were episodic and most often given only to the politically well-connected.

The justice of God, in contrast with the justice of empire, has as its astonishing outcome divine acquittal for everyone, Jew and Gentile alike. This is so contrary to expectations! The divine judge sides with the guilty, acquits regardless of merit. Mercy is now the norm. The only condition is that the accused should accept the offer of pardon and let it take effect in their lives. The result is truly stunning. Anyone who feels burdened with guilt can lift up their heads with joy, for "There is therefore now no condemnation for those who are in Christ Jesus" (Rom 8:1).

Clara. Today's theologies of liberation use the experience of becoming free as a basic reference point. Is this related to the metaphors we have already considered?

Elizabeth. You are right to point to this connection. The metaphors we already discussed, including being restored to health, victory over the powers that oppress, reconciliation from fractured relationships and the anguish that attends broken mutuality, redemption from slavery or bondage of any kind, acquittal from legal accusation and punishment: these all have the theme of liberation running through them. Interpreting the gospel in contemporary contexts of oppression, liberation theologians have lifted up what we might call this submerged metaphor and given it a powerful new lease on life. The oppression now being addressed may be spiritual or psychological, but it is more likely to be political, economic, social, cultural, or any combination thereof. The whole of the ministry, death, and resurrection of Jesus shows that God wants burdens lifted and people who are being crushed to be set free. The community of disciples today is called to speak and act as Jesus did, ringing cadences of liberation in the midst of conflict with the debilitating powers of this age: "For freedom Christ has set us free" (Gal 1:5).

4.5   *Cultic and sacrificial metaphors*

Clara. Blood and death: given the nature of sacrificial rituals in the Jerusalem temple, many of which included killing animals and sprinkling, smearing, or pouring their blood around the altar, it is no wonder the disciples drew metaphors from that arena to interpret the bloody death of Jesus on the cross. It would have been kind of unbelievable if they hadn't, wouldn't it?

Elizabeth. Yes, it would. While neither Jews nor Christians in our day sacrifice live animals as an act of worship, this practice was widespread in all the ancient religions of the Mediterranean world. The ritual was ready to hand for their use.

It is critically important to appreciate the Jewish understanding of these sacrificial rituals as discussed in biblical and Second Temple sources, because this core meaning came with the metaphor when the disciples applied animal sacrifice to the cross. Handing over precious animals, as well as other offerings such as cereal grain, fruits, and incense, was not done to appease an angry God or to pay a debt owed because of disobedience to divine law. Quite the contrary. Performed according to the law, these rituals expressed a desire to live in right relationship with God, and deepened or reset that relationship at certain key moments in the life of a person or the community. Sacrifices were offered to give thanks for a particular blessing, to mark significant life-cycle events, to repent from sin, to be purified from defilement, and to celebrate festivals.

In the case of animals, the law gave consideration to what people could afford. For example, on the Day of Atonement when the whole community repented of sin, a bull along with other animals needed to be sacrificed. On other occasions a lamb or goat would do. Poor people could bring doves or pigeons. Recall how when Mary and Joseph brought their firstborn to the temple, "they offered a sacrifice according to what is stated in the law of the Lord, a pair of turtledoves or two young pigeons" (Lk 2:24).

Usually the person making the offering, or sometimes a temple attendant, would kill the animal and collect the blood. A priest would sprinkle or pour out the blood around the altar, a symbol of God's presence, while music and prayers expressed a sense of relationship being strengthened between God and the one making the offering. Why the focus on blood? Blood is identified with life itself; without blood, an animal dies. Killing an animal and pouring its blood around the altar signified that its life was given back to YHWH, who gave it life in the first place. Burning the flesh gave over its life even further as the smoke ascended toward heaven. For many types of sacrifice, though not for sin-offerings, a portion of the flesh was given back to be shared with family in a kind of communion. Through these steps of offering something valuable, the life of the person or community giving up the animal was also symbolically given over to God.

Clara. Some of the prophets were harshly critical of sacrificial rituals, weren't they?

Elizabeth. They saw how superficial the practice could become, giving rise to a false confidence. If persons offering the sacrifice did not have the right sentiments, or if they violated the ethics of the covenant, especially regarding their neighbor, the ritual was worse than useless. One great oracle has YHWH say:

> I hate, I despise your feasts,
> and I take no delight in your solemn assemblies.

> Even though you offer me your burnt offerings and
>   grain offerings,
>   I will not accept them;
> and the offerings of your fatted animals
>   I will not look upon.
> Take away from me the noise of your songs;
>   I will not listen to the melody of your harps.
> But let justice roll down like waters,
>   and righteousness like an ever-flowing stream.
>   (Amos 5:21–24)

Clara. It sounds like prophetic criticism tried to keep sacrifice on the right track, preventing it from becoming self-serving and forgetful of God's heart.

Elizabeth. Every institutional religion needs this kind of bracing critique. When entered into with the right spirit, however, these rituals could have the intended effect of deepening relationships between the covenant people and their God. On balance, the sacrificial system was understood in this way as a means of communion, purification, and rededication.

Clara. With that background in view, how did the disciples use animal sacrifice as a metaphor for the cross?

Elizabeth. First and foremost they drew on the annual sacrifice of lambs at the feast of Passover. This had nothing to do with repentance for sin, but everything to do with the celebration of freedom from slavery in Egypt. Recall how on the eve of their escape Moses instructed the people to procure a lamb for a final meal, relaying careful instructions about its preparation, including that "you shall not break any of its bones" (Ex 12:46). They were to smear its blood over their lintels and doorposts; this would protect inhabitants of the house when the angel of death passed over Egypt.

In subsequent centuries Passover became one of the great pilgrimage feasts. Thousands of people traveled to Jerusalem to celebrate. Among other preparations, each family grouping had to pro-cure a lamb and have it sacrificed in the temple before sitting down to the Passover meal with all its traditions. The Passover sacrifice of lambs, as it is described in ancient sources, was part of a joyful ritual of remembrance and belonging in a celebrating community. According to one ancient description: "The people of Israel who were in Jerusalem kept the festival of Unleavened Bread with great gladness for seven days; and the Levites and the priests sang the praises of YHWH day after day, accompanied by loud instruments. . . . So the people ate the food of the festival for seven days, sacrificing communion offerings and giving thanks to the God of their ancestors" (2 Chron 30:21–22). Festivity, loud music, good meals, the social vibe of a people rejoicing, all thankful for freedom in the name of God: sacrifice had its place in this setting.

So too with Jesus. The early disciples quickly saw in the passover lamb a symbol for Jesus whose death and resurrection was bringing about liberation from bondage of all kinds. How better to proclaim this than to declare, "For Christ, our paschal lamb, has been sacrificed" (1 Cor 5:7)! The symbolism is dense with meaning, and making a one-to-one correspondence ruins the metaphor. It summons up the whole joyful feast.

Toward the end of the first century John's gospel alluded to the same animal by noting that when Jesus was crucified, "it was the day of preparation for the Passover, and it was about noon," the hour coinciding with the time thousands of passover lambs were being killed in the temple (Jn 19:14). The connection becomes more explicit after Jesus died when the soldiers pierced his side with a lance rather than breaking his legs: "These things occurred so that the scripture might be fulfilled, 'none of its bones shall be broken'" (Jn 19:36).

Clara. So the image of Jesus as the Lamb of God is based on the many lambs that were killed and eaten to celebrate Pass-over. As you said, the meaning of this ritual connotes belonging to a joyful community stemming from an event of liberation, not repentance for sin.

Elizabeth. Before leaving the story of the Exodus, I want to mention one other event in the founding story of Israel that also provides a metaphor of sacrifice with no connection to sin. Leading the escaped Israelites through the wilderness, Moses came to Mount Sinai. There he encountered the Holy One who communicated the desire to forge a deep and lasting bond, a covenant, with the people whereby "they will be my people and I will be their God" (paraphrased by Jer 32:38). When the people heard this they agreed, and a formal ritual marked the occasion. An altar was built; oxen were sacrificed; their blood was collected. What followed is quite graphic. "Moses took half of the blood and put it in basins, and half of the blood he dashed against the altar." Next he read out the terms of the covenant, to which the people wholeheartedly agreed. Then "Moses took the blood and dashed it on the people and said, 'See the blood of the covenant that YHWH has made with you in accord with all these words'" (Ex 24:4–8). Visually the people were connected with the altar, both splashed bloody red in a living bond of covenant union.

So too with Jesus. The disciples figured that the blood of his body spilled in death forged a new covenant, one written on the heart, as the prophet Jeremiah had envisioned. This theme comes to the fore in the different accounts of Jesus' words over the bread and wine at the last supper. Paul passed on an early version: "In the same way he took the cup also, after supper, saying, 'This cup is the new covenant in my blood'" (1 Cor 11:24). The Christian ritual of the Eucharist came to be understood as a sacrifice patterned partly on the covenant ritual, with the blood of the crucified Jesus signifying a covenant relationship, in analogy with the oxen at Sinai that were "sacrificed as offerings of well-being to YHWH" (Ex 24:5).

Clara. This kind of sacrifice was a ritual that established relationship between people and God. Like the sacrifice of the passover lambs, it was not done to repent for sin. I can see how interpreting the blood of the cross using these rituals probably worked well for people who were used to worshiping God by means of animal sacrifice. And it shows again how literalizing a metaphor fails to plumb its depths. But for myself, I find this repugnant.

Elizabeth. Hold onto that response until we take note of two more sacrificial rituals, both of which do in fact involve repentance for sin. These are the sin-offerings that occurred daily in the temple and the once-a-year sacrifice on the Day of Atonement.

Zeroing in on these rituals, it is vital to keep in mind the meaning of temple sacrifice as described above. Sin disrupted the covenant relationship with God and defiled the individual, the community, the land, even the temple. As shown throughout the scriptures, the God of Israel, gracious and merciful, held steady with the initiative to wipe out sin and heal offenses. Seeking to repent, people engaged in formal ritual practices to act out symbolically that they were returning to God, that purification was taking place, that everyone and everything was being consecrated anew. Animals were sacrificed, their blood poured out, prayers said. Through these religious gestures, people understood that their covenant relationship was reset. Purified from sin they went forward in restored communion, with resolve to live henceforth more fully for God.

Clara. This reminds me a little bit of the sacrament of reconciliation. It's not that going to the priest and confessing your sins makes God merciful to you, because God is already merciful. But when you go through the ritual of confessing, and express sorrow, receive absolution, and do penance, it changes something in you. The ritual makes you open to the grace of forgiveness in a concrete way and sets a new mood going forward.

Elizabeth. That is a very astute comparison. The important thing to keep in mind is that the ancient practice of sacrifice for sin, rather than intended to placate God, was performed according to the sacred law of the community in response to divine mercy. In the words of biblical scholar James Dunn, "Properly speaking, in the Israelite cult, God is never propitiated or appeased. The objective of the atoning act is rather the removal of sin, that is, either by purifying the person or object, or by wiping out the sin."

Clara. If I understand this correctly, it's not that sacrifice pays back something that persuades God to be merciful, because as you said, God holds steady. But it functions to reset the relationship on the human side.

Elizabeth. Good. God did not need sacrifice in order to forgive sin. Such rituals could even, in their own way, distort the free gift of divine mercy if people thought they were earning it *quid pro quo*. But when a person approached with a sincere heart to repent, then an animal's life poured out in its blood could function to seal the giver's re-commitment. He, she, or they left cleansed and rededicated; their relationship to God, broken by their own misdeeds, was restored.

Clara. So this happened every day in the Jerusalem temple. Numerous people came forward with animals to be sacrificed in repentance for sin. This practice of sin-offering was normal to the early disciples. How did they draw on it to interpret the cross?

Elizabeth. They interpreted Jesus' death as a sacrifice in accord with the ancient Jewish theology and ritual of the sin-offering. He was like a lamb on the altar of God, ritually sacrificed in repentance for sin. Paul writes, Jesus is the one "whom God put forward as a sacrifice of atonement by his blood, effective through faith" (Rom 3:25). The word atonement, *hilasterion* in Greek, is sometimes translated as expiation, with the same meaning. Note that God is the one making the offering (to whom? the metaphor doesn't work if you get too literal); Jesus is the animal; his blood poured out becomes a symbol of his life given over to purify and consecrate. The Roman Catholic liturgy uses this sacrificial metaphor every day in its communion ritual: "Behold the Lamb of God who takes away the sin of the world" (Jn 1:29).

Clara. Not to digress, but I enjoy ancient descriptions of how much cleaning up the priests had to do, scrubbing away the blood in the sanctuary and washing down the whole area every evening. They worked barefoot, with the sleeves of their tunics tightly laced, but still ended up spattered with blood from hundreds or even thousands of animals. It is hard to imagine.

Elizabeth. Yes, and most likely even harder to do. Let me call attention to one final sacrifice for sin performed annually on the Day of Atonement, Yom Kippur. On this day of strictly observed rest and fasting, the whole community prayed for forgiveness in accord with the Torah. The ritual performed by the high priest in the temple was the central feature of the day. After sacrificing a bull and other animals in the outer part of the court, he went with their blood through the hanging veil into the Holy of Holies, the sacred inner sanctum where God most assuredly dwelt, entered only once a year on this day. There he sprinkled the blood on the ark of the covenant, or, after the exile, on the raised part of the floor where it had once stood, offering these lives in repentance for his own sins and the sins of all the people. The ceremony made visibly concrete how seriously the Jewish people took their breaking of the covenant and how intent they were on re-establishing right relations with their all-holy, loving, and faithful covenant Partner. The ritual with accompanying prayers and music was a deeply religious experience of the mercy of God that re-centered the whole community for another year.

So too with Jesus. There was nothing in his life as a layman from Galilee that led anyone during his lifetime to think he was a priest, let alone a high priest. In actual fact, he wasn't. When he was crucified there were no priests or altars or temple prayers, just soldiers executing a condemned man.

With the cultic metaphor, however, the disciples imagined him in the role of the high priest as well as the multiple roles of the sacrificed animals, the curtain of the Holy of Holies, and the blood of the sin offering on Yom Kippur. This plays out most strongly in the letter to the Hebrews, where Jesus is portrayed as "a merciful and faithful high priest in the service of God, to make a sacrifice of atonement for the sins of the people" (2:17). The sacrifice he made was himself, entering into the Holy of Holies "not with the blood of goats and calves, but with his own blood, thus obtaining eternal redemption" (9:12). Sympathizing with our weakness, he gives us courage to approach the throne of grace with boldness, "for if the blood of goats and bulls, with the sprinkling of the ashes of a heifer, sanctifies those who have been defiled so that their flesh is purified, how much more will the blood of Christ, who through the eternal Spirit offered himself without blemish to God, purify our conscience from dead works to worship the living God!" (9:14).

Clara. So as with the animals, Christ's blood is meant to sanctify humans, not placate God! I am struck by two things. All of these overlapping sacrificial images provided rich material ready to hand for the disciples' interpretation of the cross and resurrection, which in their experience had brought them into a new kind of saving relationship with God. I can see that. But this seems so foreign and even repellent to many of us today.

Elizabeth. Along with many other contemporary theologians, I think you are making a valuable point. Speaking of the sacrificial image of blood poured out for us, Karl Rahner observes that while it worked well in the New Testament milieu, "this notion offers little help to us today towards the understanding we are looking for." Better to start with the significance of the resurrection for salvation, he proposes, and from there try to clarify the salvific meaning of Jesus' death within the limits of the New Testament context. Edward Schillebeeckx, too, asks whether we are bound by these references to expiation, atonement, and sacrifice. He thinks not. Like the first Christians we need to reflect out of our own background. Then the loving service of Jesus' entire life that came to a climax in his death "may have to be expressed for us in an articulation containing different emphases and distinctions from the interpretations in the New Testament, conditioned as they were by already given cultural and religious concepts."

Clara. In other words, we are not bound by these ancient sacrificial metaphors.

Elizabeth. In truth, not only is the sacrificial system no longer plausible to people's everyday reality, but the bloodiness of the sacrificial metaphor repels many today since it seems to validate violence in a world wracked by bloodshed, as if killing someone could be of benefit. There is the further concern today about the ethics of killing and eating animals.

Apart from the cultural lack of resonance and the ethical issues, both of which have damaging pastoral implications, I see a knotty problem in the way Christian theology distorted the cultic metaphor's connection between sacrifice and sin. Despite the Jewish interpretations that give priority to God's mercy, the past centuries of Christian theological writing and liturgical prayers slipped into the idea that sacrifice has some placating force, that Jesus' death has some appeasing effect on God's wrath. Similar to the way Anselm's question set up the presumption that Jesus had to die, so too the temple practice of sacrificial sin-offering, when applied to Jesus, over time has made it seem as if his death caused divine forgiveness of sin. It didn't, of course. The mercy of God is not dependent on the death of Jesus. But overuse of the cultic metaphor has caused it to lose its poetic resilience. It has been interpreted literally, giving rise to a terrible misunderstanding.

Clara. It's odd to realize how this imagery has survived in Christian ritual, theology, and spirituality, while Jewish ritual sacrifice of animals as sin-offering has not been practiced for two thousand years.

Elizabeth. Doesn't this show the power of metaphor!

4.6   *Family metaphors*

Clara. How did the experience of belonging to a family provide yet more metaphors for interpreting salvation?

Elizabeth. Ordinarily in the ancient Mediterranean world, a person did not function in isolation but as an interdependent part of an *oikos*, the Greek word for household or home, a center of human relations with a strong economic component. Belonging to a family allowed a person to share in household goods such as food, clothing, and shelter. Just as significantly, it gave one a social identity, a way of being alive in the world as a member of this group. Unlike the individualistic notion of the self in Western democracies but very much like the sense of self in contemporary Latino/a and Native American cultures and many traditional societies, the sense of self was collective, interwoven with family and community belonging.

The ordinary way of joining a family was by being born into it through the pregnancy and labor of a female member. The head of household could also adopt someone into the family; at times this would happen with a favored slave. Being without affiliation with a family left one socially homeless, truly adrift in that cultural milieu.

The disciples drew on this familiar, vital reality to articulate what had been accomplished in the life, death, and resurrection of Jesus Christ. In a word, this event allowed people to become beloved children in the family of God. Henceforth they could partake of the goods of the household and participate in its activities while being bathed in mutual affection. The community shared the gift of the Spirit of the risen Christ who enfolded them with love: "the love of God has been poured into our hearts through the Holy Spirit given to us" (Rom 5:5). The experience of being children of God enabled a way of life based on loving as Jesus does, thanks to the fundamental grace of belonging.

Clara. So how do we become members of this family?

Elizabeth. The apostle Paul used the metaphor of adoption to describe the process. Writing to the Galatians he declares that God sent his Son to redeem us, "so that we might receive adoption as children. And because you are children, God has sent the Spirit of his Son into our hearts, crying 'Abba, Father.' So you are no longer a slave but a child, and if a child then also an heir, through God" (4:5–7). Note the elements entailed in adoption. The initiative lies with God. Thanks to Christ, already a family member, the person is introduced to the family. The Spirit of Christ enables intimacy with the powerful head of household, to the point of trustfully using a colloquial name. The adopted child enjoys a very different status from that of a household slave. And the child stands to inherit, which ensures a beneficial future. The metaphor works to express the good news of salvation by appeal to the change in status from being a slave to being a family member, part of a circle of caring and great blessing.

Paul insisted on these inestimable benefits, as in this extended passage from Romans: "For all who are led by the Spirit of God are children of God. For you did not receive a spirit of slavery to fall back into fear, but you have received a spirit of adoption. When we cry, 'Abba! Father!' it is that very Spirit bearing witness with our spirit that we are children of God, and if children, then heirs, heirs of God and joint heirs with Christ" (Rom 8:14–17). We share with Christ all the goods that come with belonging to the divine household.

Clara. Besides adoption, how else might we become part of God's family?

Elizabeth. We can be born into it. The idea that community members are "born of God" runs like a thread through the gospel and letters of John. In being brought to a new way of living, imbued with God's own Spirit, people are born again as children of God. When the Pharisee Nicodemus came to see Jesus by night, he was incredulous at the very idea. "How can anyone be born after having grown old? Can one enter a second time into one's mother's womb and be born?" Rather than backing off, Jesus counseled him not to be astonished at the idea of being "born from above." It is the work of the Spirit of God, not fully explainable. It happens like the wind blowing where it will, coming from where you know not and going somewhere else you do not know. "So it is with everyone who is born of the Spirit" (Jn 3:1–8).

The Nicodemus story expands upon the idea of birth from God that was already dramatically announced in the opening prologue of John's gospel. Jesus, the Word of God, has come into the world, a light shining in the darkness. To those who believe, "he gave power to become children of God." This happened as they "were born, not of blood, or of the will of the flesh, or of man, but of God" (Jn 1:12–13). Born of God: members of the community are gifted with a new life that is beyond human ability to produce. They are brought to birth as God's very own children. Through the power of grace the relationship is that organic.

The writer of the Johannine letters uses the same metaphor multiple times over. "Beloved, we are God's children now" (1 Jn 3:2); "Those who have been born of God do not sin" (1 Jn 3:9); everyone who believes in Christ "has been born of God" (1 Jn 5:1). Being children of God, born of God, becomes a personal, spiritual identity that shows itself in interior dispositions as well as in actions that benefit others. One powerful text expresses the result in memorable terms: "Beloved, let us love one another, because love is from God; everyone who loves is born of God and knows God" (1 Jn 4:7). The reason propelling this dynamic is that "God is love" (1 Jn 4:16): like mother, like child.

Clara. Born of God: this metaphor raises the evocative image of God engaged in the female work of carrying in the womb and giving birth. It reminds me of Second Isaiah's image of the redeeming God as a woman in labor crying out, groaning, panting to bring forth the new creation (42:14), or Deuteronomy's image of God as a pregnant woman birthing a people (32:18).

Elizabeth. The verb used in the Johannine texts, *gennao*, can have either a man or a woman as the acting subject. While it can refer to male begetting, it clearly has women as its life-giving subject when it refers to Elizabeth's childbearing in her old age (Lk 1:13, 57) and to Mary's conceiving Jesus (Matt 1:20). In a long discourse Jesus also employs the verb with unmistakable female meaning: "When a woman is in labor, she has pain, because her hour has come. But when her child is born, she no longer remembers the anguish because of the joy of having brought a human being into the world" (Jn 16:21). The metaphor of being born of God carries unmistakable female resonance.

Clara. Is it in line with this tradition when in the fourteenth century Julian of Norwich used the metaphor of giving birth to meditate upon the cross? She sees that Jesus' suffering was like the pain of childbirth, complete with blood and water flowing from the body.

Elizabeth. Hear how eloquently she unpacks the metaphor using the female experience of birthing, nursing, and raising a child. "We know that all our mothers bear us for pain and for death, O what is that! But our true Mother Jesus, he alone bears us for joy and for endless life, blessed may he be. So he carries us within him in love and travail, until the full time when he wanted to suffer the sharpest thorns and cruel pains that ever were or will be, and at the last he died," enduring the suffering of labor and a death that gives us birth. Going further, she reveals that his love was not finished at birthing but continues with the nourishment of the Eucharist: "The mother can give her child to suck of her milk, but our precious Mother Jesus can feed us with himself, and does so, most courteously and most tenderly, with the blessed sacrament, which is the precious food of true life." Like a mother who lays her child on her breast, guards and protects her baby, and in later years teaches and disciplines the growing child, so too with our tender Mother Jesus who through it all says, "See how I love you." Julian's riffs on the Johannine metaphor of being "born of God" show the possibility of growing this biblical metaphor of salvation beyond its first-century usage. Whether by adoption or birth, the grace offered in Christ enables believers to be part of the family of God, with all the benefits that ensue.

4.7   Metaphor of new creation

Clara. How did the book of Genesis offer yet another startling metaphor?

Elizabeth. The surprising change that the Spirit of the risen Christ brought into the disciples' lives led to the thought that the world was starting over again, this time on a better footing. The exuberance of this feeling bursts out in exclamations such as, "If anyone is in Christ, there is a new creation; everything old has passed away; see, everything has become new!" (2 Cor 5:17). The theme becomes more specific in a lovely connection between the coming of Christ and the first day of creation: "For God who said, 'Let light shine out of darkness' has shone in our hearts" with the light of Jesus Christ (2 Cor 4:6, paraphrasing Gen 1:3). The new world coming into being includes all things in heaven and on earth, gathered into glory by the lavish gift of God.

The metaphor of a new creation underlies a famous comparison between Adam and Christ crafted by Paul. In the Genesis story of the first human couple in the garden, their original idyllic life unravels due to their wrong choice, which leads to a world of trouble. Salvation in Christ has turned this around, starting off a new creation. To argue this case, Paul drew an extended analogy comparing the first human being Adam, "the man of dust," with the human being Jesus Christ, "the man of heaven." Every human being is affected by what each of them does. Adam's disobedience brings sin, condemnation, and death into the world. Christ's obedience brings grace, justification, and new life.

The good news is that the two are not equal. "For if the many died through one human being's trespass, much more surely has the grace of God and the free gift of the one human being, Jesus Christ, abounded for the many" (Rom 5:15). Where sin abounds, grace does superabound. The scales are tipped toward salvation. There is a power in God's mercy shown in Jesus Christ that starts a new chapter for the human race, so to speak, awash in love and the hope of eternal life.

Clara. This is a fine analogy for its own day, but I find it problematic because Jesus of Nazareth was an actual historical human being whereas Adam is a figure in a religious myth of origins, not a real person. In addition, we know that death was in the world for millions of years before human beings evolved. I know what you are going to say—that in the first century no one practiced biblical scholarship or scientific investigation as we do today, and we must respect their own cultural context. But the problem comes when people take this comparison literally and try to make sense of it in their own lives. And I know what you are going to say about this too, that it shows ever more clearly the importance of interpretation.

Elizabeth. You are right on both counts! If you let the idea of a new start shine through, with the power of good stronger than evil, then this metaphor will be doing its work.

4.8   "Your holy servant Jesus" (Acts 4:30)

Elizabeth. Early Christians engaged in yet another creative interpretation. They drew on the Servant poems in Second Isaiah to understand Jesus' mission and death. This mapped the crucified Jesus onto an unnamed figure who not only bore terrible suffering and was ultimately exalted, but whose suffering was for the sake of others.

Clara. As I recall, the figure of the servant in all four poems was generally taken to personify the whole covenant community of Israel. Now the servant came to be identified with one of its members, Jesus Christ.

Elizabeth. Mind you, it is not the case that Second Isaiah was making predictions about Jesus. The link was forged in reverse. The disciples saw connections between Jesus and the servant, just as they did with the paschal lamb, the blood of the covenant, Adam, and the Torah-regulated practice of redeeming a relative.

Clara. Were all four of the servant poems used to interpret Jesus?

Elizabeth. Indeed they were. The first one appears almost verbatim in Matthew's gospel to interpret Jesus' healing mission:

> "Here is my servant, whom I have chosen,
>   my beloved, with whom my soul is well pleased.
> I will put my Spirit upon him,
>   and he will proclaim justice to the nations. . . .
> A bruised reed he will not break,
>   and a smoldering wick he will not quench,
> until he brings justice to victory."
>   (Matt 12:18–21, citing Isa 42:1–4)

The second song's emphasis on bringing light to the Gentiles is applied in Luke's gospel to Jesus in his infancy via the canticle of Simeon (Lk 2:30–32), and again to justify expanding the Christian mission from the Jews to include all the nations (Acts 13:47, citing Isa 49:6).

Clearly the Servant Song with the most impact was the fourth (Isa 52:13–53:12). Filled with terrible descriptions of suffering, its main contribution lies in going beyond the traditional theme of the righteous sufferer whom God vindicates. What the fourth song uniquely says is that the servant's suffering benefits others.

Clara. Did this help the disciples see that the cross was *for us*, for many, for all?

Elizabeth. It surely did. The third song already hints at trouble when the servant who faithfully teaches and comforts the weary is beaten, insulted, and spat upon, all the while trusting in God for vindication: this is the traditional theme of the righteous sufferer. But then the fourth song amplifies the impact of the servant's suffering with the radical claim that "by his bruises we are healed" (53:5). This final song of the servant is replete with suffering. Marred in appearance, despised and rejected, "a man of sorrows and acquainted with grief," wounded, despised, rejected, oppressed, and afflicted, counted among the transgressors, cut off from the land of the living by a perversion of justice, buried among the wicked although he had done no violence, this servant figure had an obvious, profound resonance with the early Christian community's memory of Jesus tortured, crucified, and buried.

In view of this crushing pain, the song ends with abrupt vindication: "See, my servant shall prosper; he shall be exalted and lifted up" (52:13); he shall live a long life and see his offspring; and "out of his anguish he shall see light" (53:11). The difference from other Old Testament texts about the vindicated sufferer comes when this torment is seen somehow to help others. "The righteous one, my servant, shall make many righteous, and he shall bear their iniquities.... [H]e poured out himself to death, and was numbered with the transgressors; yet he bore the sin of many, and made intercession for the transgressors" (53:11–12). As Daniel Berrigan observes, there is great irony here. The servant has been denied justice, but brings others to justice. His love is in service to others; he "invites the unjustified to the justice of God, that is to say, to holiness, to the all but unimaginable possibility of love."

Some scholars think that the persecution of the Jews under Antiochus IV in the second century BCE first prompted interpretation of Isaiah's fourth servant song in the direction of suffering borne for the good of others. In those days people faithful to the law were being abused and even killed. Hope arose that they would be lifted up after death to shine like the stars, as the book of Daniel put it, and that in some way their suffering would bring blessing upon the community. One text praised the revered elder priest Eleazar and the faithful mother with her seven sons because their courageous witness to the faith preserved the nation; they became "as it were, a ransom for the sin of our nation. And through the blood of those devout ones and their death as an atoning sacrifice, divine providence preserved Israel that had previously been mistreated" (4 Macc 17:21–22).

Clara. Don't miss the "as it were." Again, not a literal connection between their blood and a ransom for sin. What you are saying is that Christian interpretation took this already existing Jewish idea and applied it to their new circumstances. Here was a pattern of thinking that allowed them to acknowledge the pain of the cross and, in light of the resurrection, to find blessing for the transgressing world. It offered, so to speak, a key to interpreting the horrific event.

Elizabeth. Yes. The spiritual depth of this move comes to light in an observation Edward Schillebeeckx made, obviously out of his own piety. The effort to understand Jesus' death and resurrection through the lens of the suffering Servant of God has deep roots in Jewish spirituality, he suggests. "The Christians of the earliest local churches were apparently able to overcome the embarrassment they continued to feel because of Jesus' execution only by prayerful meditation on the sacred Scriptures, the Old Testament." Just imagine the insights that flowed when they made the connection between the servant and Jesus. Only contemplative grappling with the scriptures could elucidate for them the salvific implications of his suffering, and then only to a limited extent. Not rational analysis but prayerful reflection moved them to the insight that the cross was something undergone "for us."

As in the Jewish scriptures so also in the Christian, there is no explanation of how innocent suffering works to bring about salvation. But a metaphorical link is forged that gives faith a language to express good news.

Clara. The story of the Ethiopian eunuch trying to figure out the fourth poem brings this insight to joyful expression. An African official is riding in his chariot along the road to Gaza, reading aloud about the humiliation of the servant being led like a sheep to slaughter. The apostle Philip draws alongside and gets invited to hop in. "The eunuch asked Philip, 'About whom, may I ask you, does the prophet say this, about himself or about someone else?' Then Philip began to speak, and starting with this scripture, he proclaimed to him the good news about Jesus" (Acts 8:34–35). This good news led to the Ethiopian being baptized and he went on his way rejoicing.

Elizabeth. Note the joy in this story. There is no dolorism or dwelling on pain, but only the gospel message that the gracious, liberating God of Israel, God of the Exodus and return from exile, had acted again in an unimaginable way to restore new life out of someone's unjust execution, which spills over into blessing for all: the good news about Jesus.

Clara. How does this fourth servant poem show up in other New Testament writings?

Elizabeth. The community adapted its structure, which moves from the depths of the servant's suffering to the heights of exaltation, in significant ways. In one of the most telling instances, Paul writes that he is handing on what he had received from the young community, namely, "that Christ died for our sins in accordance with the scriptures, and that he was buried, and that he was raised on the third day in accordance with the scriptures"(1 Cor 15:3–4). Died for us—was raised: the pattern of the servant song was worked out early on and repeats with regularity: Christ "was handed over to death for our trespasses and was raised for our justification" (Rom 4:25).

The influential hymn in Philippians about Jesus' self-emptying was likely also constructed on the same pattern of the servant poem in Isaiah. Be like Christ, they sang, who emptied himself, becoming obedient to death on a cross, for which reason God has highly exalted him. The kenotic phrase "he emptied himself" (Phil 2:7) closely renders the text in the fourth servant song "he poured himself out" to death (Isa 53:12); and then he was exalted.

The servant motif appears in the words over the bread and the cup at the Last Supper: "given for you" (Lk 22:19). It appears in the synoptic gospels: "he took our infirmities and bore our diseases" (Matt 8:17, citing Isa 53:4), and in the later epistles: "by his wounds you have been healed" (1 Pet 2:24, citing Isa 53:5). Jesus lived out the vocation of the servant unto death, for our benefit. Such was the interpretation of the cross through the lens of the servant poems.

Clara. I start to get nervous with this emphasis on suffering, as if it were of benefit in its own right. Too many women, for example, have endured violence in their home only to be told by clergymen that they should submit to their husbands and suffer like Christ who opened not his mouth . . . and should do so for the sake of the children. No joy of the coming kingdom here.

Elizabeth. Applying this metaphor indiscriminately can oppress and even punish persons who are without power in a violent situation. But there is another angle that comes to the fore in a different context. In El Salvador Jesuit theologian Jon Sobrino has spotlighted the deep human good that emerges in a community when someone freely suffers in the struggle for justice. "As often occurs in Latin America," he writes, "in the presence of the martyrs, when human beings understand there has been love, they understand it as good news, as something deeply humanizing. It is good for us that Archbishop Romero spent time on earth." Of course, it would have been better had he not been murdered. But his suffering out of love for the people invites and inspires others to reproduce in their turn a similar service. This is the service of the Servant, called by God, bearing the sin of the world, killed for establishing right and justice, but being a light to the nations, like Jesus.

Clara. It is hard to imagine what Christian interpretation would have been like without Second Isaiah.

4.9   Let the satisfaction theory retire

Clara. Medical, military, diplomatic, financial, legal, liberative, sacrificial, and familial metaphors, along with deeply rooted themes drawn from creation and servant texts: from this walkabout through some key biblical motifs used to interpret the cross I think we have learned three things. First, the language of salvation was diverse and varied, with many different metaphors in play. Second, it was culturally specific, reflecting life in first-century Jewish and Hellenistic circles. Third, it was a colorful, evocative, poetic language, not intended to explain or prove anything comprehensively but to preach the good news. And all of these images are in the canonical Bible.

Elizabeth. Talk about creativity! The disciples drew ideas from the scriptures, especially Genesis, Exodus, the psalms, and the prophets. They made analogies from temple worship and the annual cycle of Jewish feasts. And they crafted new metaphors from everyday spheres of life.

Many of these metaphors speak dynamically of an experience of a changed relationship to God thanks to Jesus Christ. They describe the grace of going from sick to healthy, from enemy to friend, from estranged to reconciled, from bound to free, from indicted to not guilty, from slave to beloved child, from lost to found, from poor to rich, from oppressed to liberated, from alien to citizen, from old creation to new creation, from death to life. The metaphor of blood from animal sacrifice bespoke purification, forgiveness, rededication. Isaiah's servant was reconfigured to the cross with the intuition that one person's suffering can heal others of their infirmities.

If any further evidence were needed that none of these motifs gives a theoretical explanation of how Jesus' cross and resurrection is a saving event, the mixing of metaphors makes it obvious. A classic example is Romans 3:23–25. See if you can spot the metaphors: "[S]ince all have sinned and fall short of the glory of God, they are now justified by his grace as a gift, through the redemption that is in Christ Jesus, whom God put forward as a sacrifice of atonement by his blood, effective through faith."

Clara. It seems Paul is combining ideas of judicial acquittal, financially buying someone's freedom, and cultic sacrifice. They tumble over each other in one sentence to show how great is the gift.

Elizabeth. Good. Such blending and conflating of metaphors can be found throughout the New Testament, which presents a rich yet hardly coherent matrix of interpretive motifs. Another telling example: the goodness of God our Savior poured out the Spirit on us through Jesus Christ, "so that, having been justified by his grace, we might become heirs according to the hope of eternal life" (Titus 3:7).

Clara. Here the forensic and familial come together in gratitude for the blessing of baptism.

Elizabeth. The point is that the early Christian communities rose with panache to the challenging task of interpreting Jesus' death. Just think of the effort it took! They were in a fundamentally new situation, different from the days of Jesus' ministry. This was unchartered territory; the cross fit no standard script. In the light of resurrection faith they used a rich and hope-filled range of metaphors to speak about Jesus' life given for others. No theories were offered for how any of the metaphors worked. They were announcing that through this Jesus whom they loved, and who had met a terribly negative end, the gracious and merciful God of Israel was doing something profoundly good for the world.

They interpreted the cross in the mystery of God, as Jon Sobrino quietly declares. The way God grapples with evil folly is unfathomable. But in the light of Jesus Christ they do say this: absurdity and death do not have the last word. The goodness and loving-kindness of God our Savior takes initiative to save a world in trouble, as with the Exodus and as with the return from exile. This goodness is what is ultimate. Empowered by the Spirit, they formed communities around the crucified and risen Jesus Christ to preach the good news and carry on his mission in the world.

Clara. When seen against this rich and multi-faceted biblical background, Anselm's satisfaction theory does seem inadequate.

Elizabeth. That is putting it mildly. Its core assumption is in error. Even though it argues for mercy in that God's own Son became human in order to die and pay the debt, its argument that satisfaction is a condition for forgiveness contradicts the mercy of God as revealed in the scriptures. Recall the forensic metaphor. We are declared not guilty (bang the gavel!) not because anything was paid to assuage divine honor but because of the sheer goodness of God who through Christ pours out grace as a free gift. No explanation of a redemptive mechanism is given or required. Notice how this differs from Anselm's view. Notice, too, how it accords with the biblical understanding of divine mercy: "I blot out your transgressions for my own sake" (Isa 43:25).

Clara. I think what happened is that once the satisfaction theory took root in the West, people began to read most of the New Testament metaphors in its light. Instead of taking these motifs in their own context, people fit them into the rational theory, and before you know it everything started to sound like a kind of atoning satisfaction, in the medieval sense.

Elizabeth. Even if the satisfaction theory were correct, which it isn't, its dominance as a theory has crowded out the rich array of biblical metaphors that announce salvation. Like a cloud blocking the sun it has cast these motifs into shadow. In thrall to this theory, theology in the West has spun out untold explanations of its finer points. It is as if one instrument were playing, when we should be hearing an entire orchestra.

Clara. Dare I conclude that we contemporary folk should feel free to let the satisfaction theory go dormant in our spirituality and in what we pass on to our children? That we should turn from its focus on Christ's death alone, its assumption that God needs payment for sin, and, despite Anselm's intent, its warped view of divine mercy? The language about salvation in the New Testament, with its core in the Christian Old Testament and creative use of everyday transactions, does have its limits. But savoring its various metaphors in the framework of the gospels would ground us in the original experience of salvation in Christ. Then we could do for our age what the early disciples did for theirs, and interpret salvation in metaphors that make sense to people of our particular time and place.

Elizabeth. An excellent suggestion. The satisfaction theory needs to bow out into a well-deserved retirement. Some might want to grant that as an early medieval explanatory theory of how salvation occurs, it served its purpose in its own context. But even if it did, the world has moved on. It is worth repeating a point made earlier, namely, that the church has never officially defined any one specific way of understanding salvation, never opted for one biblical metaphor or one theological theory over another. New creative initiatives are possible and even necessary for a vibrant faith in our day.

The core truth is this: after a vibrant ministry Jesus' death in failure and disgrace met the living God's creative power in the resurrection, which gave his whole life and ministry divine affirmation. Empowered by the Spirit of God, Christians follow Jesus on the path of discipleship, loving God and letting love for neighbor shine in practical ways where suffering and injustice hold sway. This becomes a vital, ongoing way the grace of the merciful God who liberates from slavery, brings exiles home, forgives sin, accompanies those who suffer, and raises the dead can pervade the world with redeeming love.

Book V

God of All Flesh: Deep Incarnation

5.1 Solidarity in spades

Clara. In opening Anselm's theory to examination and setting down an alternative based in scripture, your goal has been to reclaim the mercy of God so that all creation can be included in a theology of salvation. The approach you have taken so far is historical, tracking how faith in God's liberating mercy developed through time. Starting with the Jewish people's experience of the Exodus from Egypt and the new exodus of their return from Babylonian exile, you explored Jesus' life and ministry, and his death due to the unjust power of empire, which was met by the creative power of God. You then traced how the early Christian disciples interpreted the saving grace they were experiencing in the light of this paschal mystery. As I understand it, you are using these steps to construct a path around the satisfaction theory toward what might loosely be called a narrative theology of God's accompaniment that brings salvation.

Elizabeth. You are right, of course. But let me caution that scripture is too pluriform to narrow its richness down to any one theology. In addition, the dominance of the satisfaction theory for centuries makes me leery of proposing only one way of thinking for the global church. What we are working out here is but one among several ways to understand the cross in the context of God's vast and lavish salvific will, a way that can enlighten people today and inspire their practical lives, including care for the whole natural world.

A theology of accompaniment focuses on the saving presence of the gracious and merciful God, freely and faithfully given through thick and thin: "[F]or I am with you to deliver you, says YHWH" (Jer 1:8). So far, we have traced out a double-edged solidarity at its core: a solidarity of the ministering and crucified Jesus with the human race, and a solidarity of God with him, and through him with his sisters and brothers, aimed at resurrection.

Clara. But you are not limiting this solidarity to the human race, are you? Bringing creation into the picture, it is not hard to see how such an accompaniment theology can also embrace the natural world. Today's science has made abundantly clear that a deep relationality runs through the whole cosmos. Thanks to the evolution of life, human beings are genetically related in kinship to all other species on our planet, and this whole living community is composed of chemical materials available on planet Earth, material that in turn condensed from debris left by the death of a previous generation of stars. As John Muir wrote, "When we try to pick out anything by itself, we find it hitched to everything else in the Universe." So when an early Christian hymn sings that Christ is "the firstborn of all creation," and again "the firstborn of the dead" (Col 1:15–18), we can see not only the human dead but the dead of all creation, every species, included. Would this be right?

Elizabeth. You have caught the inner logic of this theology so far with great precision.

Clara. Based on the way you phrase that, you seem to think there is even more to be said.

Elizabeth. There is. Step back for a moment and look at how today's theology identifies two different ways of thinking about Jesus Christ, two patterns of doing christology. One way starts on earth with his life, ministry, and death, and traces his resurrection into glory, which moves him into heaven, so to speak, from where as Lord and Christ he sends the life-giving Spirit. This kind of christology has an upward arc. Given its starting point, it is called a christology from below. You can find this pattern in the gospel of Mark, which starts on earth with Jesus' baptism, and the gospels of Matthew and Luke that start with his conception and birth. The other type of christology starts in heaven with God as Word creating the world, and traces this Word's descent into the world in Jesus Christ to dwell among people, full of grace and truth. This kind of christology has a downward arc and, as you no doubt surmise, is called a christology from above. Its classic locale is the Gospel of John, whose opening prologue starts with the Word who is God creating all things and comes to a fine pitch with the declaration that "the Word became flesh and dwelt among us" (1:14). There are not absolute differences between the two ways; they exist in dialectic interaction. But this can be a helpful clarification.

In a classic essay sorting out the strengths and weaknesses of each type, Karl Rahner explained that the historical approach from below is the firm basis and necessary condition for the church's understanding of Jesus Christ, while the more metaphysical approach from above is an inspired interpretation. Viewing the differences pastorally, he suggests that while both types are legitimate and necessary, christology from below fits better with the cultural mind-set of people today. It is an historical narrative, based on an actual person who lived and was remembered by disciples, and who catches our imagination more easily. To even get to the starting point of a descending christology one has to accept the authority of the church and its doctrinal teaching and, given the way the early councils and creeds articulated Christ's identity, be able to think in Hellenistic categories that do not come easily to the contemporary mind.

So far in this exploration we have been following the arc of christology from below. Now we are switching gears to christology from above. In the course of the first century the disciples came to believe that in Jesus Christ the unfathomable God of gracious love had personally joined the flesh of the world with its vulnerability and death in order to save. In other words, in Jesus God is not only *with* and *for* human beings but is present *as* a human being. The logic of accompaniment that becomes so beautifully clear in the history of Israel and the story of Jesus gains in unutterable depth when explored through this belief.

Clara. You are speaking about the doctrine of incarnation.

Elizabeth. Yes, from the Latin *in* (into) and *caro/carnis* (flesh). This is the belief, wildly radical on the face of it, that Jesus is Emmanuel, God with us. It holds that in him God joined earthly life as a participant, possessing a history, a time, and a death that constitute a profoundly personal, novel divine relationship to the world that hadn't existed before.

Clara. You say this understanding developed in the course of the first century. In other words, it was a post-resurrection insight, not one that the disciples had during Jesus' actual earthly life?

Elizabeth. That's right. It is a faith interpretation that came to full flower over time. Once the idea took hold, it was retrojected back into memories of Jesus' actual life, and then could be told as the opening chapter of his life as we do today when we celebrate Christmas.

Clara. As you say, this is a radical belief, hard for many to fathom.

Elizabeth. It helps to remember that the major setting for such insight was the community of disciples gathered together in prayer. Inspired by the Holy Spirit they read the scriptures, recounted memories of Jesus' words and deeds, shared his presence through eucharistic bread and wine, and sang hymns praising him for the gifts poured out through the Spirit who had raised him from the dead. Their lives were changed, charged with a new kind of hope and joy. Their relationship to God opened up with powerful experiences of access to divine graciousness. They were forming a dynamic community, at first within Judaism. Their mission then expanded in exciting and challenging ways from Jewish to Gentile people. Jesus Christ was at the center of all this. Josephus was right that those who loved him did not cease. The tribe of those who loved him came to see him as the embodied presence of God, God's own personal self-utterance spoken into the flesh.

Clara. "The Word was made flesh and dwelt among us." Before tracing the meaning of incarnation for an ecological theology of salvation, it would help to have a fuller picture of two things: "flesh," because in my experience an opposition between God and the flesh is what is often taught; and "Word," about which I have no idea at all.

5.2   *The rainbow gives assurance*

Elizabeth. In the Christian Old Testament the main Hebrew word for flesh, *basar*, takes its primary meaning from the material substance of which earthly creatures are made, in other words, from the body, a soft, meaty kind of stuff with tissue and fluid. Then in the way of useful words, flesh expands to include a range of meanings. It can refer to a human person as a psychosomatic individual, to kinfolk or relatives (my flesh and blood), or to all humankind. Beyond humans it can also refer to animals, to meat for eating or sacrificing, and very broadly to all living beings.

Rooted in the experience of how physical flesh changes, *basar* also moves off from concrete creatures to signify the universal quality of being vulnerable, perishable, transitory. Yes, flesh is beautiful, delightful, strong, and can even praise God. But it waxes and wanes, and then is gone. This quality of inconstancy, blooming like the flowers of the field and then fading, is picked up in a religious sense when flesh refers to human beings as sinful or erring. While the term can sometimes be used to mean hostility to God, most often in scripture it refers not to sin but to finitude, to being limited and mortal, which in itself is not sinful.

Clara. What an interesting distinction, between sin and finitude.

Elizabeth. The distinction opens up space where we can

think of flesh in a positive way. All living creatures are limited in strength, understanding, and life-span, including human beings. We cannot live more than 168 hours in a week, or do everything we would hope, or know everything in depth; as we age, we slow down and then die. This finitude is natural. Sin, on the other hand, is not natural, but a failure to act and live as moral, loving beings. We sin by actions that alienate us from ourselves, our fellow-creatures, and God. Over time collective wrongs get shaped into social structures that affect future generations and wreak havoc with people's lives. Broken relationships and their bitter fruit litter our history. We are responsible for sin, not for finitude.

Clara. Flesh: with its multi-faceted meanings the word conjures up the vigor and finitude of life in all its glorious transience, which inevitably ends in death. I can see that this is a most useful word, really, to describe a fundamental condition of all creatures that are alive on this planet.

Elizabeth. You mentioned hearing about an opposition between God and the flesh. Think about the creation story in Genesis for a moment. Does it portray such an antagonism?

Clara. As a matter of fact, it doesn't. God created the world of flesh and saw that it was good. The swarms of creatures dwelling in earth, sea, and sky, the plants, fish, winged birds, cattle, creeping things, wild animals, and humans, all have their common origin in the generosity of the Creator who gives them life in the flesh and blesses them. Not only that, but God gifts them with the power of fertility: bring forth! be fruitful and multiply! This is obviously a function of the flesh—and God saw that it was very good.

So God creates and loves not only spiritual beings or humans insofar as they exist with a spiritual dimension, but creates and loves all flesh.

Elizabeth. Exactly. Another ancient story filled with symbolism, the Genesis story of the great flood, adds an extraordinary dimension to the relationship between God and all creatures.

Remember that this story like others in the first eleven chapters of Genesis uses narratives of what happened "in the beginning" in order to teach religious truths. Their literary genre is what scholars would call antiquarian history, or primeval narratives, or myths of origins. Knowing this, we should neither read them literally nor dismiss them as useless fiction, but allow the tales to teach their religious truth in their own way. A number of ancient civilizations who were neighbors to Israel had stories of an ancient flood, and the author of the Noah story borrowed the story's main contours. One big difference in the biblical version is the way it ends. God makes a covenant with all creatures of flesh upon the earth.

Clara. God covenants with animals? I thought covenants were made with people of faith: with the ancestor Abraham, with the people of Israel led by Moses, with the memorable king David, and with Jesus' community in the New Testament.

Elizabeth. Yes, but the one with Noah and fleshy creatures is the first. Before the flood, lest there be any doubt about leaving some animals behind, Noah is instructed thus: "And of every living thing, of all flesh [*basar*], you shall bring two of every kind into the ark, to keep them alive with you; they shall be male and female" (6:19). The text goes on to include explicitly every kind of winged bird, every kind of creature that creeps on the ground, wild animals, domestic animals, every fleshy thing that moves on the earth.

When the deluge recedes, covenant-making begins. In an unexpected way God commits to a future free from universal destruction, saying to Noah, "I am establishing my covenant with you and your descendants after you, and with every living creature that is with you, the birds, the domestic animals, and every animal of the earth with you." The sign of this special relationship will be the rainbow, set in the clouds "as a sign of the covenant between me and the earth." When the rainbow appears, God will remember the covenant "that is between me and you and every living creature of all flesh" (9:15).

It is interesting to note that as the story ends, the human person recedes as an individual and becomes blended into the relationship between God and the other covenant partners who are creatures of flesh: "When the bow is in the clouds, I will see it and remember the everlasting covenant between God and every living creature of all flesh that is on the earth. God said to Noah: 'This is the sign of the covenant that I have established between me and all flesh that is on the earth'" (9:16–17).

Clara. This is kind of amazing. God makes an *everlasting* covenant with every living creature of all kinds of flesh, whether furred, feathered, or finned, establishing a covenant "between me and all flesh that is on the earth."

Elizabeth. Such a close, loving bond generates prophetic promises of future blessing for all creatures as part of YHWH's salvation of Israel: "I will pour out my spirit on all flesh" (Joel 2:28). And it gives rise to a stunning title of divine self-definition: "I am YHWH, the God of all flesh" (Jer 32:27).

This does not make the flesh divine; it remains finite and transient. The point for our purpose is that the "flesh" that the Word became is part of this continuum of good, fragile, mortal stuff created, appreciated, covenanted, and blessed by God.

5.3   Flesh misunderstood and disrespected

Clara. But later in the New Testament, doesn't Paul emphasize a connection between flesh and sin? As I recall, he often contrasts life "according to the flesh" with life "according to the spirit," the former being sinful and the latter being virtuous.

Elizabeth. Without saying that flesh is sinful in and of itself, Paul often uses it as a symbol of human weakness that allows evil to take over. He makes the sphere of the flesh, now *sarx* in Greek, stand for alienation from God through sinful tendencies and behavior. Be very clear, though, that Paul is not saying that the body as such is sinful or evil. When he lists the "works of the flesh" he includes not only indulgent sexual activity and drunkenness, which you might expect, but also hatred, jealousy, outbursts of anger, selfish ambition, and other behaviors that destroy relationships and the fabric of community life. If you live by the flesh you are oriented by such destructive drives. Living by the spirit, to the contrary, means being guided by the Spirit of Christ. The fruits of the spirit are love, joy, peace, generosity, faithfulness, kindness, and self-control, which build up the community and promote the flourishing of others (see Gal 5:13–26). Notice that these are all embodied qualities lived out in relationships; they only ever happen in the flesh, taken in a generic, not a negative sense.

In context, this construct of flesh vs. spirit is Paul's preferred tool to explore the condition of believers who are baptized into a redeemed existence in Christ. They no longer live by the flesh but by the spirit, since the Spirit of God dwells in them and is transforming them into a new creation. Certain behaviors should follow.

Clara. Unfortunately, despite this explanation, when I read or hear these Pauline texts, they sound so anti-body. Flesh vs. spirit is often understood as body vs. soul. Nuance gets lost, and I feel that being a sexual creature is somehow wrong in God's eyes.

Elizabeth. Any time you hear texts that seem to disparage the body and material reality, remember the rainbow. But you are right that to our contemporary ears, the nuance of Paul's thought gets lost. Similar to the way that using the contrast of light and dark to mean good and bad implicitly casts aspersions on people of dark skin in our culture, with prejudicial results, using flesh and spirit as a contrasting pair to mean sinful and good ends up disparaging the body.

Clara. But it is not just Paul, rightly or wrongly understood. If God creates, loves, and covenants with the flesh, why do we inherit a tradition in theology that speaks so vehemently against it?

Elizabeth. The opposition you speak of crept into theology when Christianity moved from its Jewish origins into the wider Hellenistic world. As is its practice, theology began to use ideas indigenous to this new culture to explain the faith. One key idea in Greek philosophy was the distinction between spirit and matter, the two principles that form the identity of all existing things. Spirit stood for the mind, the soul, rationality, the ability to act, to lead and stay on course; it was light, leading toward divinity. Matter stood for the body and its overpowering passions, emotions, receptivity, fickle fleshly changes; it was darkness leading to death.

Clara. Given such descriptions, I suppose it made sense that this philosophy clearly privileged spirit *over* matter as being closer to the divine. And if Christians wanted to be understood in that culture, they had to use a way of thinking familiar to their hearers. But that does not mean, does it, that *we* have to accept that culturally conditioned way of talking?

Elizabeth. We do not. We are not shackled to the thought forms of any particular culture. This becomes particularly important when we see that not only did Greek philosophy elevate spirit and denigrate matter, but using those ideas it made the cosmos into one great hierarchy of being. At the lowest level lies inanimate substances like rocks, simply matter. Plants rank next up the ladder since they enjoy a certain spirit of life. Animals are higher yet, because the matter of their body is animated by a greater spirit that gives them locomotion and instincts. Humans with powers of soul including intelligence and free will rank highest on earth. Above humans rank the angels, who are pure spirits without any bodies at all.

Clara. Within each level of being, did the hierarchy of spirit over matter make further distinctions?

Elizabeth. Applied to human beings as individuals, this binary view defined a person as a composite of two substances, body and soul, rather than as an indivisible unit of enfleshed spirit; the soul, of course, was of greater importance. Applied to the human community, spirit was thought to characterize the masculine principle while matter identified the feminine. Hence men were naturally superior to women and ruled over them according to the natural order of things. Hierarchies multiplied. Elite men had rule over slaves and other people thought to be ethnically inferior, and on and on. Applied to the natural world, humans had the right to rule over other creatures that being more matter than spirit were naturally of lesser worth. There were of course important nuances; this is an impossibly brief synopsis.

Clara. Yes it is. But the pattern is there.

Elizabeth. Christian theology never adopted this philosophy wholesale. Holding firmly to the biblical affirmation of the goodness of creation, it rejected heresies in the early centuries that saw matter in the extreme as not just distant from God but also as evil. Nevertheless, the overall pattern held, and has imbued the church's worldview, value system, and practices to this day.

Clara. If you lived with such a worldview, you would tend to be suspicious of the material pole, or at least think that it is of lesser importance. This would include your own body, and women, and also the natural world. I would say this philosophy has outlived its usefulness.

Elizabeth. So has the spirituality it has generated. Notice how perfection in this view is shaped by the metaphor of ascent: to be holy a person must flee the material world and its delights, including one's own body and sexuality, and rise to the spiritual sphere where the light of divinity dwells.

It is noteworthy that in the encyclical *Laudato Si'* ("Praise Be to You" with the subtitle "On Care for Our Common Home"), Pope Francis rendered a severe judgment on this tradition. To begin with, he wrote, it is important to know that Jesus was not an ascetic set apart from the world, nor an enemy to the pleasant things of life. As the gospels show, he was far removed from philosophies that despised the body, matter, and the things of the world. In fact, he was criticized for being a drunk and a glutton.

But the developing tradition swerved away from this wholesome attitude toward creation and worked instead with the dichotomy between matter and spirit. "Such unhealthy dualisms left a mark on certain Christian thinkers in the course of history and disfigured the Gospel" (*LS* 98).

Clara. Disfigured the gospel! That is strong language indeed. But what the pope criticizes feels sadly familiar to some degree from all my years as a Christian. By contrast, I belong to a choral group, and when we sing a chorus from Handel's "Messiah" it gives me so much hope: "And the glory of the Lord shall be revealed, and all flesh shall see it together." I've always taken heart from this line. It conjures up a peaceable kingdom of animals of all kinds including humans, with the light of glory reflected on every face, all flesh "together." It seems so promising for all creatures in the cosmos and myself, too, made of flesh, and liking it!

Elizabeth. That chorus verbalizes a line from the beginning of the scroll of our friend Second Isaiah. Recall that God speaks words of comfort: rescue is on its way; a straight path will lead the people home through the wilderness. "Then the glory of YHWH shall be revealed, and all flesh shall see it together" (40:5). The promise of redemption is given not for human beings alone but embraces all creatures in their unfathomable enfleshed otherness, mortal like us.

Clara. So if I get this right, the flesh in John's prologue does not stand for something sinful. It refers to finitude, to the vulnerable, mortal condition of all creatures whom God creates, loves, covenants with, and redeems.

Elizabeth. To this list of verbs, the prologue dramatically adds, and joins.

5.4   *She is more beautiful than the sun and the stars*

Clara. If flesh is one end of the dynamic pair united in the incarnation, the Word who was with God in the beginning and was God, as John's gospel puts it, is the other. Is there any way, besides taking advanced courses in theology, that anyone can understand this?

Elizabeth. No such course will ever be able to explain the incarnation in a clear manner to the satisfaction of our logical minds. For one thing, the Creator God, loving Redeemer and Savior of the world, is a mystery beyond human comprehension. For another, how such infinite Love could personally bond with a transient scrap of human flesh is beyond imagination. When speaking about the Word made flesh, it is crucial to remember this limit and not act as if we are clearly explaining such a union.

Clara. This is a good reminder, to counter any tendency to reduce incarnation to something simple.

Elizabeth. At the same time divine identification with the flesh in Jesus is not unbelievable, given all the other things we think God can do.

Clara. Like create the world.

Elizabeth. Precisely. Keeping this in view, let us track what John's prologue means by the Word. Remember how the figure of the Suffering Servant helped shape the disciples' interpretation of Jesus' suffering? More than simply the travail of the righteous sufferer, the cross was something endured "for us." In a similar way there was another figure in the scriptures that nurtured their understanding of Christ's cosmic significance and divine character. This was the figure of Wisdom, *hochmah* in Hebrew, *sophia* in Greek.

Clara. It wasn't the Word?

Elizabeth. Behind every line about the Word (*logos* in Greek) in John's prologue lies the story of Wisdom.

Clara. So in order to understand the meaning of the vital line "and the Word became flesh and dwelt among us," we need to know about holy *Sophia*.

Elizabeth. Yes. To begin with, try for a moment to solve this dilemma. How do you speak about divine presence and activity in the world without compromising the unimaginable transcendence of the all holy God?

Clara. Mmmmm.

Elizabeth. The Christian Old Testament does this by means of poetic figures. Functioning somewhat like circumlocutions, these figures are ways of picturing divine outreach in the world while God still remains absolutely Other.

God's spirit, for example, breathes the world into being, dwells in all things, quickens love into flame, inspires the prophets, and renews the face of the earth.

God's word is also powerfully creative. It blesses, commands, judges, promises, reveals, and saves; like the rain that makes things grow, it "will not return to me empty, but will accomplish my purpose and succeed in the thing for which I sent it" (Isa 55:11).

Scripture also speaks of divine glory that shines in the fields and makes radiant the faces of the just; divine power that liberates; divine wings that shelter; even angels who convey messages from heaven.

Biblical authors made use of these poetic figures to convey the conviction that while the all holy God was completely different from the world, being its Creator who held it in existence at every moment, this same gracious God was also immanent in the world, close by and involved. Spirit, word, glory and other figures of speech helped keep both aspects in tension.

The most highly developed of these poetic symbols of divine immanence is the Jewish figure of personified Wisdom. Standing for divine outreach in creating and saving the world, she bears a more distinctive face and has a more developed character than either spirit or word.

Rabbis of the period before Christ, taking a clue from late biblical writing, had already made an interesting move. They taught that holy Wisdom who moved throughout all creation as a pure emanation of the glory of God had come to earth and dwelt among the people of Israel in the specific form of Torah. Now the early disciples made a parallel move. They taught that holy Wisdom had come to earth and dwelt among people in the specific form of their beloved Jesus.

Clara. But wait a minute. Isn't Wisdom a female figure of power and might? How could they connect Jesus with her?

Elizabeth. It shows you that in this case gender was not of the essence. What mattered was the role divine Wisdom played in creating, redeeming, and guiding the world, and making people holy and just.

Clara. Could you be more specific?

Elizabeth. Texts are abundant; let us linger with Proverbs. Before the world was created YHWH brought Wisdom forth. In her words, "Ages ago I was set up, at the first, before the beginning of the earth" (8:23). Existing before time, Wisdom became an agent in creation: "YHWH by wisdom founded the earth" (3:19). When there were as yet no springs of water, no mountains or bits of soil, she was there. When the creating began she was beside the Creator, working like a master craftsperson to bring the earth into being. And when the work was finished, she positively exulted, delighting in God's company and rejoicing to be with human beings.

Once the world and its inhabitants were in motion, Wisdom offered generous instruction to people about how best to live. At the crossroads, before the city gates, from high places, she cried out her teaching with authority. Everyone who listened received an extraordinary promise: "Whoever finds me finds life, and obtains favor from YHWH" (8:35). Because her path is one of righteousness, society is well-ordered: "by me kings reign, and rulers decree what is just" (8:15). Not just kings but all who seek and find her will receive blessings worth more than fine gold.

In one evocative passage Wisdom builds a house and prepares a banquet of wine and rich food. She sends out her servant girls to shout the message, "Come, eat of my bread and drink of the wine I have mixed. Lay aside immaturity and live, and walk in the way of insight" (9:5–6). She is the way, the truth, and the life. Feast on her teaching and find your way to God.

Clara. Amazing. I am not familiar with these texts, but it is clear that Wisdom is a life-giving, godly kind of figure with transforming power. I must say this sounds a bit like the Holy Spirit in Christian theology. Is there yet more?

Elizabeth. In later writings of the Christian Old Testament, Wisdom takes on the functions and attributes of YHWH in an ever clearer manner.

The book of Wisdom calls her not just the master craftsperson of creation but the "mother" and "fashioner of all things" (7:22) who knows the secrets of the seasons, the motion of the constellations, the tempers of wild animals, and the virtues of healing roots because she made them all. She not only creates but also redeems. To illustrate that people "were saved by Wisdom" (9:18), this book goes on to recount the familiar Genesis and Exodus stories, only this time with Wisdom as the acting agent. When the earth was flooded, for example, "Wisdom again saved it, steering the righteous man by a paltry piece of wood" (10:4). Inspiring Moses to leadership, she freed the people from slavery: "A holy people and blameless race wisdom delivered from a nation of oppressors. . . . She brought them over the Red Sea, and led them through deep waters; but she drowned their enemies, casting them up from the depth of the sea" (10:15–19). Omnipresence is hers, for her intelligent and loving holy spirit, more mobile than any motion, pervades all things (7:22–24). Omnipotence is hers, for "she can do all things" (7:27). Hers, too, is the power to sanctify, making people friends of God, and prophets.

The godly qualities come to a pitch when the author of this book characterizes Wisdom as a breath of the power of God, a pure emanation of divine glory, a reflection of eternal light, a mirror of the working of God, an image of divine goodness (7:25–26). Divine beauty shines forth from her: "She is more beautiful than the sun and excels every constellation of the stars" (7:29) The clincher comes with the radical statement that "against wisdom evil does not prevail" (7:30). Only the living God is more powerful than evil, so the divine identity of Wisdom is clear. Thus it is not surprising that Wisdom providentially rules the whole world: "She reaches mightily from one end of the earth to the other, ordering all things sweetly and well" (8:1).

Clara. What an extraordinary passage. But it sounds as if Jewish monotheism has broken apart and the people were referring to another god or a goddess. Was this the case?

Elizabeth. You raise an issue that vexed rabbis of a later period. Their debates about the meaning of Wisdom concluded that Jewish monotheism held firm. These texts were actually referring to the one God of Israel but in female rather than male language. God, of course, is beyond gender, and creates both male and female in the divine image, so this kind of God-talk can be justified, though it is not common.

Clara. I'm curious as to what prompted this development.

Elizabeth. In many religions of the wider Mediterranean world, goddesses such as Isis or Athena played central roles and were worshiped with moving prayers and ceremonies. Scholars speculate that the attraction of such practices, along with the political advantage of belonging to a goddess cult in some places, led rabbinic sages of the diaspora to emphasize the figure of Wisdom. Within strong monotheistic belief, she is neither a replacement for nor an addition to YHWH but an alternative way of speaking about the one unfathomable God of Israel who creates and redeems the world.

For our purposes, it is important to remember that the wisdom tradition also carried the impulse to bring Wisdom to earth where she sets up her tent to live among people. The book of Sirach declares that the Creator chose the place, and it was the people of Israel: "Make your dwelling in Jacob . . . and so I was established in Zion . . . and in Jerusalem was my domain. I took root in an honored people" (Sir 24:8–11). In a similar way, the book of Baruch notes that after creating the stars who shine in gladness and respond "Here we are!" to the One who made them, God gave Wisdom to his servant Jacob and to Israel whom he loved; and so "she appeared on earth and lived with humankind" (Bar 3:37). This is an intensely poetic way of expressing the immense gift of divine nearness while keeping in view the transcendent otherness of God. Early Christians pressed it into service to tell of the significance of Jesus.

5.5 Jesus the Wisdom of God

Clara. I see what happened. Drawing once again from their rich Jewish tradition, the disciples who loved and believed in Jesus and felt the ongoing impact of his presence through the Spirit in their community, interpreted him as the person in whom God as Wisdom came to dwell bodily on earth.

Elizabeth. That's right. It started slowly, with some evocative references in Paul (1 Cor 8:6), and grew stronger in the gospels, which portrayed him doing Wisdom's deeds, saying her words, taking on her roles, and in fact being her embodiment on earth. See this fascinating comparison between Luke and Matthew. In response to messengers from John the Baptist querying whether he is the one who is to come, Jesus points to his deeds of healing the sick and bringing good news to the poor. Luke's version ends with Jesus taking note of his critics and saying, "Nevertheless, wisdom is vindicated by all her children" (7:35). Here the evangelist presents Jesus as a child of Wisdom, her envoy whom she supports because his words and actions show people her ways.

Matthew's version is significantly different. Its final words are, "Yet wisdom is vindicated by her deeds" (11:19). Here the evangelist takes the step of identifying Jesus with Wisdom herself.

"The deeds of the Christ" (11:2) with which this passage opens are filled in with descriptions of Jesus' own loving, prophetic actions, which are criticized by his opponents, and are then justified as Wisdom's own deeds. Wisdom is justified by her deeds. For this gospel writer, Jesus is personally Wisdom in action.

Clara. It is fascinating to see how a change of one word, from "her children" to "her deeds" can open up Jesus' portrayal to the point where it is saturated with intimations of divinity.

Elizabeth. The identification of Jesus with Wisdom flowered in the later part of the first century. The hymns of Colossians (1:15–20) and Hebrews (1:2–3) and the gospel of John just about take it for granted. The importance of this connection cannot be overstated. It configured a limited historical figure, Jesus, the crucified prophet from Nazareth, to Wisdom's universal role in creating, saving, and making holy the world. The Wisdom tradition is a major route the early church took to the belief that Jesus Christ is the embodiment of the Creator God's own personal outreach and saving presence to the world. No other poetic biblical figure had such strong resonance with divine character and action, or came to dwell among the people on earth in a specific place. In the clear words of James Dunn concluding an extensive study of the Wisdom-Jesus link, "Herein we see the origin of the doctrine of the incarnation."

Clara. It occurs to me that the Advent hymn "O come, O come, Emmanuel," draws on this connection; in the second stanza we sing:

> O come, thou Wisdom from on high, who orders
>   all things mightily;
> to us the path of knowledge show, and teach us in
>   her ways to go.
> Rejoice, rejoice, Emmanuel shall come to thee, O Israel.

Even today the Christian community calls to Jesus as Holy Wisdom. *Elizabeth*. The connection has never disappeared. One of the most magnificent churches of the ancient world, Hagia Sophia (Holy Wisdom) in Constantinople, now called Istanbul, was dedicated to Jesus Christ under this title, and numerous theologians of East and West have made use of wisdom motifs.

Clara. This adds another dimension beyond thinking about Jesus as a holy prophet inspired by the Spirit. It leads to language about his deity or divinity, doesn't it?

Elizabeth. Indeed. Once the disciples interpreted Jesus as the human being whom God as Wisdom became, belief in incarnation took root in the Christian tradition. They came to see with the eyes of faith, so to speak, that this one human being revealed the holy mystery of God through the medium of the flesh. They came to believe that God was dwelling on earth as Jesus; that full of grace and truth, Jesus was in person the historical sacrament of God's merciful love; that he personally embodied divine presence and action in the world for human salvation and creation's renewal. Within the inevitable limits of his historical era, geographical location, culture, gender, ethnicity, class, and every other particular that necessarily marks an individual life, his story inscribes in time a revelation of the heart of God.

Clara. But let me raise an objection. John writes "the Word became flesh and dwelt among us." Why the Word, and not Wisdom?

Elizabeth. For reasons no one is sure of, the author of the prologue tells the story of Wisdom while shifting the acting subject from Wisdom to Word, from *sophia* to *logos*. Virtually every attribute and activity of the Word in the prologue come from rich Wisdom sources in the Christian Old Testament, whereas the Word is a much less developed figure. The prologue, we might say, transposes into the key of *logos* the music that was originally written in the key of *sophia*.

Clara. Could it have been because of gender? In a patriarchal culture it might be off-putting to say he, a human being, became the person she, who is divine, became.

Elizabeth. Perhaps. In Greek *logos* is a grammatically masculine noun and lends itself more readily to the idea of a divine Word being uttered as a human man. The switch might also be due to the overwhelming influence of Hellenistic culture, where *logos* was a pivotal term in Greek philosophy. Then too, "the word of the Lord" was a phrase frequently used by the prophets. Yet another pressure might have come from the apostolic mission itself, whose purpose was to "preach the word," or the good news of the gospel, to the whole world.

Whatever the reason, the understanding made possible by the link between Jesus and Wisdom was subsequently carried forward in theological language about the Word. Jesus is the Word of God, God's self-utterance, God's own self-expression in the flesh.

Clara. But even before the coming of Christ, God was present in the world, right? What difference does the incarnation make, if any?

Elizabeth. You are right to say that the transcendent God who creates all things is always everywhere present, relating to creation in loving, liberative, salvific ways.

Incarnation bespeaks a different form of divine presence marked by an unimaginable intensity of intimacy. It is presence in the flesh. The omnipresent God is now present in and as a living, breathing human being. Through the incarnation the ineffable God acquires a genuine human life, a story in time, even a death, and does so as a participant in the history of life on our planet. Consequently, Jesus' life now forms part of the story that Christians tell about God.

With the incarnation God's presence abides not only in and for the world but goes deep down to the point of identity as *part* of the world. An unimaginable act of loving solidarity, it enacts the kind of divine love that not only blesses people benevolently but also enters empathetically into their experience, self-identifying with the glory and agony of human life from within, befriending even the godless and the godforsaken. In Jesus Christ the unfathomable God has now joined the mess, as one of my colleagues puts it.

In a particular way, incarnation places the crucified God on the side of the tortured and dispossessed, rather than in alliance with the powerful who crush the life out of others in myriad ways. The cross is where believers in Christ find their God, vulnerable to the brutality and power of the privileged. This raises a strong challenge. As theologian Shawn Copeland preached in prophetic cadences, "We can stand with our God only insofar as we stand beside and wait in active and compassionate solidarity with children, women, and men who suffer concretely, unbeautifully, and actually in our world which is God's world. . . ." In solidarity with such a vulnerable God, Christians place their shoulders to the wheel of transforming the world with an unquenchable hope. In the words of Jeannine Hill Fletcher,

> Even as his body is lifted in torture, pierced by the soldier's sword, bleeding from his thorn-torn brow and nail-punctured hands and feet, Christian faith is placed in the triumph over destruction that resurrection promises. The affirmation that God resides in Jesus is the affirmation that resident within the body broken and bloodied by the weight of the world, God abides with the tortured, and transforms death to new life.

Clara. This is an evocative and awesome belief. But here is one of my problems. The church teaches that being incarnate, Jesus Christ has two natures, human and divine, in his one person. This makes him seem like a divided person, not a real human being at all. Pardon the image, but the two natures seem like two slices of bread put together to make a sandwich.

Elizabeth. You should understand that after the New Testament period a contentious history ensued for several centuries during which the Christian communities around the Mediterranean argued over how best to articulate the identity of Jesus Christ as Savior. As a result of this lengthy and complex struggle, the church established formal teachings about the Trinity, which is the Christian form of monotheism, and about the inner constitution of Christ. Early councils taught that Jesus is fully human and fully divine, both natures being united without mixing and without separation in one and the same person of the divine Son.

Expressed in official language, these doctrines about God and Christ used core concepts and patterns of thinking from the Hellenistic world that were vibrantly alive in their own day and carried profound meaning, but are by and large foreign to contemporary minds.

Clara. How then can we grasp the incarnation?

Elizabeth. Here is where the incomprehensibility of God can function as an aid to understanding. Our finite human minds cannot grasp the essence of divine nature. God is the holy mystery of love, unfathomable, and always in saving relation to the striving, evolving world. If this unimaginable Love who creates the world, covenants with all creatures of flesh on the earth, hears-sees-knows what oppressed people are suffering and burns to liberate them, leads exiles home, keeps on renewing the face of the earth, and promises to wipe away all tears, if this all-holy, dynamic God wishes to personally join the very flesh of the earth, then God can choose a specific bit of human flesh and do so.

Clara. If I get this right, then, we should not think of human nature and divine nature as two versions of the same thing, namely nature, just as apples and oranges are two forms of fruit. They are not commensurate at all, human nature being what we are in our finite ways, and divine nature escaping comprehension as the mystery of love that encompasses the world.

Elizabeth. That is one way to put it. Incarnation holds that God who is always and everywhere active in loving relation to the world (recall spirit, word, wisdom) has chosen to express divine mystery as this human being. Full of grace and truth, this one personal human life reveals the holy mystery of God through the limited medium of the flesh.

Clara. This is a core intuition of faith, right?

Elizabeth. Yes. The inner relation between Jesus and God cannot be proven by historical methods, nor can it be established in biological or philosophical ways. The precise "mechanism" of incarnation, if I may call it that, is not open to scrutiny, as is also true of God's creating, raising from the dead, and other divine actions.

At one point Paul, using an early hymn, employs the metaphor of divine self-emptying; Matthew sees Wisdom embodied in Jesus who does her words and deeds; John speaks of the divine Word becoming flesh and pitching a tent among us. These expressions all seek to express the community's experience of God's being truly "with us" in the person of Jesus. They bespeak the experience that God chose to be present on earth as this person and is revealed through his life, death, and resurrection to such a degree that believers can say "God was manifested in the flesh" (1 Tim 3:16).

Even with that, it is interesting to note that some in the early community did not agree with this interpretation. The second letter of John warns against deceivers "who do not confess that Jesus Christ has come in the flesh" (2 Jn 1:7). They thought that to contaminate the all-holy God with messy, mortal flesh was beyond disrespectful. For Greek-speaking Gentiles, the uniting of the spiritual and material would have been an unhappy union of two opposed realms. For adherents of Platonic philosophy, it was scandalous even to contemplate. Therefore, some people rejected one or other pole of the union. They either denied that Jesus was the Word of God, or, affirming that he was God, denied that his body was real flesh; it only seemed to be.

Clara. But if you can affirm that the Word became flesh and dwelt among us, even if you can't understand exactly how, then Jesus becomes someone who truly reveals the hidden God, as far as is possible in one human life.

Elizabeth. To cite a catchy phrase: If this is God, then thus is God. Note that what we learn about God from Jesus is not contrary to what had already been revealed about the loving-kindness and fidelity of God through the history and scriptures of Israel. It is communicated differently, however, through one particular human being who chose to care for the sick, poor, and marginalized folk of his society, and who taught about God's abundant mercy to the point where sinners were welcome at his table. The last shall be first: many of us still don't get it.

Clara. If this is God, then thus is God: I like that. This would mean that following Jesus, taking up his values and practicing his way of life, is a sure path to God.

Elizabeth. Jesus as the revealer of God and as teacher of the Way who is himself the way, the truth, and the life (all wisdom motifs): these beliefs are rooted for Christians in the incarnation.

Clara. And this is the same God of liberating power and compassion revealed in Israel's Exodus and return from exile, right?

Elizabeth. Of course. With the advent of Jesus, Christians write another chapter in the story of this God's merciful involvement with the world. It is a chapter that tells of God's own union with the finitude of the flesh in order to walk with it through death to life.

Clara. At this point T. S. Eliot's lines about the impossibility of language to describe the ineffable come to my mind with verve:

Words strain,
Crack and sometimes break, under the burden,
Under the tension, slip, slide, perish,
Decay with imprecision, will not stay in place,
Will not stay still.

Elizabeth. Thank you for this reference, which is right on target. The point for our purpose is that belief in Jesus as the incarnate Wisdom and Word of God has a powerful contribution to make to a theology of salvation in which God's saving accompaniment includes the whole natural world.

5.6 Deep incarnation

Clara. I must say that given my own questions, it is fascinating to find out where the idea of the incarnation came from and how it developed. This makes me understand it differently, and gives a certain intellectual strength to the confession of faith. But now can we turn back to the whole natural world, and see the relevance of the incarnation for the bear, the squid, the wetlands, and the bugs?

Elizabeth. The natural world is a complex, evolving place, rife with interactions, with beautiful new forms emerging, new individuals always being born, and death all around. It is a world of flesh in the biblical sense. Human beings, of course, are a part of this web of life, having recently emerged along one line of mammals. In this context, scholars who are attuned to the ecological pattern of life today hear something in John's prologue that has not surfaced before: "And the Word became flesh and dwelt among us."

Clara. Flesh!

Elizabeth. Yes. The text does not say that the Word became a human being, although there is a perfectly good word for this in

Greek (*anthropos*), let alone that the Word became a man, meaning a male human being (*aner*). But the Word became flesh, *sarx* in Greek, which translates the Hebrew *basar*. Taking the ancient themes of God's covenanting with flesh and dwelling among the people of Israel a step further, the prologue affirms that in a profoundly saving event the Word became *flesh*, entered personally into the natural sphere of what is fragile, vulnerable, perishable, the very opposite of divine glory, in order to shed light on all from within.

Clara. But isn't the type of flesh we are talking about here precisely human flesh?

Elizabeth. Indeed it is. But as you have already noted, human beings are part of an interconnected whole. Scientific knowledge today is repositioning the human species as an intrinsic part of the evolutionary network of life on planet Earth, which in turn is a part of the solar system, which itself formed out of the dust and gas of ancient exploding stars. The landscape of our imagination expands when we realize that human connection to nature is so deep that we can no longer completely define human identity without including the great sweep of cosmic development and our shared biological ancestry with all organisms in the community of life.

We evolved relationally; we exist symbiotically; our existence depends on interaction with the rest of the natural world. Relocating anthropology in this broader context provides the condition to rethink the scope and significance of the incarnation in an ecological direction. The flesh that the Word of God became as a particular human being is part of the tree of evolving life on earth, which in turn is part of the vast body of the cosmos.

Clara. So, like a pebble thrown into a pond, the incarnation ripples outward with saving ramifications for all flesh, including flesh that is other than human.

Elizabeth. To catch this broad meaning, the Danish theologian Niels Gregersen has coined the phrase "deep incarnation." It is starting to be used in theology to indicate the radical divine reach in Christ through human flesh all the way down into the living web of organic life with its growth and decay, amid the wider processes of evolving nature that beget and sustain life. As he writes, "In Christ, God enters into the biological tissue of creation in order to share the fate of biological existence. . . . In the incarnate One, God shares the life conditions of foxes and sparrows, grass and trees, soil and moisture." The saving God became a human being, who was part of the wider human community, which shares the membrane of life with other creatures, all made from cosmic material, and vulnerable to death and disintegration.

Clara. So if we take flesh at its most inclusive meaning, the flesh assumed in Jesus Christ connects the living God with all human beings; this has been said for centuries. But it also connects the creating God who saves with all biological life and the whole matrix of the material universe down to its very roots; this is the new vision.

Elizabeth. That's right. You can argue this point from John's prologue itself. It starts with the same words as the opening chapter of Genesis, "In the beginning," thereby evoking the story of creation. The prologue's next verses put the whole gospel that follows in a cosmic context as it speaks of the divine Word making "all things," nothing excluded (Jn 1:1–3). Then the Word joins what has been made.

Clara. As you pointed out, new backing also comes from scientific understanding of the evolutionary world.

Elizabeth. Yes. In becoming flesh the transcendent God as Wisdom/Word lays hold of matter in the form of a human being, a species in which matter has become conscious of itself and deliberately purposive. This matter emerged from the history of the cosmos and is not detachable from the history of the living world. Think of it this way. As a creature of earth, Jesus was a complex living unit of minerals and fluids, an item in the carbon, oxygen, and nitrogen cycles. The atoms comprising his body were once part of other creatures. The genetic structure of the cells in his body were kin to the flowers, fish, frogs, finches, foxes, the whole community of life that descended from common ancestors in the ancient seas. And by the nature of living things he was going to die.

Clara. A lot depends, doesn't it, on seeing humans as part of a greater whole.

Elizabeth. I have long enjoyed a passage from Charles Darwin's *On the Origin of Species* that puts this with sharp concreteness: "What can be more curious than that the hand of a man formed for grasping, the paw of a mole for digging, the leg of a horse, the paddle of the porpoise, and the wing of the bat, should all be constructed on the same pattern, and should include the same bones, in the same relative positions?" In the view of those who think God created every animal species individually, he argues, we can only say that it has so pleased the Creator to construct each animal this way. But if we suppose an ancient progenitor had its limbs arranged this way, then all descendants inherit the pattern. The bones might be enveloped in a thick membrane to form a paddle to swim, or a thin membrane to form a wing to fly, or they may be lengthened, shortened, or separated into fingers for some profitable purpose, but there will be no tendency to alter the framework. Indeed, naturalists give the same names to these bones in widely different animals. "What a grand natural system," Darwin exclaims, "formed by descent with slight modifications!"

Deep incarnation understands John's gospel to be saying that the *sarx* that the Word of God became not only weds Jesus Christ to other human beings in the human species; it also reaches beyond us to join the incarnate one to the whole evolving biological world of living creatures and the cosmic dust of which they are composed.

Clara. What I'm realizing is that as the early disciples used the best understandings in their culture to talk of Jesus Christ and his significance, so should we employ the best understandings in our culture to articulate what Jesus is and does. Hence, as scientists have uncovered the links among all flesh, all biological organisms, so we can see that the Word made flesh is inextricably linked with all of them.

Elizabeth. Well said. As a densely specific expression of the love of God already poured out in creation, the incarnation brings God near in a different way to the whole of earthly reality in its corporal and material dimensions—all of earth's ecosystems, plants and animals, and the cosmos in which planet Earth dynamically exists.

For Christian faith, the one ineffable God who creates the heavens and the earth is free enough to participate personally in the created world this way, and loving enough to want to do so.

5.7   Deep cross and resurrection

Clara. If we understand the cross and resurrection of Jesus in the light of deep incarnation, then the ecological world of nature is affected by the paschal mystery, right? Maybe not the same way as humans are, but nevertheless as creatures of flesh who die?

Elizabeth. You open up an intriguing line of thought. Let us begin with our own species. The cross is a mysterious and profound sign that God enters into the darkest trials of human suffering, death, and near-despair. In solidarity with the human race, Jesus crucified and risen abides in intimate contact with all people who walk through the valley of the shadow of death. His presence in the Spirit can comfort, strengthen, and bring hope to everyone in their suffering and dying. So Christians have long believed.

Clara. To put this in terms of the incarnation, Jesus' cross inscribes divine participation in pain and death into the historical human world.

Elizabeth. Christian devotion has always drawn on this insight, feeling that God with us in Jesus can sympathize and pour out compassion on people in their suffering.

Clara. But is the suffering solidarity of God in Christ limited to human beings? Or does it extend to the whole community of life of which human beings are a part? Deep incarnation would seem to imply that God-in-Christ is with all flesh that suffers and dies, not just human beings. Let me give a concrete example: deep incarnation seems to say that God in Christ is with every field mouse caught and eaten by a hawk.

Elizabeth. You are right on track here. The logic of deep incarnation gives a strong warrant for extending divine solidarity from the cross into the groan of suffering and the silence of death of all creatures.

Clara. Because nature suffers without ceasing. . . .

Elizabeth. The story of life on earth is a marvelous tale of new forms emerging from old. The diversity of life that so beguiles us today is the outcome of a long struggle in which organic life keeps breaking through to life forms that are more complex and beautiful. But the cost is terrible. Over thousands of millennia new species arise, thrive, and go extinct. Billions and billions of sentient creatures with nervous systems suffer unto death. Yes, new life comes from death. But this does not lessen the hard truth that pain and death are woven into the very fabric of life's evolutionary history on earth. As some scholars would have it, nature is cruciform.

Jesus' anguished death places him among this company of creatures of the flesh. Such a location allows divine solidarity to reach to all who are made of flesh and are perishing, not disdaining them in their distress. It is as if by inhabiting the inside of the isolating shell of death, Christ crucified brings divine life into closest contact with disaster, setting up a gleam of light for all other creatures who suffer in that same annihilating darkness. In their suffering and dying, they are never left alone. "Understood in this way," proposes Gregersen, "the death of Christ becomes an icon of God's redemptive co-suffering with all sentient life as well as the victims of social competition."

Clara. During his ministry Jesus taught that not even a sparrow falls to the ground without God's knowing and caring. The cross now seems to bring vital divine presence even closer to every dead bird.

Elizabeth. Seen through the lens of deep incarnation, Calvary graphically shows that the God of suffering love abides in solidarity with all creatures, bearing the cost of new life through endless millennia of evolution, from the extinction of whole species to, yes, every sparrow that falls to the ground.

Clara. To tell the truth, I can't see that the presence of God with creatures in their suffering and death makes much difference. They still die.

Elizabeth. In one sense you are right. The natural world moves on according to its own processes, and rightly so. But think what it means to affirm the compassionate presence of God in the midst of death. Seemingly absent, the Creator of all flesh is silently present with creatures in their pain and dying. They remain connected to the God of life despite what is happening; in fact, in the depths of what is happening. This unfathomable divine presence means they are not alone but knowingly accompanied in their anguish and dying with a love that does not snap off just because they are in trouble. The cross gives warrant for locating the compassion of God right at the center of their affliction. The indwelling Spirit of God, the Spirit of the crucified Christ, does not abandon them in the moment of trial but companions them into death. The field mouse does not die alone.

Clara. Can this be true? This would be deeply significant, if so.

Elizabeth. Biologically speaking, new life continuously comes from death over time. Theologically speaking, the cross signals that God is present in the midst of anguish, bearing every creature and all creation forward with an unimaginable promise. This does not solve the problem of suffering in a neat systematic way. It does make a supreme difference in what might come next.

Clara. It would seem to connect all creatures with resurrection, yes?

Elizabeth. Recall that what resurrection means in the concrete is not seriously imaginable to us who still live within the time-space grid of our known universe. Yet the empty tomb stands as an historical marker for the God of creation who can act with a power that transfigures biological existence itself. The Easter narratives witness that the crucified Jesus did not die into nothingness but into the embrace of the ineffable God who gives life, the first fruits of all the human dead. His destiny means that our hope does not merely clutch at a possibility, but stands on the irrevocable ground of what has already transpired in him.

Clara. And now this hope can be widened to include hope for all creatures.

Elizabeth. As the first fruit of an abundant harvest, the risen Jesus Christ pledges a future for all the dead, not only the dead of the human species but of all species. In Jesus crucified and risen, God who graciously gives life to the dead and brings into being the things that do not exist will redeem the whole cosmos. As Ambrose of Milan in the fourth century preached, "In Christ's resurrection the earth itself arose."

The reasoning runs like this. This person, Jesus of Nazareth, Wisdom incarnate, was composed of star stuff and earth stuff; his life formed a genuine part of the historical and biological community of Earth; his body existed in a network of relationships drawing from and extending to the whole physical universe. As a child of the earth he died, and the earth claimed him back in a grave. In the resurrection his flesh was called to life again in transformed glory. Risen from the dead, Jesus has been reborn as a child of the earth, radiantly transfigured. Karl Rahner's dramatic words spell out the dynamism of the result: "His resurrection is like the first eruption of a volcano which shows that in the interior of the world God's fire is already burning, and this will bring everything to blessed ardor in its light. He has risen to show that this has already begun." The evolving world of life, all of matter in its endless permutations, will not be left behind but will be transfigured by the resurrecting action of the Creator God.

Clara. The New Testament holds to this idea, doesn't it? I am thinking of the colorful passage where all creation is depicted groaning in the pain of childbirth, waiting to be set free from bondage and obtain redemption (Rom 8:18–25).

Elizabeth. Right. So does the great hymn in Colossians (1:15–20) which draws on the Wisdom tradition and the history of Jesus in equal measure to proclaim Christ as "the firstborn of all creation." The drumbeat of "all things" repeated five times in this short text, coupled with references to "all creation," "everything," the encompassing "things visible and invisible," and "all things whether on earth or in heaven," drives home the blessing of new life that flows to all creatures from the crucified and risen Christ.

It is little noted, but the author of this letter goes on to encourage believers to stay faithful, "without shifting from the hope promised by the gospel that you heard, which has been proclaimed to every creature under heaven" (1:23).

Clara. The gospel is meant for every creature under heaven! Recently I have become aware through friends in the Orthodox church that the ancient tradition of the church in the East has always understood the death and resurrection of the incarnate Christ to mean salvation for the whole cosmos.

Elizabeth. Without denying the human need to be redeemed from sin, the Eastern church did not concentrate on sin in the obsessively juridical way that has so characterized the church in the West. Rather, it thought that what all creatures also needed to be delivered from was death and its corruption. Consequently, Eastern theologies of redemption have had a more cosmic scope, announcing good news for all creatures that die. Like the Orthodox doctrine of icons, this teaching is based upon an understanding of the incarnation: Christ took flesh, something from the material order, and so his resurrection has opened the door to the redemptive metamorphosis of all creation.

Clara. Back to my field mouse: much of this theological language seems kind of abstract, talking about matter, creation, creatures in general. Can we include actual concrete plants and animals?

Elizabeth. It would hardly make sense to speak of the risen Christ ensuring a blessed future for the whole world and then leave something out, would it?

Clara. People will ask: will I see my dog in heaven?

Elizabeth. Stay aware of the danger of literalizing, or reducing "heaven" to life on earth as we know it, only on a grander scale. The transformation to come escapes our imagination. It is true to say, though, that deep resurrection encourages us to include every creature of flesh in the hoped-for future. Each will be blessed according to its own nature as part of the whole creation that will be made new. Some years ago when I was teaching in South Africa, an article critical of my lectures appeared in a local newspaper with the headline, "Salvation Even for Elephants?" If you are focused on a cosmocentric rather than a narrowly anthropocentric view of incarnation, the answer is assuredly yes.

Clara. As Jesus said, not even a dead bird is forgotten by God.

Elizabeth. Pope Francis writes beautifully along these lines in *Laudato Si'*. In the days of his flesh, "the gaze of Jesus" looked on the natural world with an attention full of fondness and wonder. Now risen from the dead, Christ, who took unto himself this material world, is intimately present to each creature, "surrounding it with his affection," illuminating it, and directing it toward fullness in God. Indeed, "The very flowers of the field and the birds which his human eyes contemplated and admired are now imbued with his radiant presence" (*LS* 96–100). Speaking oracles of promise like the prophets of old, Francis proposes a wonderful vision of where this is all going. "At the end we will find ourselves face to face with the infinite beauty of God." Rather than enjoying this by ourselves, "eternal life will be a shared experience of awe in which each creature, resplendently transfigured, will take its rightful place." All creation "will share with us in unending plenitude" (243). The fullness of God will be our common home, "our" referring here to humans and all other species together, just as now in time our common home is the earth.

Clara. Awesome.

Elizabeth. And because God has been united to the earth in incarnation and loves this place intensely, Francis concludes, we are called to a generous commitment to care for our planet with a similar love.

Clara. This would seem to be the basis for an ecological ethic.

Elizabeth. The general sweep of Christian doctrine certainly provides this basis, once our eyes are opened to ecological reality, but the life, death and resurrection of Jesus Christ incarnate is undoubtedly the dynamic core.

Clara. Christ, the firstborn of all the dead of Darwin's tree of life.

Elizabeth. Since God who creates and empowers the evolutionary world also joins the fray in Christ, personally drinking the cup of suffering and going down into the nothingness of death, affliction even at its worst does not have the last word. Hope against hope springs from divine presence amid the death. One with the flesh of the earth, Jesus Christ risen embodies the ultimate hope of all creatures in creation. The coming final transformation of history will be the salvation of everything, including the groaning community of life, brought into communion with the God of love.

Clara. Interpreting the cross this way foregrounds the meaning of salvation as God's accompanying the whole troubled, sinful, agonized, and dying world into the depths of agony and death and beyond. Mercy upon mercy.

Book VI

Conversion of Heart and Mind: Us

6.1   *Conversion in the spirit of the burning bush*

Clara. I have been imagining a trail of stepping stones to describe our exploration up to this point. We crossed over from the long-established path of Anselm's theory that the cross was necessary for salvation toward a different understanding of divine mercy. Major flagstones on this alternate path were the liberating history of the people of Israel, the story of Jesus, the varied metaphors interpreting his cross and resurrection, and the incarnation with its salvific meaning for the whole interconnected network of life. You might say we have walked through the Christian Old Testament, the synoptic gospels, the epistles, and the Gospel of John. Advancing along this path, our imagination gently and surely left behind any idea that the living God needed a death in order to be merciful. Step by step we came to a vista of divine compassion engaged with the whole suffering world, including humanity in our sinfulness, not because some debt was paid or punishment endured but because this is the character of God. Having come this far, what step remains to be taken?

Elizabeth. Conversion. The flagstones we have already walked upon, to use your image, bring us to the profound step of conversion to the earth as God's beloved creation. This is a turning that will impact our whole lives. It will expand our understanding of the God we are called to love with all our heart and soul, mind and strength, making clear that the Creator is also the Redeemer who accompanies the whole natural world with saving compassion. It will also expand the neighbor we are called to love as ourselves, since the beaten-up traveler left by the side of the road whose wounds we must tend to includes needy and poor human beings along with natural ecosystems and all their creatures. Doctrine, ethics, and spirituality now become ecological as we deal with pressing human concerns in a broader planetary perspective.

Clara. I can see how such conversion would affect the lives not only of individuals but also of whole church communities. If we start thinking differently about redemption, then we will start acting differently too, and that will deepen our understanding even further.

Elizabeth. A simple, strong statement about this interaction appears in *Laudato Si'* where Pope Francis notes how faith convictions can offer Christians ample motivation to care for the most vulnerable of their poor brothers and sisters as well as for the earth. It will be downright beneficial for humanity and the earth together, he proposes, "when we believers better recognize the ecological commitments which stem from our convictions" (*LS* 64). Note the flow from convictions to actions for ecological well-being. If the two are not organically connected, practical commitments can easily dry up in the face of difficulties.

Clara. But will merely shifting our beliefs necessarily stimulate change in behavior? It seems to me that there is frequently a disconnect between our intellectual positions and our concrete actions. I think of Elder Zosima in Dostoevsky's *The Brothers Karamazov* who distinguishes between "love in dreams," which is an abstract commitment to the well-being of others, and "active love" that is the tough, unremitting work for the good of the neighbor in need. How can a shift in beliefs move anyone beyond "love in dreams" to sustained action?

Elizabeth. You have to understand that faith convictions entail more than intellectual beliefs. As a worldview that offers a road map for one's life, they also involve the heart and a lived spirituality. Recall the powerful sequence of verbs at the burning bush, how God sees, hears, and knows what people are suffering. Recall how "knowing" in this text is broader than cognitive knowledge but indicates a participation in what is known, like Adam "knowing" his wife. Unless we know like this, with felt compassion, we are ignorant of the living God, no matter how accurately we can recite creed or catechism. Opening up our faith convictions to the all-merciful God who loves the earth, therefore, becomes a conversion with not only intellectual but also emotional, spiritual, and ethical dimensions.

One sign that our minds and hearts are turning toward creation in a blessed way, Pope Francis writes, is that we will start to "feel intimately united with all that exists" (*LS* 11). Once such compassionate knowing begins to occur, it will propel a raft of spiritual practices. As he describes it, we will:

— approach the natural world with awe and wonder;
— realize that everything is connected;
— develop bonds of affection with other creatures;
— grow in a deep sense of communion.

If love for the earth develops this way, beneficial actions will flow from faith convictions. If love remains stunted, then the cold indifference and ruthless exploitation that mark our time will sink whatever good intentions we might have.

The encyclical is clear about the fact that the earth is being mistreated because of human sin. Driven by greed, economic systems promote gross consumerism based on the lie that there is an infinite supply of the world's goods. Profit-making deprives both human poor peoples and endangered species of what they need to survive, while serving the interests of certain powerful groups. Accompanied by unrestrained delusions of grandeur, people engage in self-aggrandizing economic practices that create gross injustice, not least to the rights of future generations.

In the face of such ingrained behavior it will not do to attend only to this or that source of pollution or this or that ravaging of a forest, though such specific actions are vitally necessary. In face of the threat to the planetary community, we need a distinctive way of looking at the whole world that will cherish it and, together with a prophetic lifestyle and mystical spirituality, will generate resistance to the ecological assault.

Clara. I know many people who believe in God's mercy in Christ but find it difficult to connect this faith with the ecological world, despite our discussion here. You can spell out the implications of creation, liberation, cross, resurrection, and incarnation all you want, but it feels like a giant seismic shift to rearrange the faith furniture in their head to see that all creatures are embraced by God's mercy.

Elizabeth. We have already discussed a major reason for this, namely, the Western philosophy that holds humans are superior to the material world, which, in turn, is made for our use. The problem resides in a tyrannical anthropology. We loom so large in our own minds that we block out the others around us. The last part of our trail, therefore, will be made up of small stepping stones that fitted together can walk us toward conversion not only by thinking more inclusively but also by feeling kinship with other creatures and singing God's praise with them. The goal is to be converted in the spirit of the burning bush, to see, hear, and "know" the world in a godly sense, and thereby be moved to action. Toward that end, I propose that we engage in five thought experiments. Together their cumulative effect may rejuvenate our imagination so that faith convictions of mind and heart can flow to practical ecological commitments.

Clara. This could be very interesting. What is the first thought experiment?

6.2   *Blue marble: the community of creation*

Elizabeth. To start with, bring to mind the picture of our planet taken from the moon. There it is, a beautiful blue marble spinning against the vast black background of space. Now imagine that under its shielding atmosphere there exists a network of living creatures ranging in size from wee microorganisms to giant sequoias and massive blue whales, including humans toward the larger end of the scale, all interacting with the land, water, and air of their different ecosystems. In scientific terms this enveloping skein of life is called the biosphere. In faith terms it is called the community of creation. Picture yourself as an indigenous member of this community.

The basis for this sense of community, of course, is the belief that the whole world comes from the hand of the one gracious God who created everything out of love. Not only that, but throughout time every creature with its relationships is held in existence by the same vivifying Giver of life. At the end, all will be gathered into a new heaven and a new earth by the same divine, ineffable love. Such is the doctrine of creation in its threefold fullness.

Clara. Originating, sustaining, and completing: God's creative work is active in everything from the beginning, in the present, and into the future.

Elizabeth. Ponder how this conviction weaves all creatures into one community. Biblical Hebrew uses a special word, *bara*, to create, to refer to God who creates. A verb of singular majesty, it is used of no other agent, since it bespeaks an unimaginable outpouring of divine power and care like unto nothing else. At the same time a remarkable range of other verbs render divine creating with picturesque images. God forms the world like a potter with clay, stretches out the heavens, firms up the earth, adorns the world with beauty; causes by speaking a word like a royal fiat that brings order out of chaos; brings forth like a parent: "You were unmindful of the Rock that bore you [paternal verb]; you forgot the God who gave you birth [maternal verb]" (Deut 32:18). Whatever the model used, whether artistic rendering, material production, royal command, or the process of birthing, among others, they all point to life-giving love at the heart of the universe that touches every creature. "The earth is YHWH's and all that is in it, the world and all who dwell therein" (Ps 24:1). *All.* Undergirding the tremendous variation among creatures lies the shared identity of belonging to God.

All creatures, furthermore, share in the gift of being passionately cared for by the Creator who acts not with raw power but with a particular ethic. Note how this plays out in Psalm 146, which encourages trust in God,

> who made heaven and earth,
>   the sea, and all that is in them;
> who keeps faith forever;
>   who executes justice for the oppressed;
>   who gives food to the hungry. (6–7)

Wanting the beloved world to flourish, the creative power of God has a relentless ethical dimension that is active in compassionate care for all creatures, with a specific eye for those who are oppressed or in need. This is how God keeps faith forever.

Coming from the same Source and being loved with the same ineffable affection, all species form together "one splendid universal communion" (*LS* 200).

Clara. The opening chapters of Genesis can surely trigger this picture, with God creating all types of creatures, including humans, and seeing that all together it is very good. It's instructive to notice that we humans do not even rate a day of our own, but have to share the sixth day with cattle, creeping things, and wild animals of every kind.

Elizabeth. The last book of the Bible also creates a sense of community with its imaginative visions of the earth and skies transformed by the grace of the bright morning star, Jesus Christ. In the midst of this beauty the author writes, "Then I heard every creature in heaven and on earth and under the earth and in the sea, and all that is in them, singing" (Rev. 5:13). Along with the human saints, all creatures are singing the praises of God.

Clara. If the Bible begins and ends this way with the religious picture of one universal community of creation, there must be evidence of this community all through these sacred books, right?

Elizabeth. A communal vision permeates the Bible. One particularly lovely text in Job advises people to ask the beasts, birds, plants, and fish to teach us the true nature of things. They will reveal that the life of every living thing as well as the breath of every human being is in God's hands (Job 12:7–10).

Clara. It's an interesting move, to think the animals and plants can teach us something about God. It's like accessing the theological witness of the world.

Elizabeth. The biblical vision of the community of creation is profoundly theocentric. Rather than starting out with human beings, this vision sees that in its origin, history, and goal, the whole world with its innumerable relationships is ultimately grounded in the creative, redeeming God of love. Neither plants, animals, nor human beings; neither land, sea, nor air; neither sun, stars, nor galaxies would exist apart from the life-giving and sustaining power of the Creator. When broken down to its most basic element, the community of creation bespeaks the truth that all beings in this evolving world are in fact *creatures*, sustained in life by the Creator. All share this same non-negotiable character.

To put this in dramatically simple terms, human beings and other species on earth have more in common than what separates them. This does not mean they are all the same; of course they are not. But in their beautiful, terrible, fragile, and vulnerable lives, they share the fundamental identity of being creatures of the same generous God.

Clara. We have more in common than what separates us: what a startling idea! In trying to imagine this, the scientific discoveries of our day are immensely helpful, because they arrive at the same insight by other means, don't they? Astronomy demonstrates that the solar system including our earth is part of one magnificent, evolving universe; just look at the pictures from the Hubble telescope. And evolutionary biology establishes that all life on our planet descends from original ancestors in the ancient seas; all species, including *homo sapiens*, continue to be embedded in and dependent upon biospheric processes. Darwin drew the variety of species as different branches on the one tree of life.

Elizabeth. Nice to have science and religion in sync on this point. Be careful, however, not to conflate the two. Scientists arrive at their understanding by a tremendously careful process of trial and error, testing hypotheses and accepting observed results if they are repeatable and predictive. Thanks to their discoveries numerous people in our day, including scientists themselves, stand in awe and wonder at the network of life of which humans are a part.

Appreciating the same cosmic phenomenon, faith sees through to a deeper dimension, its origin and goal in God. Attributing the world with all its creatures to their Source, faith calls it not "nature" but "creation," a religious word that bespeaks a relationship. The mystery of God is love beyond imagining. This creative mystery brings forth a universe with power to develop according to its own inner dynamics, which has brought the world to its present, still unfinished configuration. Such faith conviction is not meant to supplant science. "Belief in God the creator is never an explanation, nor is it meant to be. This belief is good news," writes Schillebeeckx, with insight that deserves a great deal of thought. Faith sees the whole world that science discovers as a free gift of the living God, gives thanks, and steps up to love this neighbor as ourselves.

This first thought experiment will succeed if we picture our blue marble of a planet and grasp in mind and heart that we humans really do form with all others one splendid community of creation.

6.3   From pyramid to circle

Clara. What is the second thought experiment?

Elizabeth. This exercise aims to remove a key obstacle that prevents us from carrying out the first one successfully. So imagine yourself stepping down from the tip of a pyramid of human privilege and rejoining other creatures as their kin in the circle of life on earth.

This pyramid was constructed by the philosophy we've already discussed that saw the world organized according to a hierarchy of being, with human beings (actually elite human men) at the pinnacle. It promotes the idea that due to our innate superiority humans have the right to command and control the natural world, which is created to serve our purposes. Instead of lording it over other creatures from a pinnacle of power, imagine redrawing the structure of relationship into one of kinship with others in a circle of mutual relations.

Clara. Even before trying this experiment, I have to raise an objection. Doesn't the creation story in Genesis have God telling the first human couple to "have dominion" over fish and birds and all other creatures (1:28)?

Elizabeth. Indeed it does. But what does this mean? Let us track what dominion means in its own story, what it means in the context of the whole Bible, and what shape it took in the course of tradition. Then it will be clear how this second thought experiment reinforces the first.

Common lines of biblical interpretation today interpret "dominion" in at least two ways. It could mean that humans had permission to carve out a safe living space amid a large and hostile natural world; remember, there were lions roaming in Israel! The dominion role can also be traced to a custom of the ancient royal court. If a ruler had a large territory to govern, he would appoint representatives to oversee distant regions in his name. Such officials would be said to have "dominion" over that part of the kingdom, meaning they were charged to see that the ruler's wishes were carried out.

Read Genesis in light of this royal custom. God has just created all creatures, blessed them, and pronounced them good. The human couple is entrusted with "dominion" over them, which means they are representatives of the Creator charged to see that the divine will is carried out. And what is the divine will? Be fruitful! multiply!! flourish!!! Far from giving humans permission to exploit the natural world, dominion in the name of the creating God makes them responsible to see that it thrives.

Clara. Still, the idea of human dominion as power-over has had such influence! Maybe because it is in the opening story of the Bible, embedded in the rhetoric of a majestic prose poem. But there is a second version of creation, isn't there?

Elizabeth. In Genesis chapter 2 creation starts all over again, obviously signaling a different literary tradition of origins. First God forms an earth creature (*adam*) out of the dust of the earth (*adamah*), and breathes the spirit of life into its nostrils. Then comes a garden with pleasant trees; a river runs through it; the earth creature is told "to till and keep it." Next come animals and birds, formed from the same dust and inspirited with the same breath of life, and finally the earth creature is sexually differentiated into male and female.

This account underscores the earthy solidarity women and men have with each other and with the rest of creation. Far from being placed over the natural world, they are made of the same stuff, immersed in a web of reciprocal relations with the land and other creatures, and charged to reverence and serve, to carefully use and responsibly protect them. Already the second creation story enfolds the dominion mandate of the first chapter of Genesis into a more mutual pattern of relationship.

Tracking creation through the rest of the Bible makes it clear that dominion is not at all the primary model for the relation between humans and the natural world. Except for Genesis 1 and Psalm 8, there are precious few other references to this model. Instead, biblical authors consistently place human beings within, not over, the interdependent community of creation, whose center and encompassing horizon is the generous creating God.

Ponder the magnificent Psalm 104. Here one does not find the duality of humans and nature or the emphasis on dominion typical of Western tradition. Rather, in cascades of ecologically attuned poetry this prayer puts all creatures including human beings on a plane of equality in the wonderful order of God's creation. Seen first of all as fellow-creatures, humans serve and praise God along with other living beings within a sphere of relations that are reciprocal rather than top-down. Numerous other biblical texts have this same vision, leading scholars today to argue that the major biblical paradigm is not dominion but the community of creation. Today's ecological concerns offer a fresh opportunity to recover this understanding.

Clara. I'm just so used to thinking that human beings are meant to rule over nature that I suspect later tradition had a lot to do with how the biblical view was interpreted.

Elizabeth. Yes, once Christian thought adopted a dualistic philosophy with the hierarchy of spirit over matter, it subordinated the religious importance of the natural world, accounting for the tenacious human-centeredness that pervades most theologies.

This view turned really vicious in the fifteenth and sixteenth centuries when European nations began to colonize other continents. A hierarchically structured philosophy done amidst this aggressive entrepreneurial culture interpreted *dominion* to mean *domination* over nature. Such interpretation allowed Genesis 1 to be read with an imperialist slant. Resources in other lands were there to be extracted and brought back to the ruler in the home country. Plants and animals were means of profit. Not to be missed is the way elite peoples also applied the idea of dominion to other human beings: white Europeans, at the top of the pyramid within the human species, or so they thought, had the right to dominate and enslave darker, indigenous peoples. Tragically and sinfully, the official church and most European theology supported this position. I find it daunting to realize how deeply this view of human beings as masters and rulers of nature has shaped Christian belief and practice. It has clearly forged our own country's lifestyle and business practices. With deep roots in classical tradition, dominion as domination has largely erased the community of creation from consciousness, opening the door to unbridled exploitation of nature without ecclesial protest.

Clara. The churches have started to come around on this issue, haven't they? Other religions as well?

Elizabeth. They have indeed. In addition to grassroots movements by now several decades old, religious leaders have begun to speak out and multifaith cooperative ventures are multiplying. To take but one pertinent example, in blunt language *Laudato Si'* criticizes the assumption that humans are the pinnacle of creation, saying this is not only "inadequate" but frankly "wrong." In view of the church's long acceptance of matter-spirit dualism and the paradigm of domination, Pope Francis recognizes that he is contributing something new to Catholic teaching by emphasizing that even if "we Christians have at times incorrectly interpreted the Scriptures, nowadays we must forcefully reject the notion that our being created in God's image and given dominion over the earth justifies absolute domination over other creatures" (*LS* 67). Instead, we are meant to live in relationships of mutual responsibility with the natural world, sharing together in one community embraced by the love of God. Think kinship rather than domination. Think circle of life rather than pyramid of privilege and subordination.

Clara. Stepping down from the pinnacle of privilege is not easy. We have to deconstruct and reconstruct the architecture of our imagination and the feelings of our heart.

Elizabeth. It can also be frightening. One audience member stood to raise this challenge after I gave a lecture on the subject: "All my life I've seen myself at the tip of the pyramid. If it dissolves or changes shape, where am I?"

Clara. Maybe this worrier would benefit from a visit to the American Museum of Natural History in New York City. There you can walk a Cosmic Pathway that spirals from the high ceiling down to the lower floor. You start at the top with a re-enactment of the Big Bang, and then each step downward covers tens of millions of years of the universe's more than thirteen billion years of development. Exhibits along the side help you visualize what was going on, from galaxies forming to life beginning on earth. At the bottom you step over all of human history in a line as thin as a human hair. That walk always gives me such a good sense of being part of a greater whole.

Elizabeth. Getting concrete about the timeline can only increase that healthy realization. In approximate terms, how old is the universe?

Clara. 13.8 billion years old.

Elizabeth. When did our solar system of sun and planets take shape?

Clara. About 5 billion years ago.

Elizabeth. When did life begin on our planet Earth?

Clara. Around 3.5 billion years ago.

Elizabeth. When did modern *homo sapiens* emerge?

Clara. About 200,000 to 100,000 years ago on the African savanna.

I've always liked the timeline suggested by Carl Sagan, which helps us grasp the enormous stretches of time involved. If the Big Bang took place on January 1, our solar system formed on September 1. Life on earth started on September 25. Human beings emerged on December 31 at ten minutes to midnight.

Elizabeth. We humans have only recently arrived. Apex of the pyramid? Or part of the circle of life on an evolving planet?

What a need there is to reimagine ourselves as a species! Certainly we are distinct from other species in the circle, as indeed they are from each other. But we are also kin. We have magnified the distinction and forgotten the kinship. If we reimagine ourselves as part of God's good creation, then we could grow into a new way of being human that enhances rather than diminishes the life of other creatures.

6.4   "A value of their own in God's eyes" (LS 69)

Clara. What is the third thought experiment?

Elizabeth. This experiment and the next are the flip side of the previous one. Once we reposition our human selves as genuinely part of the community of creation, we can look with fresh eyes at other creatures. So, to use technical language that is quite serviceable, this third experiment asks us to imagine that other creatures have intrinsic value in their own right, not just instrumental value for human use.

Clara. You mean we should picture them as good in themselves just because God created (*bara*) them, and not only because they are good for us?

Elizabeth. Yes. *Laudato Si'* offers largely unnoticed help in refashioning imagination in this direction. In the introduction to this encyclical Pope Francis lists what will be its recurrent themes. Along with salient issues such as the interconnectedness of everything in the world and the intimate relation between poor people and the fragility of the planet, he names "the value proper to each creature." There is no single section with its own heading where this is treated, but it pops up throughout the encyclical in striking ways.

Clara. Go ahead and cherry-pick, to get our imaginations rolling.

Elizabeth. "We are not God" (67). I think this is one of the greatest lines ever written in an encyclical; it grounds the teaching that follows. We do not own the earth; it is God's; it was here before us and is a gift. Our responsibility is to live in mutual relations with nature, benefitting from its bounty and protecting its life. Against this theological background, the drumbeat of intrinsic value begins to sound. "Because all creatures are connected, each must be cherished with love and respect" (42). Clearly the Bible has no place for a monopoly of human beings unconcerned for other creatures. Instead, "we are called to recognize that other living beings have a value of their own in God's eyes" (69).

Clara. Saying "we are called" makes this part of the Christian vocation. Saying other creatures "have a value of their own in God's eyes" redefines upward what Western philosophy had assessed as of lesser worth. Imagine seeing other creatures with God's eyes!

Elizabeth. The encyclical continues forthrightly on this point. "In our time the Church does not simply state that other creatures are completely subordinate to the good of human beings, as if they had no worth in themselves and can be treated as we wish" (69). Rather, "They have an intrinsic value independent of their usefulness" (140). And why? Because God loves them. "Even the fleeting life of the least of beings is the object of God's love, and in its few seconds of existence, God enfolds it with affection" (77).

Clara. Even mayflies that live for less than a day!

Elizabeth. As part of the community of creation, "every creature has its own value and significance" (76). The whole universe shaped by open systems with countless forms of relationship and participation is pervaded, as Dante saw, by "the love that moves the sun and the other stars" (77). This infinitely gracious love embraces every creature. Without impinging on its autonomy, "God is intimately present to each being" (80).

Clara. I have to think about this, God being present to every bug.

Elizabeth. The encyclical ratchets up the religious role of creatures in view of their intrinsic value. Other species are a source of revelation: each one "reflects in its own way a ray of God's infinite wisdom and goodness" (69), and can teach us about the Creator. They are also a sacrament of communion, being a place where we can encounter God: since "the Spirit of life dwells in them" they are a "locus of divine presence," calling us into relationship (88).

Ultimately, we human beings have the responsibility to care for all other species because "the final purpose of other creatures is not to be found in us. Rather, all creatures are moving forward, with us and through us, towards a common point of arrival, which is God" (83).

Clara. Would you say this tremendous sense of the intrinsic value of all creatures helps to explain the pope's intense dismay at the ecological damage being done in our day?

Elizabeth. Certainly. He writes so that we will become "painfully aware, to dare to turn what is happening in the world into our own personal suffering and thus to discover what each of us can do about it" (19). If we really felt our connection to the world, we would "feel the desertification of the soil almost as a physical ailment, and the extinction of a species as a painful disfigurement" (89). The news that other species are going extinct at a rapid rate would register as more than intellectual knowledge. Their destruction would awaken a painful emotional response in our heart and spur us to action.

Clara. It would be like a death in the family that causes intense sorrow. I have long been struck by Thomas Merton's words about divine identification with people who are crushed: through "murder, massacres, revolution, hatred, the slaughter and torture of the bodies and souls of men, the destruction of cities by fire, the starvation of millions, the annihilation of populations and finally the cosmic inhumanity of atomic war: Christ is massacred in his members, torn limb from limb; God is murdered in men."

Elizabeth. God is murdered in women, men, and children of the human species. And in polar bears, baobab tress, and frogs on the verge of mass extinction.

Clara. When something you treasure is destroyed, it kills something in you too. Imagine if preachers took this to heart and drew attention to local pollution or the loss of a local species as a sin that causes us to suffer and disfigures the whole body of Christ.

Elizabeth. We can all do this, based on the intrinsic worth of every creature in God's eyes.

6.5 *"You save humans and animals alike"* (Ps 36:6)

Clara. What is the fourth thought experiment?

Elizabeth. This mental move helps to make the previous one more concrete. Imagine the birds and the bees with their own relationships to the creating, merciful God, interacting in mutual relation.

Most of the time theology focuses on the relationship between God and human persons, and on divine action in the lives of human communities and their history. But if all creatures are beloved of God, this is insufficient. The Creator of the heavens and the earth is intimately related to all creatures, addresses them, blesses them, and calls them by name. In response they look to God in their need, rejoice in divine gifts, and give praise. Imagine this relationship in the case of one particular creature. It can put a chink in the tyranny of human-obsessed spirituality.

Clara. Right off, I think of the symbolic and narrative language of Genesis 1 that presents the Creator talking to the birds of the air, the fish of the sea, and the cattle, creeping things, and wild animals of the dry land. God blesses them, and tells them to be fruitful and multiply, all the while seeing how good they are. Are there other biblical examples that can make this thought experiment more effective?

Elizabeth. There are many more than can be cited here, but savor these to get a taste of what is in store. Start with the skies. For biblical faith the sun, moon, and stars are not gods as in other ancient religions, but beautiful creatures. They return the favor of being created by proclaiming the weighty radiance of God's presence:

> The heavens are telling the glory of God,
>   and the firmament proclaims his handiwork.
> Day to day pours forth speech,
>   and night to night declares knowledge. (Ps 19:1–4)

The skies of day and night speak in a voice that goes out through all the earth.

Staying with the stars for a moment, see how organically the psalmist enwraps humans and stars together as recipients of divine compassion:

> YHWH heals the brokenhearted
>   and binds up their wounds;
> He determines the number of the stars
>   and gives to all of them their names. (Ps 147:3–4)

Clara. How cool is that, that God heals human grief and names the stars in one fell swoop? I recall how earlier we discussed Baruch's delightful description of the relation between the Creator and the stars: "The stars shone in their watches, and were glad; God called them, and they said, 'Here we are!' They shone with gladness for the One who made them" (3:34).

Elizabeth. It is not just the heavens that interact with their Creator. "Comfort," that magnificent verb that opens the scroll of Second Isaiah promising God's mercy toward a disheartened, exhausted group of exiles is also promised to the natural world in distress. "For YHWH will comfort Zion, will comfort all her waste places;" her desert will bloom like the garden of Eden; together people and land will rejoice and sing thanks (Isa 51:3).

Clara. What a way to think about cleaning up polluted areas, to *comfort* them!

Elizabeth. And the natural world often needs comfort, because its devastation results from human sins, such as stealing and violence, which break out again and again: "Therefore the land mourns and all who live in it languish; together with the wild animals and the bird of the air, even the fish are perishing" (Hos 4:3).

By contrast, on that coming day of God's redemption, joy will be characteristic of the land itself: "The wilderness and the dry land shall be glad, the desert shall rejoice and blossom; like the crocus it shall blossom abundantly, and rejoice with joy and singing" (Isa 35:1–2). Caves and hills will not be able to contain themselves: "shout, O depths of the earth; break forth into singing, O mountains, O forest, and every tree in it, for YHWH has redeemed Jacob" (Isa 44:23).

Clara. The skies telling forth, the earth lamenting and being comforted or rejoicing and blossoming, the sea and all that swims in it roaring, the mountains and fields exulting, the trees clapping their hands. What kind of thinking would have occasioned this language? Surely these and other texts help us see that the natural world is more than a scenic backdrop in the eyes of God, more than a stage for the human drama, but a created participant to whom God speaks and toward whom God acts with compassion. Can we get more specific about animals?

Elizabeth. No aspect of the community of creation exists in which the Creator is not intimately involved, including animals. Notice this rationale for divine interest:

> For every wild animal of the forest is mine
> and the cattle on a thousand hills.
> I know all the birds of the air
> and all that moves in the field is mine.
> (Ps 50:10–11)

All animals, from cattle chewing grass to young lions roaring for their prey, cry to God; they "look to you to give them their food in due season" (Ps 104:27). And when they are satisfied, they give thanks: "All your works give you thanks, O YHWH, and all your faithful ones bless you" (Ps 145:10).

God covenants with all creatures of flesh, as we saw in the Noah story with its covenant sign of the rainbow. Made of flesh, animals are vulnerable to pain and death, in need of God's redeeming care. One psalm makes this explicit in startling language: "you save humans and animals alike, O YHWH" (Ps 36:6).

Clara. God saves the animals!

Elizabeth. The great theophany from the whirlwind in Job attends in detail to ravens hunting, mountain goats giving birth, wild asses ranging the mountains, ostriches flapping their wings trying to fly, horses snorting, and eagles nesting on high cliffs: all these display knowledge of being workable creatures of God; in all of them God takes delight (chapters 38–39).

Clara. "The creator loves pizzazz," as Annie Dillard wrote.

Elizabeth. Along with the rest of creation, animals are summoned to praise God's holy name:

> Praise YHWH from the earth,
>> you sea monsters and all deeps,
> fire and hail, snow and frost,
>> stormy wind that fulfills his command!
> Mountains and all hills,
>> fruit trees and all cedars,
> Wild animals and all cattle,
>> creeping things and flying birds! (Ps 148:7–10)

Clara. Recently I've become aware that when this psalm is used as a responsorial psalm in the Mass, these verses are left out; we skip from sun and moon to the people. But this can be changed, right?

Elizabeth. The omission is an unfortunate decision by a committee; it can be rectified, along with many other omissions of the natural world in future liturgical texts. The pressing ecological issues of our day bring to the fore how the relation between God and creation has been made invisible by the reductionism of church theology and liturgy.

Clara. The animals also show up in the biblical view of redemption, don't they?

Elizabeth. The extraordinary promise of a renewed creation includes shalom for people and the whole natural world together. In Isaiah's oracle the sound of weeping will cease; people will live long and fruitful lives "like the days of a tree," and their offspring will be blessed. At the same time, "The wolf and the lamb shall feed together, the lion shall eat straw like the ox. . . . They shall not hurt or destroy on all my holy mountain" (Isa 65:17–25).

Clara. What a good sign of the transformation of the world into God's peaceful reign, that the wolf and the lamb shall feed together. It's like maximum security for the weakest in its own habitat.

Elizabeth. The ironic ending of the book of Jonah offers yet another explicit example of God's care for the beasts. Angry that his mission to Nineveh had succeeded so well that the city would be spared destruction, and even angrier that a little bush that gave him shade had withered, leaving him to bake in the sun, Jonah wanted to die.

> Then YHWH said, "You are concerned about the bush, for which you did not labor and which you did not grow; it came into being in a night and perished in a night. And should I not be concerned about Nineveh, that great city, in which there are more than a hundred and twenty thousand persons who do not know their right hand from their left, and also many animals?" (4:10–11).

Clara. "Should I not be concerned about the animals?" That's a terrific divine line. We have been so blind to this characteristic of divine love.

Elizabeth. And let us not forget Jesus' teaching about God's care for even one dead sparrow.

Clara. The Bible certainly gives us food for thought about the mutual relation between God and all living beings. I'm thinking that to perform this thought experiment successfully, it's probably best to look upon a single creature and try to fathom its relationship with God. Converse with a cat, contemplate a tree, marvel at a crow. Whether we settle on predator or prey, and many creatures are both, we need to feel our way into the community of creation and its relationship to God.

Elizabeth. Let our imagination be guided by this mantra-like verse: "God is good to all, and compassionate over all that has been made" (Ps 145:9).

6.6   Expanding the heart: us

Clara. And the fifth thought experiment?

Elizabeth. With this imaginative move we come full circle, back to the round blue earth with humans and all creatures together as a community of creation, and we bring this kinship relation to expression in pronouns. If the previous experiments have succeeded, if we imagine our human selves as part of the community of creation, come down from the pinnacle of privilege to rejoin the circle of life, acknowledge the intrinsic value of other creatures, and see their interaction with the living God, then we should be able to include them with ourselves at appropriate moments. In order to create a stronger and more enduring sense of connection with the more than human world, this experiment invites us to reimagine "us." Try to expand the boundaries of the community of "us" when you think, speak, pray, teach, preach, read, or propose actions, in order to include the rest of creation.

Clara. This could also be done with "we" or "you," couldn't it?
Elizabeth. Indeed it could. The expansion cannot be done in all instances. In some biblical passages, for example, the pronoun obviously refers to a particular human group: "YHWH brought us out of Egypt with a mighty hand and an outstretched arm" (Deut 26:8). But to stay with the Bible for this experiment, there are many passages about God's gracious involvement with the world where rightly imagining other creatures included in the "us" will help bonds of affection grow.

Clara. We humans already have enough trouble expanding "us" to include people of other races, nationalities, religions, sexual orientations, political opinions, and so on, different from our own. What you propose pushes the envelope across the species line, which is more difficult yet. I'm thinking that if we succeed, perhaps this practice can expand our hearts to make more room for others of our own species. Can we try this here, to see how it would work?

Elizabeth. Since prayer has power to change the heart, let us start with Psalm 67, a short song of thanksgiving. It begins, "May God be gracious to us and bless us." Who is the "us" in this prayer? As the psalm progresses, the "us" is marvelously elastic. In its opening line the "us" originally referred to the people of Israel. But the psalm believes that divine blessing on Israel is the means God uses to reveal divine blessing on all the nations. Mid-psalm this starts to happen: "Let the nations be glad and sing for joy," for God guides them with justice and faithfulness. By the end, a good harvest has come in and now the blessing extends to the whole earth:

> The earth has yielded its increase;
> God, our God, has blessed us.
> May God continue to bless us;
> let all the ends of the earth revere him. (Ps 67:6–7)

Imagine the "us" expanded to the community of creation with penguins, parrots, tuna, and elephants included in the blessing, their faces lit with divine favor as they go about their business. "May God continue to bless us" would mean all of us creatures, from the Arctic to the Antarctic ends of the earth.

Clara. Since I first came upon it I have loved the American naturalist Henry Beston's description of animals as other nations. Living in the early years of the twentieth century, he was critical of how urban civilization caused people to distort the reality of animals' lives:

> We patronize them for their incompleteness, for their tragic fate of having taken form so far below ourselves. And therein we err, and greatly err. For the animal shall not be measured by man. In a world older and more complete than ours they move finished and complete, gifted with extensions of the senses we have lost or never attained, living by voices we shall never hear. They are not brethren, they are not underlings; they are other nations, caught with ourselves in the net of life and time, fellow prisoners of the splendour and travail of the earth.

So the nations in the psalms that are glad for God's just guidance could be all species on earth.

Elizabeth. With this imagination, we can grow the prayer for God's blessing on "us" to include the nations of the animals and plants of the tundra, the plains, the jungles, the cities, the coasts and the deep seas, all of life on earth. Doing this kind of thing habitually would make faith convictions hospitable to other creatures at a deeply spiritual level.

Clara. Many psalms are open to this way of being prayed. It would make other creatures' relationship to God more explicit in our own consciousness.

Elizabeth. Pray "The Lord has done great things for us; we are glad indeed" (Ps 126:3) with the glories of the African savanna in mind. Envision the plants and animals of the rain forest in mutual relationship with God when we pray, "Let your steadfast love, O Lord, be upon us, for we have placed our trust in you" (Ps 33:22). Acknowledge God as rock and salvation for the migrating monarch butterflies: "God is a refuge for us" (Ps 62:8). In light of ecological destruction wrought by human activity, pray the psalms that cry for deliverance from enemies with other species such as endangered orangutans in view:

> Have mercy upon us, O Lord, have mercy upon us,
> for we have had more than enough of contempt.
> Our soul has had more than its fill
> of the scorn of those who are at ease,
> of the contempt of the proud. (Ps 123:3–4)

Clara. So imagine that "us" means all of us in the community of creation. It certainly could motivate action for responsible care of the earth. This is challenging and I think it is great. But some people might object that praying this way anthropomorphizes animals. They don't have human consciousness, so how can they receive God's blessing, cry in lament, or respond with praise?

Elizabeth. To clarify understanding, let us bring in an influential principle used many times by Thomas Aquinas. Its original Latin has provided theology students with a neat tongue-twister: *Quidquid recipitur ad modum recipientis recipitur.* In English, that translates to "Whatever is received, is received according to the mode of the recipient," or more colloquially, each creature receives and responds to the love of God according to its own nature.

Clara. So expanding "us" does not collapse difference between the species.

Elizabeth. Of course not. What it does is credit every creature in the community with its own relationship to God. "Praise God all you nations . . . for great is God's steadfast love toward us"

(Ps 117:1–2). Indeed, "You are the hope of all the earth, and of the far distant seas" (Ps 65:5).

Clara. I'm sure there are many more texts from the Christian Old Testament, but what New Testament passages might we consider?

Elizabeth. In the prologue to John's gospel, we've already discussed at some length what "flesh" means, and what the "Word" means, but what about *us*? "The Word was made flesh and dwelt among *us*" (Jn 1:14). Expand your imagination of this gospel text with the whole dazzling biosphere of plants and animals in view, now under threat.

A similar awakening occurs when we read the annunciation of Jesus' birth to Joseph: "and they shall name him Emmanuel, which means 'God is with us'" (Matt 1:23). Who is the "us" God is with? In Jesus Christ the God who creates and saves is with the salmon and pine trees and bears of the Pacific Northwest, and with every ecosystem around the globe.

Clara. What a gorgeous way to interpret Christ in view of the whole planetary community.

Elizabeth. Many texts can open to such wide-ranging allusions. Read that God raised Jesus and "will also raise us by his power" (1 Cor 6:14), and see in your mind's eye Pope Francis's vision of the future when all creatures, resplendently transfigured, will enjoy with human beings the beauty of God. Hear the ringing question, "Who will separate us from the love of Christ?" in a species-inclusive manner, and the answer becomes awesome: nothing in the past, present, or future, no evil power, not even death can so separate creatures from God (Rom 8:35–39). Imagine Paul proclaiming that the God who made heaven and earth and gives breath to all mortal beings cannot be confined to a shrine; rather, this God "is not far from any one of us, for 'in him we live and move and have our being,' as some of your poets have said" (Acts 17:27–28). While the people of Athens may not have imagined their sheep and olive trees included in the "us" from whom God is not far, ecological awareness prompts us to do so.

If in faith we see that all creatures are inclusively loved by God, rich in mercy, who shows immeasurable "kindness toward us in Christ Jesus" (Eph 2:7), then our own kindness would flow to every neighbor in need, including the distressed of other species.

Clara. Mindful of the struggle that lies ahead, Pope Francis ends *Laudato Si'* with an exhortation to joy and hope, "Let us sing as we go" (244). Might this "us" also include the songs of our fellow creatures?

Elizabeth. The shared capacity to sing points to the many deep genetic connections that link humans to other living beings. In a beautiful article Rhodora Beaton eloquently states, "The image of singing as we go invites a broader vision of the journey song, one that includes the duets of gibbons, the beat-keeping dances of parrots, and the elaborate and distinctive calls of whales and other aquatic mammals." Humans do not sing alone but raise their voices with a world of singers sharing the journey of life together.

Clara. Expand "us"!

6.7   Creation and the cross

Clara. Presuming we work through these thought experiments with even a modicum of success and that the community of creation begins to reside in our minds and hearts as powerfully as it exists in reality, how shall we summarize and carry forward this treatise on creation and the cross?

Elizabeth. The best take-away for spirituality and ethics would be a lively sense of the presence of God to all creatures on planet Earth, walking with them in their joy and suffering in order to heal, redeem, and liberate, and a humbled awareness of the creating God who cares especially for the poor and oppressed among human beings and among all species. It would also mean a strong appreciation of the living God's merciful love poured out without merit on any creature's part, and a vibrant hope in God that promotes action on behalf of ecojustice for the flourishing of life. These are all outflows from a theology of salvation as accompaniment, an "I am with you to deliver you" view of God's saving work.

This book's theology, or search for understanding of the faith, supports these insights and practices by carefully setting out the pathway of divine mercy through the scriptures of the Jewish and Christian communities. Moving away from the tenacious view that Jesus had to die to save the world from sin, we walked across the flagstone of the ever-flowing mercy of God evident in the narratives of Exodus from slavery and the return of exiles. Seeing this same gracious mercy expressed in the life, death, and resurrection of Jesus in its historical context, and appreciating how early disciples interpreted these events in multiple ways as an outpouring of mercy, provided us with further steps toward the paradigm of a theology of accompaniment. The flagstone of the incarnation, interpreted deeply, brought our journey to the breathtaking vista of divine involvement with the flesh of all creation in its suffering and dying, with merciful promise of new life that only a God who creates could give. Finally, with imaginative thought experiments we jogged our minds and hearts into new pathways of inclusive love.

A theology of accompaniment holds the faith conviction that God forever companions the world with liberating, saving mercy. The living God, who in the Spirit is already in, with, and for all creation, has in Jesus Christ joined the history of the world and participates in its journey as a member of the planetary community. The Christian vocation with an inbuilt ecological commitment takes shape in this light.

Within this overall framework, we can interpret the cross as a particular event of divine solidarity with the suffering and death of all creatures. Historically it was an unjust act entailing violent death for a good human being. Theologically it places the self-giving love of God in intimate contact with every human death, every tortured unjust death, every death of creatures and species in the evolving world. Hope for the future of all creation arises with the resurrection of Jesus from the dead by the power of the Spirit. The cross of the risen Christ indelibly impresses a blessed future into the history of the world and all its creatures.

Clara. In other words, if we zoom out and place the cross in a cosmic context, it becomes an historically accessible, tormented moment that reveals that God walks with all creatures in their living and dying, including human beings with our fierce power to build and destroy, in order to save. Where does sin stand in this accompaniment theology?

Elizabeth. Sin is a terribly powerful reality in the world and has become systemic, built up over time into the very infrastructure of human exchanges with each other and the earth. The cross dramatizes the terrible destruction humans can foster, as well as holds up indelibly what Christians see as the epitome of divine participation in the ensuing suffering and death. This is the dangerous memory *par excellence* that shakes lovers of God out of complacency and calls them to attend with vigor to their suffering neighbors, human and more-than-human, especially those relegated to the margins.

Terms such as forgiveness of sin and practices that express repentance are necessary to keep the whole picture of human adversarial wrong-doing in view, with a commensurate need for reconciliation. Without them, talk about divine mercy in creation becomes unreal. But these need to be understood as part of the bigger story of God's ongoing creative, saving activity with the world.

Clara. To underscore the main point, the path we have walked leads to a different end-point than the long-held idea that the cross was necessary in order for God to forgive sin.

Elizabeth. Scripture testifies that the cross did not begin the outpouring of divine mercy to the world. It has been present from the beginning and endures forever. No one threw a switch to turn off its flow, though one might think so, given the way preaching and teaching have labeled the cross as the event that triggered divine forgiveness. Gracious and compassionate, God has always been acting mercifully.

The cross of Christ brings this infinitely merciful love into a different kind of personal intimacy with the pain and death of creatures. In view of Jesus' death the words of divine solidarity at the burning bush, "I know well what they are suffering," can be announced with unexpected resonance. Together with the resurrection from which it cannot be separated, the cross anchors divine saving love historically in the flesh of the world's evolving life. In its light we see that saving mercy accompanies all creatures in the world's beautiful, terrible journey through time to final fulfillment. The grace of this presence empowers life to emerge anew, rebuilds broken relationships, forgives wretched human sin, and embraces all the dead into their future, promised but unknown.

Loudly and clearly, one more time, the mercy of God is not dependent on the death of Jesus. Divine mercy does not require the torture and violence of crucifixion. To phrase this in reverse, the death of Jesus is not necessary in order for God to forgive sin. The fact that Jesus died an agonizing death on the cross is indeed part of the story of salvation Christians tell, but not because he had to appease an angry God or pay some kind of debt. Salvation does not require that kind of transaction.

Grasping the cross in a more biblical light will allow an ecological view to emerge that sees God accompanying creation through time with mercy, which in our day encompasses a planet in peril. Not incidentally, this understanding can circle back to include human beings within a more holistic theology of salvation as part of a wider world.

Clara. It's fascinating how the ecological crisis has opened up this perspective, perhaps new to us but ancient in its origin.

Elizabeth. The signs of our time propel the living tradition forward. The biosphere of our blue marble of a planet is under severe duress. The atmosphere is heating up. Populations of songbirds, pollinators, and amphibians, mammals from bats to moose, and many aquatic species are plummeting. Every year multiple species go extinct (gone forever!) at an alarming rate due to human actions. This raises a new question about the will of God for the world, or more explicitly, about the merciful intent of God for all creatures and their ecosystems. Since salvation means making life whole, liberating, healing, forgiving, restoring, cleansing, opening up new possibilities, belief in a God who saves is obviously germane to the polluted, ravaged, depleted natural world. Comfort! A theology of accompaniment sees God's redeeming action always present and active in service of the flourishing of a world that is currently suffering reversals and death in a horrific way.

To sum up, the living God, gracious and merciful, always was, is, and will be accompanying the world with saving grace, including humans in their sinfulness, and humans and all creatures in their unique beauty, evolutionary struggle, and inevitable dying. The cross does not change this truth, or occasion a shift in God's attitude from betrayed honor to willingness to forgive. It does make the compassionate love of God's heart blazingly clear in an historical event. "The death of Christ becomes an icon of God's redemptive co-suffering with all sentient life as well as the victims of social competition," to recall Gregersen's insight. In Jesus Christ crucified we are gifted with an historical sacrament of encounter with the mercy of God, which impels us toward conversion to the suffering earth, sustained by hope for the resurrection of the flesh of all of us.

Clara. I feel very at home with this interpretation of the cross and its cosmic view.

Elizabeth. As with any theology, the path laid down here will prove its worth if the faith convictions it generates motivate individuals and communities to passionate, ethical, practical commitments to the natural world in tandem with all the earth's poor and marginalized people. A whole agenda arises when we realize that for this conversion to take root it needs to find expression in church liturgies and eucharistic prayers, in religious art and music, in public preaching and teaching, and in private prayers and spirituality, and devotional writing. There is a long road ahead before such generous commitment to the earth becomes commonplace. But many are making a beginning.

Clara. Maybe by the twenty-second century?

Elizabeth. I'm sorry to say that as a planetary community of life we do not have that much time. But an important step will be taken if Christians see that the grace of the crucified and risen Christ washes over all creation, to practical and critical effect.

Clara. I am struck that the path we have been following brings us to the same place Anselm arrived at when, after pondering the cross with Boso, he found that the compassion of God was "incomparably greater than anything that can be conceived" (II.20).

Elizabeth. On that we are agreed, though obviously we have arrived at this core insight by a vastly different route. To conclude our conversation, I would like to quote this same medieval thinker on one more shared point of agreement, but with a twist. Anselm writes that God's merciful ways with the world have an "indescribable beauty." Aware of this, let us give thanks to God "with all our heart, praising and proclaiming the ineffable height of divine compassion, which acts beyond our expectation in such astonishing ways, showing such exceeding love and tenderness toward us" (I.3)—toward all of us in the community of creation.

Notes

Introduction

Joseph Ratzinger, *Introduction to Christianity* (San Francisco: Ignatius Press, 1990/2004), 233.

I am using the translation of Anselm's *Cur Deus Homo* by S. N. Deane, published in *Saint Anselm: Basic Writings* (LaSalle, IL: Open Court Pub., 1962); references are given by Book number (I or II) followed by chapter number (e.g., I.3).

Book I

1.6

Joseph Ratzinger, *Introduction to Christianity* (San Francisco: Ignatius Press, 1990/2004), 281.

Edward Schillebeeckx, *Christ: The Experience of Jesus as Lord* (New York: Seabury, 1980), 700.

James Cone, *The Cross and the Lynching Tree* (Maryknoll, NY: Orbis Books, 2011), 150.

Delores Williams, *Sisters in the Wilderness: The Challenge of Womanist God-Talk* (Maryknoll, NY: Orbis Books, 1993), 165.

Ignacio Ellacuría, "The Crucified People," in *Mysterium Liberationis: Fundamental Concepts of Liberation Theology,* ed. Ignacio Ellacuría and Jon Sobrino (Maryknoll, NY: Orbis Books, 1993), 580–603.

Rita Nakashima Brock, *Journeys by Heart: A Christology of Erotic Power* (New York: Crossroad, 1988), 50.

Mark Heim, "Christ Crucified," *Christian Century* 118 (March 7, 2001), 12–17, at 14.

1.7

John Muir, "Thoughts on Finding a Dead Yosemite Bear" in *The Wilderness World of John Muir*, ed. Edwin Way Teale (New York: Houghton Mifflin, 2001), 317.

Book II

Unless otherwise specified, in this chapter all biblical quotations are from the book of Isaiah. I am using the *New Revised Standard Version* translation of the Bible.

2.1

Abraham Heschel, *The Prophets* (New York: Harper & Row, 1962), 147.

2.2

Walter Brueggemann, *Theology of the Old Testament: Testimony, Dispute, Advocacy* (Minneapolis: Augsburg Fortress Press, 1997), 216.
Barbara Summers, ed., *I Dream a World: Portraits of Black Women Who Changed America* (New York: Stewart, Tabori, & Chang, 1989), editor's note, n.p.
Beverly Harrison, "The Power of Anger in the Work of Love," *Union Seminary Quarterly Review* 36 (1980–81): 41–57.
Abraham Heschel, *The Prophets* (New York: Harper & Row, 1962), 284.

* R. S. Sugirtharajah, ed., *Voices from the Margin: Interpreting the Bible from the Third World* (Maryknoll, NY: Orbis Books, 2016). This 25th anniversary edition presents critical, post-colonial readings of the Exodus from Latin American, Asian feminist, Palestinian, Native American, Filipino American, and African American perspectives.

2.3

Phyllis Trible, "Journey of a Metaphor," in her *God and the Rhetoric of Sexuality* (Philadelphia: Fortress Press, 1978), 31–59.

2.8

Walter Brueggemann, *Theology of the Old Testament: Testimony, Dispute, Advocacy* (Minneapolis: Augsburg Fortress Press, 1997), 178.

Douglas Knight and Amy-Jill Levine, *The Meaning of the Bible: What the Jewish Scriptures and Christian Old Testament Can Teach Us* (New York: HarperCollins, 2011), 135.

Brevard Childs, *Biblical Theology of the Old and New Testaments* (Minneapolis: Fortress Press, 1992), 358.

Book III

3.2

Josephus, *The Jewish War*, 5.450.

3.3

Ada María Isasi Díaz, "Christ in Mujerista Theology," in *Thinking of Christ*, ed. Tatha Wiley (New York: Continuum, 2003), 157–76.

Edward Schillebeeckx, *Jesus: An Experiment in Christology* (New York: Seabury, 1979), 115.

3.5

James Dunn, *Christology in the Making: A New Testament Inquiry into the Origins of the Doctrine of the Incarnation* (Philadelphia: Westminster, 1980), 30.

3.7

Josephus, *The Jewish War*, 1.88.

Philo, *On The Embassy of Gaius*, Book XXXVIII, 299–305.

Paula Fredriksen, *From Jesus to Christ* (New Haven, CT: Yale University Press, 2000), 125.

3.8

Karl Rahner, *Foundations of Christian Faith* (New York: Seabury, 1978), 284.

3.9

Walter Kasper, *Jesus the Christ* (New York: Paulist Press, 1976), 145.

Karl Rahner, *Foundations of Christian Faith* (New York: Seabury, 1978), 264–84.

3.10

David Tracy, *The Analogical Imagination: Christian Theology and the Culture of Pluralism* (New York: Crossroad, 1981), 282.

3.11

Jon Sobrino, *Jesus the Liberator* (Maryknoll, NY: Orbis Books, 1993), 255.

Edward Schillebeeckx, *Christ: The Experience of Jesus as Lord* (New York: Seabury, 1980), 729.

Book IV

4.1

Josephus, *The Jewish Antiquities*, 18.3.3 (63–64).

4.2

William Shakespeare, *Romeo and Juliet*, Act 2, scene 2.

* The debate was triggered by Hans Conzelmann, *The Theology of St. Luke* (New York: Harper & Bros., 1960), and it continues to reverberate.

4.3

Gustaf Aulén, *Christus Victor* (New York: Macmillan, 1969).

4.4

Andrie du Toit, "Forensic Metaphors in Romans and Their Soteriological Significance," in *Salvation in the New Testament*, ed. Jan van der Watt (Leiden: Brill, 2005), 242.

4.5

James Dunn, *The Theology of Paul the Apostle* (Grand Rapids, MI: Eerdmans, 1998), 214.

Karl Rahner, *Foundations of Christian Faith* (New York: Seabury, 1978), 282.

Edward Schillebeeckx, *Jesus: An Experiment in Christology* (New York: Seabury, 1979), 319.

4.6

Julian of Norwich, *Showings* (New York: Paulist Press, 1978), Long text, ch. 60, 297–99.

4.8

Daniel Berrigan, *Isaiah: Spirit of Courage, Gift of Tears* (Minneapolis: Fortress Press, 1996), 153.

Edward Schillebeeckx, *Jesus: An Experiment in Christology* (New York: Seabury, 1979), 290.

Jon Sobrino, *Jesus the Liberator* (Maryknoll, NY: Orbis Books, 1993), 230.

4.9

Jon Sobrino, *Jesus the Liberator* (Maryknoll, NY: Orbis Books, 1993), 220.

Book V

5.1

John Muir, *My First Summer in the Sierra* (Boston: Houghton Mifflin, 1911), on page 110 of the Sierra Club Books 1988 edition.

Karl Rahner, "The Two Basic Types of Christology," *Theological Investigations* 13 (New York: Seabury Press, 1975): 213–23.

5.3

Pope Francis, *Laudato Si', On Care for Our Common Home* (Libreria Editrice Vaticana, 2015); hereafter cited as *LS* with paragraph number.

5.5

James D. G. Dunn, *Christology in the Making: A New Testament Inquiry into the Origins of the Doctrine of the Incarnation* (Philadelphia: Westminster, 1980), 212.

Shawn Copeland, homily preached on Palm Sunday 2017, online at *Catholic Women Preach*.

Jeannine Hill Fletcher, *The Sin of White Supremacy: Christianity, Racism and Religious Diversity in America* (Maryknoll, NY: Orbis Books, 2017), 135.

T. S. Eliot, "Burnt Norton," *Four Quartets* (New York: Harcourt, Brace & World, 1971), part V.

5.6

Niels Henrik Gregersen, ed., *Incarnation: On the Scope and Depth of Christology* (Minneapolis: Fortress Press, 2015), 18.

Charles Darwin, *On the Origin of Species* (New York: Barnes & Noble Classics, 2004), 343.

5.7

Niels Henrik Gregersen, "The Cross of Christ in an Evolutionary World," *Dialog* 40, no. 3 (2001): 192–207, at 205.

Ambrose of Milan, *PL* 16:1354.

Karl Rahner, "Easter: The Beginning of Glory," in *The Great Church Year*, ed. Albert Raffelt and Harvey Egan (New York: Crossroad, 2001), 191.

Book VI

6.2

Edward Schillebeeckx, "I Believe in God, Creator of Heaven and Earth," in his *God Among Us: The Gospel Proclaimed* (New York: Crossroad, 1983), 91.

6.4

Thomas Merton, "A Body of Broken Bones" in *New Seeds of Contemplation* (New York: New Directions, 2007), 71.

6.5

Annie Dillard, *Pilgrim at Tinker Creek* (New York: Harper & Row, 1974), 137.

6.6

Henry Beston, *The Outermost House: A Year of Life on the Great Beach of Cape Cod* (New York: Viking Press, 1962), 25.

Thomas Aquinas, *Summa Theologiae* I, q.75, a.5.

Rhodora Beaton, "Let Us Sing as We Go: Language Origins and the Sung Response of Faith," *Horizons: Journal of the College Theology Society* 44, no. 1 (2017): 79.

Works Consulted

Book I

David Brondos. *Fortress Introduction to Salvation and the Cross*. Minneapolis: Fortress Press, 2007.

Lisa Cahill. "The Atonement Paradigm: Does It Still Have Value?" *Theological Studies* 68 (2007): 418–32.

Raymond Corriveau and Alberto de Mingo Kaminouchi, eds. *Readings on Redemption*. Rome: General Secretariat for Redemptorist Spirituality, 2006.

Mark Heim. *Saved from Sacrifice: A Theology of the Cross*. Grand Rapids, MI: Eerdmans, 2006.

Theodore Jennings. *Transforming Atonement: A Political Theology of the Cross*. Minneapolis: Fortress Press, 2009.

William Loewe. "Anselm and the Turn to Theory," in his *Lex Crucis: Soteriology and the Stages of Meaning*, 71–101. Minneapolis: Fortress Press, 2015.

Barbara Reid. *Taking Up the Cross: New Testament Interpretations through Latina and Feminist Eyes*. Minneapolis: Augsburg Fortress, 2007.

Rosemary Radford Ruether. *Women and Redemption*. Minneapolis: Fortress Press, 1998.

Richard W. Southern. *Saint Anselm: A Portrait in a Landscape*. Cambridge: Cambridge University Press, 1990.

Marit Trelsted, ed. *Cross Examinations: Readings on the Meaning of the Cross Today*. Minneapolis: Augsburg Fortress, 2006.

Book II

Klaus Baltzer. *Deutero-Isaiah: A Commentary on Isaiah 40–55*. Minneapolis: Augsburg Fortress, 2001.

Bruce Birch, Walter Brueggemann, Terence Fretheim, and David Petersen. *A Theological Introduction to the Old Testament*. Nashville: Abingdon Press, 1999.

Walter Brueggemann. *Theology of the Old Testament: Testimony, Dispute, Advocacy*. Minneapolis: Augsburg Fortress, 1997.

Brevard Childs. *Biblical Theology of the Old and New Testaments*. Minneapolis: Fortress Press, 1992.

Donald Gowan. *Theology of the Prophetic Books: The Death & Resurrection of Israel*. Louisville, KY: Westminster John Knox, 1998.

Abraham Heschel. *The Prophets*. New York: Harper & Row, 1962.

Douglas Knight and Amy-Jill Levine. *The Meaning of the Bible: What the Jewish Scriptures and Christian Old Testament Can Teach Us*. New York: HarperCollins, 2011.

John Courtney Murray. *The Problem of God, Yesterday and Today*. New Haven, CT: Yale University Press, 1964.

Book III

Raymond Brown. *The Death of the Messiah*, vols. I and II. New York: Doubleday, 1994.

Paula Fredriksen. *Jesus of Nazareth, King of the Jews: A Jewish Life and the Emergence of Christianity*. New York: Knopf, 1999.

Pinchas Lapide. *The Resurrection of Jesus: A Jewish Perspective*. Minneapolis: Augsburg, 1983.

John Meier. *A Marginal Jew: Rethinking the Historical Jesus*. New York: Doubleday, 1991.

Gerald O'Collins. *Believing in the Resurrection*. New York: Paulist, 2012.

E. P. Sanders. *Jesus and Judaism*. Philadelphia: Fortress Press, 1985.

Edward Schillebeeckx. *Jesus: An Experiment in Christology*. New York: Seabury, 1979.

Elisabeth Schüssler Fiorenza. *In Memory of Her: A Feminist Theological Reconstruction of Christian Origins*. New York: Crossroad, 1983.

Jon Sobrino. *Jesus the Liberator: A Historical-Theological View*. Maryknoll, NY: Orbis Books, 1993.

Book IV

Daniel Berrigan. *Isaiah: Spirit of Courage, Gift of Tears*. Minneapolis: Fortress Press, 1996.

James D. G. Dunn. *The Theology of Paul the Apostle*. Grand Rapids, MI: Eerdmans, 1998.

Joseph Fitzmyer. *Paul and His Theology: A Brief Sketch*. Englewood Cliffs, NJ: Prentice Hall, 1989.

Paula Fredriksen. *From Jesus to Christ: The Origins of the New Testament Images of Christ*. New Haven, CT: Yale University Press, 2000.

Maria Pascuzzi. *Paul: Windows on His Thought and His World*. Winona, MN: Anselm Academic, 2014.

Edward Schillebeeckx. *Christ: The Experience of Jesus as Lord*. New York: Seabury, 1980.

Jon Sobrino. *Christ the Liberator: A View from the Victims*. Maryknoll, NY: Orbis Books, 2001.

Jan van der Watt, ed. *Salvation in the New Testament: Perspectives on Soteriology*. Leiden: Brill, 2005.

Book V

Walter Brueggemann. *The God of All Flesh*, ed. K.C. Hanson. Eugene, OR: Cascade Books, 2016.

Celia Deane-Drummond and David Clough, eds. *Creaturely Theology: On God, Humans, and Other Animals*. London: SCM Press, 2009.

James D. G. Dunn. *Christology in the Making: A New Testament Inquiry into the Origins of the Doctrine of the Incarnation*. Philadelphia: Westminster, 1980.

Denis Edwards. "Every Sparrow That Falls to the Ground: The Cost of Evolution and the Christ-Event," *Ecotheology* 11, no. 1 (2006): 103–23.

Terence Fretheim. *God and World in the Old Testament: A Relational Theology of Creation*. Nashville: Abingdon, 2005.

Niels Henrik Gregersen. "The Cross of Christ in an Evolutionary World," *Dialog* 40, no. 3 (2001): 192–207.

_____, ed. *Incarnation: On the Scope and Depth of Christology*. Minneapolis: Fortress Press, 2015.

Jürgen Moltmann. *The Crucified God.* New York: Harper & Row, 1974.

Karl Rahner. "On the Theology of the Incarnation," *Theological Investigations* IV. New York: Seabury Press (1974), 105–20.

Book VI

Richard Bauckham. *The Bible and Ecology: Rediscovering the Community of Creation.* Waco, TX: Baylor University Press, 2010.

Leonardo Boff. *Cry of the Earth, Cry of the Poor.* Maryknoll, NY: Orbis Books, 1997.

Douglas Christie. *The Blue Sapphire of the Mind: Notes for a Contemplative Ecology.* New York: Oxford University Press, 2013.

Ernst Conradie, ed. *Creation and Salvation: A Companion on Recent Theological Movements.* Berlin: LIT Verlag, 2012.

Denis Edwards. *Ecology at the Heart of Faith.* Maryknoll, NY: Orbis Books, 2006.

Christopher Irvine. *The Cross and Creation in Christian Liturgy and Art.* Collegeville, MN: Liturgical Press, 2013.

James Mackey. *Christianity and Creation.* New York: Continuum, 2006.

Sallie McFague. *Blessed Are the Consumers: Climate Change and the Practice of Restraint.* Minneapolis: Fortress Press, 2013.

Bill McKibben. *Earth: Making a Life on a Tough New Planet.* New York: St. Martin's Griffin, 2011.

Paul Waldau and Kimberley Patton, eds. *A Communion of Subjects: Animals in Religion, Science, and Ethics.* New York: Columbia University Press, 2006.

Acknowledgments

This book would not have seen the light of day without a raft of support that kept my research and writing afloat through thick and thin. My deep and lasting gratitude goes to:

— Fordham University, for granting a most welcome faculty research leave.

— My religious community, Sisters of St. Joseph of Brentwood NY, who supported the leave and this work through a thousand affirmations, large and small.

— My colleague Terrence Tilley, who performed the irreplaceable service of reading the entire work Book by Book while it was in process; with humor and keen intelligence he offered critical comments about style and content that immeasurably sharpened the text.

— James Robinson, doctoral student and my research assistant, whose library runs, tracking of sources, gifts of quotations and poetry, and excellent editorial suggestions helped shape the outcome; Jim graciously went way beyond the call of duty.

— My biblical posse Mary Callaway, Harry Nasuti, Maria Pascuzzi, Michael Peppard, and Larry Welborn, who enlightened me about Hebrew verbs and Greek nouns and kept me on track through the scriptures.

— Sarit Kattan Gribetz who generously guided my inquiries about sacrifice in the Second Temple period; Larry Kaufmann who sent resources on redemption from the Redemptorist Fathers; and Franklin Harkins who tipped me to resources about Anselm.

— Readers Jean Amore, Ave Regina Gould, Karen Gargamelli and the Benincasa Community, Roger Haight, Patricia Monahan, and Clara Santoro, whose insightful and challenging feedback along the way helped clarify Clara's voice and direct the writing.

— My editor Robert Ellsberg for excellent suggestions offered in a collegial spirit; it is a great pleasure to work with him and the whole staff at Orbis Books.

Made in United States
North Haven, CT
01 November 2022

26188399R00143